WILD

ALSO BY CHERYL STRAYED

Torch
Tiny Beautiful Things: Advice on Love and Life from Someone Who's Been There

Cheryl Strayed

WILD

A JOURNEY FROM LOST TO FOUND

Atlantic Books
LONDON

First published in the United States of America in 2012 by Alfred A. Knopf, a division of Random House Inc, New York.

First published in Great Britain in 2012 by Atlantic Books, an imprint of Atlantic Books Ltd.

This paperback edition published in Great Britain in 2015 by Atlantic Books.

10

A CIP catalogue record for this book is available from the British Library.

Paperback ISBN: 978-0-85789-776-3
E-book ISBN: 978-0-85789-777-0

OME film edition: 978-1-78239-487-7
Paperback film edition: 978-1-78239-486-0

Maps by Mapping Specialists

Atlantic Books
An imprint of Atlantic Books Ltd
Ormond House
26–27 Boswell Street
London
WC1N 3JZ

www.atlantic-books.co.uk

Printed in Great Britain by CPI Group (UK) Ltd, Croydon, CR0 4YY

For Brian Lindstrom

And for our children,
Carver and Bobbi

CONTENTS

AUTHOR'S NOTE

To write this book, I relied upon my personal journals, researched facts when I could, consulted with several of the people who appear in the book, and called upon my own memory of these events and this time of my life. I have changed the names of most but not all of the individuals in this book, and in some cases I also modified identifying details in order to preserve anonymity. There are no composite characters or events in this book. I occasionally omitted people and events, but only when that omission had no impact on either the veracity or the substance of the story.

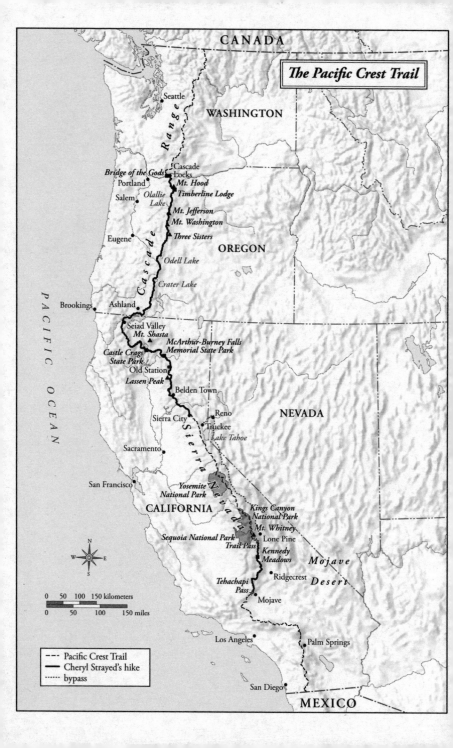

WILD

The trees were tall, but I was taller, standing above them on a steep mountain slope in northern California. Moments before, I'd removed my hiking boots and the left one had fallen into those trees, first catapulting into the air when my enormous backpack toppled onto it, then skittering across the gravelly trail and flying over the edge. It bounced off of a rocky outcropping several feet beneath me before disappearing into the forest canopy below, impossible to retrieve. I let out a stunned gasp, though I'd been in the wilderness thirty-eight days and by then I'd come to know that anything could happen and that everything would. But that doesn't mean I wasn't shocked when it did.

My boot was gone. Actually gone.

I clutched its mate to my chest like a baby, though of course it was futile. What is one boot without the other boot? It is nothing. It is useless, an orphan forevermore, and I could take no mercy on it. It was a big lug of a thing, of genuine heft, a brown leather Raichle boot with a red lace and silver metal fasts. I lifted it high and threw it with all my might and watched it fall into the lush trees and out of my life.

I was alone. I was barefoot. I was twenty-six years old and an orphan too. *An actual stray,* a stranger had observed a couple of weeks before, when I'd told him my name and explained how very loose I was in the world. My father left my life when I was six. My mother died when I was twenty-two. In the wake of her death, my stepfather morphed from the person I considered my dad into a man I only occasionally recognized. My two siblings scattered in their grief, in spite of my efforts to hold us together, until I gave up and scattered as well.

In the years before I pitched my boot over the edge of that mountain, I'd been pitching myself over the edge too. I'd ranged and roamed and railed—from Minnesota to New York to Oregon and all across the West—until at last I found myself, bootless, in the summer of 1995, not so much loose in the world as bound to it.

It was a world I'd never been to and yet had known was there all along, one I'd staggered to in sorrow and confusion and fear and hope. A world I thought would both make me into the woman I knew I could become and turn me back into the girl I'd once been. A world that measured two feet wide and 2,663 miles long.

A world called the Pacific Crest Trail.

I'd first heard of it only seven months before, when I was living in Minneapolis, sad and desperate and on the brink of divorcing a man I still loved. I'd been standing in line at an outdoor store waiting to purchase a foldable shovel when I picked up a book called *The Pacific Crest Trail, Volume 1: California* from a nearby shelf and read the back cover. The PCT, it said, was a continuous wilderness trail that went from the Mexican border in California to just beyond the Canadian border along the crest of nine mountain ranges—the Laguna, San Jacinto, San Bernardino, San Gabriel, Liebre, Tehachapi, Sierra Nevada, Klamath, and Cascades. That distance was a thousand miles as the crow flies, but the trail was more than double that. Traversing the entire length of the states of California, Oregon, and Washington, the PCT passes through national parks and wilderness areas as well as federal, tribal, and privately held lands; through deserts and mountains and rain forests; across rivers and highways. I turned the book over and gazed at its front cover—a boulder-strewn lake surrounded by rocky crags against a blue sky—then placed it back on the shelf, paid for my shovel, and left.

But later I returned and bought the book. The Pacific Crest Trail wasn't a world to me then. It was an idea, vague and outlandish, full of promise and mystery. Something bloomed inside me as I traced its jagged line with my finger on a map.

I would walk that line, I decided—or at least as much of it as I could in about a hundred days. I was living alone in a studio apartment in

Minneapolis, separated from my husband, and working as a waitress, as low and mixed-up as I'd ever been in my life. Each day I felt as if I were looking up from the bottom of a deep well. But from that well, I set about becoming a solo wilderness trekker. And why not? I'd been so many things already. A loving wife and an adulteress. A beloved daughter who now spent holidays alone. An ambitious overachiever and aspiring writer who hopped from one meaningless job to the next while dabbling dangerously with drugs and sleeping with too many men. I was the granddaughter of a Pennsylvania coal miner, the daughter of a steelworker turned salesman. After my parents split up, I lived with my mother, brother, and sister in apartment complexes populated by single mothers and their kids. As a teen, I lived back-to-the-land style in the Minnesota northwoods in a house that didn't have an indoor toilet, electricity, or running water. In spite of this, I'd become a high school cheerleader and homecoming queen, and then I went off to college and became a left-wing feminist campus radical.

But a woman who walks alone in the wilderness for eleven hundred miles? I'd never been anything like that before. I had nothing to lose by giving it a whirl.

It seemed like years ago now—as I stood barefoot on that mountain in California—in a different lifetime, really, when I'd made the arguably unreasonable decision to take a long walk alone on the PCT in order to save myself. When I believed that all the things I'd been before had prepared me for this journey. But nothing had or could. Each day on the trail was the only possible preparation for the one that followed. And sometimes even the day before didn't prepare me for what would happen next.

Such as my boots sailing irretrievably off the side of a mountain.

The truth is, I was only half sorry to see them go. In the six weeks I'd spent in those boots, I'd trekked across deserts and snow, past trees and bushes and grasses and flowers of all shapes and sizes and colors, walked up and down mountains and over fields and glades and stretches of land I couldn't possibly define, except to say that I had been there, passed over it, made it through. And all the while, those boots had blistered my feet and rubbed them raw; they'd caused my nails to blacken and detach themselves excruciatingly from four of my toes. I was done with those boots by the time I lost them and those boots were done with me, though it's also true that I loved them. They had become not so much inanimate objects to me as extensions of who I was, as had just about everything else I carried that summer—my backpack, tent, sleeping bag, water purifier, ultralight stove, and the little orange whistle that I carried in lieu of a gun. They were the things I knew and could rely upon, the things that got me through.

I looked down at the trees below me, the tall tops of them waving gently in the hot breeze. They could keep my boots, I thought, gazing across the great green expanse. I'd chosen to rest in this place because of the view. It was late afternoon in mid-July, and I was miles from civilization in every direction, days away from the lonely post office where I'd collect my next resupply box. There was a chance someone would come hiking down the trail, but only rarely did that happen. Usually I went days without seeing another person. It didn't matter whether someone came along anyway. I was in this alone.

I gazed at my bare and battered feet, with their smattering of remaining toenails. They were ghostly pale to the line a few inches above my ankles, where the wool socks I usually wore ended. My calves above them were muscled and golden and hairy, dusted with dirt and a constellation of bruises and scratches. I'd started walking in the Mojave Desert and I didn't plan to stop until I touched my hand to a bridge that crosses the Columbia River at the Oregon-Washington border with the grandiose name the Bridge of the Gods.

I looked north, in its direction—the very thought of that bridge a beacon to me. I looked south, to where I'd been, to the wild land that had schooled and scorched me, and considered my options. There was only one, I knew. There was always only one.

To keep walking.

PART ONE

THE TEN THOUSAND THINGS

The breaking of so great a thing
should make a greater crack.

WILLIAM SHAKESPEARE,
Antony and Cleopatra

1

THE TEN THOUSAND THINGS

My solo three-month hike on the Pacific Crest Trail had many beginnings. There was the first, flip decision to do it, followed by the second, more serious decision to *actually* do it, and then the long third beginning, composed of weeks of shopping and packing and preparing to do it. There was the quitting my job as a waitress and finalizing my divorce and selling almost everything I owned and saying goodbye to my friends and visiting my mother's grave one last time. There was the driving across the country from Minneapolis to Portland, Oregon, and, a few days later, catching a flight to Los Angeles and a ride to the town of Mojave and another ride to the place where the PCT crossed a highway.

At which point, at long last, there was the actual doing it, quickly followed by the grim realization of what it meant to do it, followed by the decision to quit doing it because doing it was absurd and pointless and ridiculously difficult and far more than I expected doing it would be and I was profoundly unprepared to do it.

And then there was the real live truly doing it.

The staying and doing it, in spite of everything. In spite of the bears and the rattlesnakes and the scat of the mountain lions I never saw; the blisters and scabs and scrapes and lacerations. The exhaustion and the deprivation; the cold and the heat; the monotony and the pain; the thirst and the hunger; the glory and the ghosts that haunted me as I hiked eleven hundred miles from the Mojave Desert to the state of Washington by myself.

And finally, once I'd actually gone and done it, walked all those miles for all those days, there was the realization that what I'd thought was the beginning had not really been the beginning at all. That in truth my hike on the Pacific Crest Trail hadn't begun when I made the snap decision to do it. It had begun before I even imagined it, precisely four years, seven months, and three days before, when I'd stood in a little room at the Mayo Clinic in Rochester, Minnesota, and learned that my mother was going to die.

I was wearing green. Green pants, green shirt, green bow in my hair. It was an outfit that my mother had sewn—she'd made clothes for me all of my life. Some of them were just what I dreamed of having, others less so. I wasn't crazy about the green pantsuit, but I wore it anyway, as a penance, as an offering, as a talisman.

All that day of the green pantsuit, as I accompanied my mother and stepfather, Eddie, from floor to floor of the Mayo Clinic while my mother went from one test to another, a prayer marched through my head, though *prayer* is not the right word to describe that march. I wasn't humble before God. I didn't even believe in God. My prayer was not: *Please, God, take mercy on us.*

I was not going to ask for mercy. I didn't need to. My mother was forty-five. She looked fine. For a good number of years she'd mostly been a vegetarian. She'd planted marigolds around her garden to keep bugs away instead of using pesticides. My siblings and I had been made to swallow raw cloves of garlic when we had colds. People like my mother did not get cancer. The tests at the Mayo Clinic would prove that, refuting what the doctors in Duluth had said. I was certain of this. Who were those doctors in Duluth anyway? What was Duluth? *Duluth!* Duluth was a freezing hick town where doctors who didn't know what the hell they were talking about told forty-five-year-old vegetarian-ish, garlic-eating, natural-remedy-using nonsmokers that they had late-stage lung cancer, that's what.

Fuck them.

That was my prayer: *Fuckthemfuckthemfuckthem.*

And yet, here was my mother at the Mayo Clinic getting worn out if she had to be on her feet for more than three minutes.

"You want a wheelchair?" Eddie asked her when we came upon a row of them in a long carpeted hall.

"She doesn't need a wheelchair," I said.

"Just for a minute," said my mother, almost collapsing into one, her eyes meeting mine before Eddie wheeled her toward the elevator.

I followed behind, not allowing myself to think a thing. We were finally on our way up to see the last doctor. The *real doctor,* we kept calling him. The one who would gather everything that had been gathered about my mom and tell us what was true. As the elevator car lifted, my mother reached out to tug at my pants, rubbing the green cotton between her fingers proprietarily.

"Perfect," she said.

I was twenty-two, the same age she was when she'd been pregnant with me. She was going to leave my life at the same moment that I came into hers, I thought. For some reason that sentence came fully formed into my head just then, temporarily blotting out the *Fuck them* prayer. I almost howled in agony. I almost choked to death on what I knew before I knew. I was going to live the rest of my life without my mother. I pushed the fact of it away with everything in me. I couldn't let myself believe it then and there in that elevator and also go on breathing, so I let myself believe other things instead. Such as if a doctor told you that you were going to die soon, you'd be taken to a room with a gleaming wooden desk.

This was not so.

We were led into an examining room, where a nurse instructed my mother to remove her shirt and put on a cotton smock with strings that dangled at her sides. When my mother had done so, she climbed onto a padded table with white paper stretched over it. Each time she moved, the room was on fire with the paper ripping and crinkling beneath her. I could see her naked back, the small curve of flesh beneath her waist. She was not going to die. Her naked back seemed proof of that. I was staring at it when the real doctor came into the room and said my mother would be lucky if she lived a year. He explained that they would not attempt to cure her, that she was incurable. There was nothing that could have been done, he told us. Finding it so late was common, when it came to lung cancer.

"But she's not a smoker," I countered, as if I could talk him out of the diagnosis, as if cancer moved along reasonable, negotiable lines. "She only smoked when she was younger. She hasn't had a cigarette for years."

The doctor shook his head sadly and pressed on. He had a job to do. They could try to ease the pain in her back with radiation, he offered.

Radiation might reduce the size of the tumors that were growing along the entire length of her spine.

I did not cry. I only breathed. Horribly. Intentionally. And then forgot to breathe. I'd fainted once—furious, age three, holding my breath because I didn't want to get out of the bathtub, too young to remember it myself. *What did you do? What did you do?* I'd asked my mother all through my childhood, making her tell me the story again and again, amazed and delighted by my own impetuous will. She'd held out her hands and watched me turn blue, my mother had always told me. She'd waited me out until my head fell into her palms and I took a breath and came back to life.

Breathe.

"Can I ride my horse?" my mother asked the real doctor. She sat with her hands folded tightly together and her ankles hooked one to the other. Shackled to herself.

In reply, he took a pencil, stood it upright on the edge of the sink, and tapped it hard on the surface. "This is your spine after radiation," he said. "One jolt and your bones could crumble like a dry cracker."

We went to the women's restroom. Each of us locked in separate stalls, weeping. We didn't exchange a word. Not because we felt so alone in our grief, but because we were so together in it, as if we were one body instead of two. I could feel my mother's weight leaning against the door, her hands slapping slowly against it, causing the entire frame of the bathroom stalls to shake. Later we came out to wash our hands and faces, watching each other in the bright mirror.

We were sent to the pharmacy to wait. I sat between my mother and Eddie in my green pantsuit, the green bow miraculously still in my hair. There was a big bald boy in an old man's lap. There was a woman who had an arm that swung wildly from the elbow. She held it stiffly with the other hand, trying to calm it. She waited. We waited. There was a beautiful dark-haired woman who sat in a wheelchair. She wore a purple hat and a handful of diamond rings. We could not take our eyes off her. She spoke in Spanish to the people gathered around her, her family and perhaps her husband.

"Do you think she has cancer?" my mother whispered loudly to me.

Eddie sat on my other side, but I could not look at him. If I looked at him we would both crumble like dry crackers. I thought about my older sister, Karen, and my younger brother, Leif. About my husband, Paul, and about my mother's parents and sister, who lived a thousand miles away. What they would say when they knew. How they would cry. My prayer was different now: *A year, a year, a year.* Those two words beat like a heart in my chest.

That's how long my mother would live.

"What are you thinking about?" I asked her. There was a song coming over the waiting room speakers. A song without words, but my mother knew the words anyway and instead of answering my question she sang them softly to me. "Paper roses, paper roses, oh how real those roses seemed to be," she sang. She put her hand on mine and said, "I used to listen to that song when I was young. It's funny to think of that. To think about listening to the same song now. I would've never known."

My mother's name was called then: her prescriptions were ready.

"Go get them for me," she said. "Tell them who you are. Tell them you're my daughter."

I was her daughter, but more. I was Karen, Cheryl, Leif. Karen Cheryl Leif. KarenCherylLeif. Our names blurred into one in my mother's mouth all my life. She whispered it and hollered it, hissed it and crooned it. We were her kids, her comrades, the end of her and the beginning. We took turns riding shotgun with her in the car. "Do I love you this much?" she'd ask us, holding her hands six inches apart. "No," we'd say, with sly smiles. "Do I love you *this* much?" she'd ask again, and on and on and on, each time moving her hands farther apart. But she would never get there, no matter how wide she stretched her arms. The amount that she loved us was beyond her reach. It could not be quantified or contained. It was the ten thousand named things in the Tao Te Ching's universe and then ten thousand more. Her love was full-throated and all-encompassing and unadorned. Every day she blew through her entire reserve.

She grew up an army brat and Catholic. She lived in five different states and two countries before she was fifteen. She loved horses and Hank Williams and had a best friend named Babs. Nineteen and pregnant, she married my father. Three days later, he knocked her around the room. She left and came back. Left and came back. She would not put up with it, but she did. He broke her nose. He broke her dishes. He skinned her knees dragging her down a sidewalk in broad daylight by her hair. But he didn't break her. By twenty-eight she managed to leave him for the last time.

She was alone, with KarenCherylLeif riding shotgun in her car.

By then we lived in a small town an hour outside of Minneapolis in a series of apartment complexes with deceptively upscale names: Mill Pond and Barbary Knoll, Tree Loft and Lake Grace Manor. She had one job, then another. She waited tables at a place called the Norseman and then a place called Infinity, where her uniform was a black T-shirt that said GO FOR IT in rainbow glitter across her chest. She worked the day shift at a factory that manufactured plastic containers capable of holding highly corrosive chemicals and brought the rejects home. Trays and boxes that had been cracked or clipped or misaligned in the machine. We made them into toys—beds for our dolls, ramps for our cars. She worked and worked and worked, and still we were poor. We received government cheese and powdered milk, food stamps and medical assistance cards, and free presents from do-gooders at Christmastime. We played tag and red light green light and charades by the apartment mailboxes that you could open only with a key, waiting for checks to arrive.

"We aren't poor," my mother said, again and again. "Because we're rich in love." She would mix food coloring into sugar water and pretend with us that it was a special drink. Sarsaparilla or Orange Crush or lemonade. She'd ask, *Would you like another drink, madam?* in a snooty British voice that made us laugh every time. She would spread her arms wide and ask us how much and there would never be an end to the game. She loved us more than all the named things in the world. She was optimistic and serene, except a few times when she lost her temper and spanked us with a wooden spoon. Or the one time when she screamed *FUCK* and broke down crying because we wouldn't clean our room. She was kindhearted and forgiving, generous and naïve. She dated men with names like Killer and Doobie and Motorcycle Dan and one guy named Victor who liked to downhill ski. They would give us five-dollar bills to buy candy from the store so they could be alone in the apartment with our mom.

"Look both ways," she'd call after us as we fled like a pack of hungry dogs.

When she met Eddie, she didn't think it would work because he was eight years younger than she, but they fell in love anyway. Karen and

Leif and I fell in love with him too. He was twenty-five when we met him and twenty-seven when he married our mother and promised to be our father; a carpenter who could make and fix anything. We left the apartment complexes with fancy names and moved with him into a rented ramshackle farmhouse that had a dirt floor in the basement and four different colors of paint on the outside. The winter after my mother married him, Eddie fell off a roof on the job and broke his back. A year later, he and my mom took the twelve-thousand-dollar settlement he received and with it bought forty acres of land in Aitkin County, an hour and a half west of Duluth, paying for it outright in cash.

There was no house. No one had ever had a house on that land. Our forty acres were a perfect square of trees and bushes and weedy grasses, swampy ponds and bogs clotted with cattails. There was nothing to differentiate it from the trees and bushes and grasses and ponds and bogs that surrounded it in every direction for miles. Together we repeatedly walked the perimeter of our land in those first months as landowners, pushing our way through the wilderness on the two sides that didn't border the road, as if to walk it would seal it off from the rest of the world, make it ours. And, slowly, it did. Trees that had once looked like any other to me became as recognizable as the faces of old friends in a crowd, their branches gesturing with sudden meaning, their leaves beckoning like identifiable hands. Clumps of grass and the edges of the now-familiar bog became landmarks, guides, indecipherable to everyone but us.

We called it "up north" while we were still living in the town an hour outside of Minneapolis. For six months, we went up north only on weekends, working furiously to tame a patch of the land and build a one-room tarpaper shack where the five of us could sleep. In early June, when I was thirteen, we moved up north for good. Or rather, my mother, Leif, Karen, and I did, along with our two horses, our cats and our dogs, and a box of ten baby chicks my mom got for free at the feed store for buying twenty-five pounds of chicken feed. Eddie would continue driving up on weekends throughout the summer and then stay come fall. His back had healed enough that he could finally work again, and he'd secured a job as a carpenter during the busy season that was too lucrative to pass up.

KarenCherylLeif were alone with our mother again—just as we'd been during the years that she'd been single. Waking or sleeping that summer, we were scarcely out of one another's sight and seldom saw anyone else. We were twenty miles away from two small towns in opposite directions: Moose Lake to the east; McGregor to the northwest. In the fall we'd attend school in McGregor, the smaller of the two, with a population of four hundred, but all summer long, aside from the occasional visitor— far-flung neighbors who stopped by to introduce themselves—it was us and our mom. We fought and talked and made up jokes and diversions in order to pass the time.

Who am I? we'd ask one another over and over again, playing a game in which the person who was "it" had to think of someone, famous or not, and the others would guess who it was based on an infinite number of yes or no questions: *Are you a man? Are you American? Are you dead? Are you Charles Manson?*

We played it while planting and maintaining a garden that would sustain us through the winter in soil that had been left to its own devices throughout millennia, and while making steady progress on the construction of the house we were building on the other side of our property and hoped to complete by summer's end. We were swarmed by mosquitoes as we worked, but my mother forbade us to use DEET or any other such brain-destroying, earth-polluting, future-progeny-harming chemical. Instead, she instructed us to slather our bodies with pennyroyal or peppermint oil. In the evenings, we would make a game of counting the bites on our bodies by candlelight. The numbers would be seventy-nine, eighty-six, one hundred and three.

"You'll thank me for this someday," my mother always said when my siblings and I complained about all the things we no longer had. We'd never lived in luxury or even like those in the middle class, but we had lived among the comforts of the modern age. There had always been a television in our house, not to mention a flushable toilet and a tap where you could get yourself a glass of water. In our new life as pioneers, even meeting the simplest needs often involved a grueling litany of tasks, rigorous and full of boondoggle. Our kitchen was a Coleman camp stove, a fire ring, an old-fashioned icebox Eddie built that depended on actual ice to keep things even mildly cool, a detached sink propped against an outside wall of the shack, and a bucket of water with a lid on it. Each component demanded just slightly less than it gave, needing to be tended and maintained, filled and unfilled, hauled and dumped, pumped and primed and stoked and monitored.

Karen and I shared a bed on a lofted platform built so close to the ceiling we could just barely sit up. Leif slept a few feet away on his own smaller platform, and our mother was in a bed on the floor below, joined by Eddie on the weekends. Every night we talked one another to sleep, slumber-party style. There was a skylight window in the ceiling that ran the length of the platform bed I shared with Karen, its transparent pane only a few feet from our faces. Each night the black sky and the bright stars were my stunning companions; occasionally I'd see their beauty and solemnity so plainly that I'd realize in a piercing way that my mother was right. That someday I *would* be grateful and that in fact I was grateful now, that I felt something growing in me that was strong and real.

It was the thing that had grown in me that I'd remember years later, when my life became unmoored by sorrow. The thing that would make me believe that hiking the Pacific Crest Trail was my way back to the person I used to be.

On Halloween night we moved into the house we'd built out of trees and scrap wood. It didn't have electricity or running water or a phone or an indoor toilet or even a single room with a door. All through my teen years, Eddie and my mom kept building it, adding on, making it better. My mother planted a garden and canned and pickled and froze vegetables in the fall. She tapped the trees and made maple syrup, baked bread and carded wool, and made her own fabric dyes out of dandelions and broccoli leaves.

I grew up and left home for college in the Twin Cities at a school called St. Thomas, but not without my mom. My acceptance letter mentioned that parents of students could take classes at St. Thomas for free. Much as she liked her life as a modern pioneer, my mother had always wanted to get her degree. We laughed about it together, then pondered it in private. She was forty, too old for college now, my mother said when we discussed it, and I couldn't disagree. Plus, St. Thomas was a three-hour drive away. We kept talking and talking until at last we had a deal: she would go to St. Thomas but we would have separate lives, dictated by me. I would live in the dorm and she would drive back and forth. If our paths crossed on campus she would not acknowledge me unless I acknowledged her first.

"All this is probably for nothing," she said once we'd hatched the plan. "Most likely I'll flunk out anyway." To prepare, she shadowed me during the last months of my senior year of high school, doing all the home-work that I was assigned, honing her skills. She replicated my worksheets, wrote the same papers I had to write, read every one of the books. I graded her work, using my teacher's marks as a guide. I judged her a shaky student at best.

She went to college and earned straight As.

Sometimes I hugged her exuberantly when I saw her on campus; other times I sailed on by, as if she were no one to me at all.

We were both seniors in college when we learned she had cancer. By then we weren't at St. Thomas anymore. We'd both transferred to the University of Minnesota after that first year—she to the Duluth campus, I to the one in Minneapolis—and, much to our amusement, we shared a major. She was double majoring in women's studies and history, I in women's studies and English. At night, we'd talk for an hour on the phone. I was married by then, to a good man named Paul. I'd married him in the woods on our land, wearing a white satin and lace dress my mother had sewn.

After she got sick, I folded my life down. I told Paul not to count on me. I would have to come and go according to my mother's needs. I wanted to quit school, but my mother ordered me not to, begging me, no matter what happened, to get my degree. She herself took what she called a break. She only needed to complete a couple more classes to graduate, and she would, she told me. She would get her BA if it killed her, she said, and we laughed and then looked at each other darkly. She'd do the work from her bed. She'd tell me what to type and I'd type it. She would be strong enough to start in on those last two classes soon, she absolutely knew. I stayed in school, though I convinced my professors to allow me to be in class only two days each week. As soon as those two days were over, I raced home to be with my mother. Unlike Leif and Karen, who could hardly bear to be in our mother's presence once she got sick, I couldn't bear to be away from her. Plus, I was needed. Eddie was with her when he could be, but he had to work. Someone had to pay the bills.

I cooked food that my mother tried to eat, but rarely could she eat. She'd think she was hungry and then she'd sit like a prisoner staring down at the food on her plate. "It looks good," she'd say. "I think I'll be able to eat it later."

I scrubbed the floors. I took everything from the cupboards and put new paper down. My mother slept and moaned and counted and swallowed her pills. On good days she sat in a chair and talked to me.

There was nothing much to say. She'd been so transparent and effusive and I so inquisitive that we'd already covered everything. I knew that her love for me was vaster than the ten thousand things and also the ten thousand things beyond that. I knew the names of the horses she had loved as a girl: Pal and Buddy and Bacchus. I knew she'd lost her virginity at seventeen with a boy named Mike. I knew how she met my father the next year and what he seemed like to her on their first few dates. How, when she'd broken the news of her unwed teen pregnancy to her parents, her father had dropped a spoon. I knew she loathed going to confession and also the very things that she'd confessed. Cursing and sassing off to her mom, bitching about having to set the table while her much younger sister played. Wearing dresses out the door on her way to school and then changing into the jeans she'd stashed in her bag. All through my childhood and adolescence I'd asked and asked, making her describe those scenes and more, wanting to know who said what and how, what she'd felt inside while it was going on, where so-and-so stood and what time of day it was. And she'd told me, with reluctance or relish, laughing and asking why on earth I wanted to know. I wanted to know. I couldn't explain.

But now that she was dying, I knew everything. My mother was in me already. Not just the parts of her that I knew, but the parts of her that had come before me too.

It wasn't long that I had to go back and forth between Minneapolis and home. A little more than a month. The idea that my mother would live a year quickly became a sad dream. We'd gone to the Mayo Clinic on February 12. By the third of March, she had to go to the hospital in Duluth, seventy miles away, because she was in so much pain. As she dressed to go, she found that she couldn't put on her own socks and she called me into her room and asked me to help. She sat on the bed and I got down on my knees before her. I had never put socks on another person, and it was harder than I thought it would be. They wouldn't slide over her skin. They went on crooked. I became furious with my mother, as if she were purposely holding her foot in a way that made it impossible for me. She sat back, leaning on her hands on the bed, her eyes closed. I could hear her breathing deeply, slowly.

"God damn it," I said. *"Help me."*

My mother looked down at me and didn't say a word for several moments.

"Honey," she said eventually, gazing at me, her hand reaching to stroke the top of my head. It was a word she used often throughout my childhood, delivered in a highly specific tone. This is not the way I wanted it to be, that single *honey* said, but it was the way it was. It was this very acceptance of suffering that annoyed me most about my mom, her unending optimism and cheer.

"Let's go," I said after I'd wrestled her shoes on.

Her movements were slow and thick as she put on her coat. She held on to the walls as she made her way through the house, her two beloved dogs following her as she went, pushing their noses into her hands and thighs. I watched the way she patted their heads. I didn't have a prayer anymore. The words *fuck them* were two dry pills in my mouth.

"Bye, darlings," she said to the dogs. "Bye, house," she said as she followed me out the door.

It hadn't occurred to me that my mother would die. Until she was dying, the thought had never entered my mind. She was monolithic and insurmountable, the keeper of my life. She would grow old and still work in the garden. This image was fixed in my mind, like one of the memories from her childhood that I'd made her explain so intricately that I remembered it as if it were mine. She would be old and beautiful like the black-and-white photo of Georgia O'Keeffe I'd once sent her. I held fast to this image for the first couple of weeks after we left the Mayo Clinic, and then, once she was admitted to the hospice wing of the hospital in Duluth, that image unfurled, gave way to others, more modest and true. I imagined my mother in October; I wrote the scene in my mind. And then the one of my mother in August and another in May. Each day that passed, another month peeled away.

On her first day in the hospital, a nurse offered my mother morphine, but she refused. "Morphine is what they give to dying people," she said. "Morphine means there's no hope."

But she held out against it for only one day. She slept and woke, talked and laughed. She cried from the pain. I camped out during the days with her and Eddie took the nights. Leif and Karen stayed away, making excuses that I found inexplicable and infuriating, though their absence didn't seem to bother my mom. She was preoccupied with nothing but eradicating her pain, an impossible task in the spaces of time between the doses of morphine. We could never get the pillows right. One afternoon, a doctor I'd never seen came into the room and explained that my mother was *actively dying*.

"But it's only been a month," I said indignantly. "The other doctor told us a year."

He made no reply. He was young, perhaps thirty. He stood next to my mother, a gentle hairy hand slung into his pocket, looking down at her in the bed. "From this point on, our only concern is that she's comfortable."

Comfortable, and yet the nurses tried to give her as little morphine as they could. One of the nurses was a man, and I could see the outline of his penis through his tight white nurse's trousers. I wanted desperately to pull him into the small bathroom beyond the foot of my mother's bed and offer myself up to him, to do anything at all if he would help us. And also I wanted to take pleasure from him, to feel the weight of his body against me, to feel his mouth in my hair and hear him say my name to me over and over again, to force him to acknowledge me, to make this matter to him, to crush his heart with mercy for us.

When my mother asked him for more morphine, she asked for it in a way that I have never heard anyone ask for anything. A mad dog. He did not look at her when she asked him this, but at his wristwatch. He held the same expression on his face regardless of the answer. Sometimes he gave it to her without a word, and sometimes he told her no in a voice as soft as his penis in his pants. My mother begged and whimpered then. She cried and her tears fell in the wrong direction. Not down over the light of her cheeks to the corners of her mouth, but away from the edges of her eyes to her ears and into the nest of her hair on the bed.

She didn't live a year. She didn't live to October or August or May. She lived forty-nine days after the first doctor in Duluth told her she had cancer; thirty-four after the one at the Mayo Clinic did. But each day was an eternity, one stacked up on the other, a cold clarity inside of a deep haze.

Leif didn't come to visit her. Karen came once after I'd insisted she must. I was in heartbroken and enraged disbelief. "I don't like seeing her this way," my sister would offer weakly when we spoke, and then burst into tears. I couldn't speak to my brother—where he was during those weeks was a mystery to Eddie and me. One friend told us he was staying with a girl named Sue in St. Cloud. Another spotted him ice fishing on Sheriff Lake. I didn't have time to do much about it, consumed as I was each day at my mother's side, holding plastic pans for her to retch into, adjusting the impossible pillows again and again, hoisting her up and onto the potty chair the nurses had propped near her bed, cajoling her to eat a bite of food that she'd vomit up ten minutes later. Mostly, I watched her sleep, the hardest task of all, to see her in repose, her face still pinched with pain. Each time she moved, the IV tubes that dangled all around her swayed and my heart raced, afraid she'd disturb the needles that attached the tubes to her swollen wrists and hands.

"How are you feeling?" I'd coo hopefully when she woke, reaching through the tubes to smooth her flattened hair into place.

"Oh, honey," was all she could say most times. And then she'd look away.

I roamed the hospital hallways while my mother slept, my eyes darting into other people's rooms as I passed their open doors, catching glimpses of old men with bad coughs and purpled flesh, women with bandages around their fat knees.

"How are you doing?" the nurses would ask me in melancholy tones.

"We're holding up," I'd say, as if I were a we.

But it was just me. My husband, Paul, did everything he could to make me feel less alone. He was still the kind and tender man I'd fallen for a few years before, the one I'd loved so fiercely I'd shocked everyone by marrying just shy of twenty, but once my mother started dying, something inside of me was dead to Paul, no matter what he did or said. Still, I called him each day from the pay phone in the hospital during the long afternoons, or back at my mom and Eddie's house in the evenings. We'd have long conversations during which I'd weep and tell him everything and he would cry with me and try to make it all just a tiny bit more okay, but his words rang hollow. It was almost as if I couldn't hear them at all. What did he know about losing anything? His parents were still alive and happily married to each other. My connection with him and his gloriously unfractured life only seemed to increase my pain. It wasn't his fault. Being with him felt unbearable, but being with anyone else did too. The only person I could bear to be with was the most unbearable person of all: my mother.

In the mornings, I would sit near her bed and try to read to her. I had two books: *The Awakening,* by Kate Chopin, and *The Optimist's Daughter,* by Eudora Welty. These were books we'd read in college, books we loved. So I started in, but I could not go on. Each word I spoke erased itself in the air.

It was the same when I tried to pray. I prayed fervently, rabidly, to God, any god, to a god I could not identify or find. I cursed my mother, who'd not given me any religious education. Resentful of her own repressive Catholic upbringing, she'd avoided church altogether in her adult life, and now she was dying and I didn't even have God. I prayed to the whole wide universe and hoped that God would be in it, listening to me. I prayed and prayed, and then I faltered. Not because I couldn't find God, but because suddenly I absolutely did: God was there, I realized, and God had no intention of making things happen or not, of saving my mother's life. God was not a granter of wishes. God was a ruthless bitch.

The last couple of days of her life, my mother was not so much high as down under. She was on a morphine drip by then, a clear bag of liquid flowing slowly down a tube that was taped to her wrist. When she woke, she'd say, "Oh, oh." Or she'd let out a sad gulp of air. She'd look at me, and there would be a flash of love. Other times she'd roll back into sleep as if I were not there. Sometimes when my mother woke she did not know where she was. She demanded an enchilada and then some applesauce. She believed that all the animals she'd ever loved were in the room with her—and there had been a lot. She'd say, "That horse darn near stepped on me," and look around for it accusingly, or her hands would move to stroke an invisible cat that lay at her hip. During this time I wanted my mother to say to me that I had been the best daughter in the world. I did not want to want this, but I did, inexplicably, as if I had a great fever that could be cooled only by those words. I went so far as to ask her directly, "Have I been the best daughter in the world?"

She said yes, I had, of course.

But this was not enough. I wanted those words to knit together in my mother's mind and for them to be delivered, fresh, to me.

I was ravenous for love.

My mother died fast but not all of a sudden. A slow-burning fire when flames disappear to smoke and then smoke to air. She didn't have time to get skinny. She was altered but still fleshy when she died, the body of a woman among the living. She had her hair too, brown and brittle and frayed from being in bed for weeks.

From the room where she died I could see the great Lake Superior out her window. The biggest lake in the world, and the coldest too. To see it, I had to work. I pressed my face sideways, hard, against the glass, and I'd catch a slice of it going on forever into the horizon.

"A room with a view!" my mother exclaimed, though she was too weak to rise and see the lake herself. And then more quietly she said: "All of my life I've waited for a room with a view."

She wanted to die sitting up, so I took all the pillows I could get my hands on and made a backrest for her. I wanted to take her from the hospital and prop her in a field of yarrow to die. I covered her with a quilt that I had brought from home, one she'd sewn herself out of pieces of our old clothing.

"Get that out of here," she growled savagely, and then kicked her legs like a swimmer to make it go away.

I watched my mother. Outside the sun glinted off the sidewalks and the icy edges of the snow. It was Saint Patrick's Day, and the nurses brought her a square block of green Jell-O that sat quivering on the table beside her. It would turn out to be the last full day of her life, and for most of it she held her eyes still and open, neither sleeping nor waking, intermittently lucid and hallucinatory.

That evening I left her, though I didn't want to. The nurses and doctors had told Eddie and me that *this was it.* I took that to mean she would die in a couple of weeks. I believed that people with cancer lingered. Karen and Paul would be driving up together from Minneapolis the next morning and my mother's parents were due from Alabama in a couple of days, but Leif was still nowhere to be found. Eddie and I had called Leif's friends and the parents of his friends, leaving pleading messages, asking him to call, but he hadn't called. I decided to leave the hospital for one night so I could find him and bring him to the hospital once and for all.

"I'll be back in the morning," I said to my mother. I looked over at Eddie, half lying on the little vinyl couch. "I'll come back with Leif."

When she heard his name, she opened her eyes: blue and blazing, the same as they'd always been. In all this, they hadn't changed.

"How can you not be mad at him?" I asked her bitterly for perhaps the tenth time.

"You can't squeeze blood from a turnip," she'd usually say. Or, "Cheryl, he's only eighteen." But this time she just gazed at me and said, "Honey," the same as she had when I'd gotten angry about her socks. The same as she'd always done when she'd seen me suffer because I wanted something to be different than it was and she was trying to convince me with that single word that I must accept things as they were.

"We'll all be together tomorrow," I said. "And then we'll all stay here with you, okay? None of us will leave." I reached through the tubes that were draped all around her and stroked her shoulder. "I love you," I said, bending to kiss her cheek, though she fended me off, in too much pain to endure even a kiss.

"Love," she whispered, too weak to say the *I* and *you*. "Love," she said again as I left her room.

I rode the elevator and went out to the cold street and walked along the sidewalk. I passed a bar packed with people I could see through a big plate-glass window. They were all wearing shiny green paper hats and green shirts and green suspenders and drinking green beer. A man inside met my eye and pointed at me drunkenly, his face breaking into silent laughter.

I drove home and fed the horses and hens and got on the phone, the dogs gratefully licking my hands, our cat nudging his way onto my lap. I called everyone who might know where my brother was. He was drinking a lot, some said. Yes, it was true, said others, he'd been hanging out with a girl from St. Cloud named Sue. At midnight the phone rang and I told him that *this was it*.

I wanted to scream at him when he walked in the door a half hour later, to shake him and rage and accuse, but when I saw him, all I could do was hold him and cry. He seemed so old to me that night, and so very young too. For the first time, I saw that he'd become a man and yet also I could see what a little boy he was. *My* little boy, the one I'd half mothered all of my life, having no choice but to help my mom all those times she'd been away at work. Karen and I were three years apart, but we'd been raised as if we were practically twins, the two of us equally in charge of Leif as kids.

"I can't do this," he kept repeating through his tears. "I can't live without Mom. I can't. I can't. I can't."

"We have to," I replied, though I couldn't believe it myself. We lay together in his single bed talking and crying into the wee hours until, side by side, we drifted off to sleep.

I woke a few hours later and, before waking Leif, fed the animals and loaded bags full of food we could eat during our vigil at the hospital. By eight o'clock we were on our way to Duluth, my brother driving our mother's car too fast while U2's *Joshua Tree* blasted out of the speakers. We listened intently to the music without talking, the low sun cutting brightly into the snow on the sides of the road.

When we reached our mother's room at the hospital, we saw a sign on her closed door instructing us to check in at the nurse's station before entering. This was a new thing, but I assumed it was only a procedural matter. A nurse approached us in the hallway as we walked toward the station, and before I spoke she said, "We have ice on her eyes. She wanted to donate her corneas, so we need to keep the ice—"

"*What?*" I said with such intensity that she jumped.

I didn't wait for an answer. I ran to my mother's room, my brother right behind me. When I opened the door, Eddie stood and came for us with his arms outstretched, but I swerved away and dove for my mom. Her arms lay waxen at her sides, yellow and white and black and blue, the needles and tubes removed. Her eyes were covered by two surgical gloves packed with ice, their fat fingers lolling clownishly across her face. When I grabbed her, the gloves slid off. Bouncing onto the bed, then onto the floor.

I howled and howled and howled, rooting my face into her body like an animal. She'd been dead an hour. Her limbs had cooled, but her belly was still an island of warm. I pressed my face into the warmth and howled some more.

I dreamed of her incessantly. In the dreams I was always with her when she died. It was me who would kill her. Again and again and again. She commanded me to do it, and each time I would get down on my knees and cry, begging her not to make me, but she would not relent, and each time, like a good daughter, I ultimately complied. I tied her to a tree in our front yard and poured gasoline over her head, then lit her on fire. I made her run down the dirt road that passed by the house we'd built and then ran her over with my truck. I dragged her body, caught on a jagged piece of metal underneath, until it came loose, and then I put my truck in reverse and ran her over again. I took a miniature baseball bat and beat her to death with it, slow and hard and sad. I forced her into a hole I'd dug and kicked dirt and stones on top of her and buried her alive. These dreams were not surreal. They took place in plain, ordinary light. They were the documentary films of my subconscious and felt as real to me as life. My truck was really my truck; our front yard was our actual front yard; the miniature baseball bat sat in our closet among the umbrellas.

I didn't wake from these dreams crying. I woke shrieking. Paul grabbed me and held me until I was quiet. He wetted a washcloth with cool water and put it over my face. But those wet washcloths couldn't wash the dreams of my mother away.

Nothing did. Nothing would. Nothing could ever bring my mother back or make it okay that she was gone. Nothing would put me beside her the moment she died. It broke me up. It cut me off. It tumbled me end over end.

It took me years to take my place among the ten thousand things again. To be the woman my mother raised. To remember how she said *honey* and picture her particular gaze. I would suffer. I would suffer. I would want things to be different than they were. The wanting was a wilderness and I had to find my own way out of the woods. It took me four years, seven months, and three days to do it. I didn't know where I was going until I got there.

It was a place called the Bridge of the Gods.

2

SPLITTING

If I had to draw a map of those four-plus years to illustrate the time between the day of my mother's death and the day I began my hike on the Pacific Crest Trail, the map would be a confusion of lines in all directions, like a crackling Fourth of July sparkler with Minnesota at its inevitable center. To Texas and back. To New York City and back. To New Mexico and Arizona and Nevada and California and Oregon and back. To Wyoming and back. To Portland, Oregon, and back. To Portland and back again. And again. But those lines wouldn't tell the story. The map would illuminate all the places I ran to, but not all the ways I tried to stay. It wouldn't show you how in the months after my mother died, I attempted—and failed—to fill in for her in an effort to keep my family together. Or how I'd struggled to save my marriage, even while I was dooming it with my lies. It would only seem like that rough star, its every bright line shooting out.

By the time I arrived in the town of Mojave, California, on the night before I began hiking the PCT, I'd shot out of Minnesota for the last time. I'd even told my mother that, not that she could hear. I'd sat in the flowerbed in the woods on our land, where Eddie, Paul, my siblings, and I had mixed her ashes in with the dirt and laid a tombstone, and explained to her that I wasn't going to be around to tend her grave anymore. Which meant that no one would. I finally had no choice but to leave her grave to go back to the weeds and blown-down tree branches and fallen pinecones. To snow and whatever the ants and deer and black bears and ground wasps wanted to do with her. I lay down in the mother ash dirt among the crocuses and told her it was okay. That I'd surrendered. That since she died, everything had changed. Things she couldn't have imagined and wouldn't have guessed. My words came out low and steadfast. I was so sad it felt as if someone were choking me, and yet it seemed my whole life depended on my getting those words out. She would always be my mother, I told her, but I had to go. She wasn't there for me in that flowerbed anymore anyway, I explained. I'd put her somewhere else. The only place I could reach her. In me.

The next day I left Minnesota forever. I was going to hike the PCT.

It was the first week of June. I drove to Portland in my 1979 Chevy Luv pickup truck loaded with a dozen boxes filled with dehydrated food and backpacking supplies. I'd spent the previous weeks compiling them, addressing each box to myself at places I'd never been, stops along the PCT with evocative names like Echo Lake and Soda Springs, Burney Falls and Seiad Valley. I left my truck and the boxes with my friend Lisa in Portland—she'd be mailing the boxes to me throughout the summer—and boarded a plane to Los Angeles, then caught a ride to Mojave with the brother of a friend.

We pulled into town in the early evening, the sun dipping into the Tehachapi Mountains a dozen miles behind us to the west. Mountains I'd be hiking the next day. The town of Mojave is at an altitude of nearly 2,800 feet, though it felt to me as if I were at the bottom of something instead, the signs for gas stations, restaurants, and motels rising higher than the highest tree.

"You can stop here," I said to the man who'd driven me from LA, gesturing to an old-style neon sign that said WHITE'S MOTEL with the word TELEVISION blazing yellow above it and VACANCY in pink beneath. By the worn look of the building, I guessed it was the cheapest place in town. Perfect for me.

"Thanks for the ride," I said once we'd pulled into the lot.

"You're welcome," he said, and looked at me. "You sure you're okay?"

"Yes," I replied with false confidence. "I've traveled alone a lot." I got out with my backpack and two oversized plastic department store bags full of things. I'd meant to take everything from the bags and fit it into my backpack before leaving Portland, but I hadn't had the time. I'd brought the bags here instead. I'd get everything together in my room.

"Good luck," said the man.

I watched him drive away. The hot air tasted like dust, the dry wind whipping my hair into my eyes. The parking lot was a field of tiny white pebbles cemented into place; the motel, a long row of doors and windows shuttered by shabby curtains. I slung my backpack over my shoulders and gathered the bags. It seemed strange to have only these things. I felt suddenly exposed, less exuberant than I had thought I would. I'd spent the past six months imagining this moment, but now that it was here—now that I was only a dozen miles from the PCT itself—it seemed less vivid than it had in my imaginings, as if I were in a dream, my every thought liquid slow, propelled by will rather than instinct. *Go inside,* I had to tell myself before I could move toward the motel office. *Ask for a room.*

"It's eighteen dollars," said the old woman who stood behind the counter. With rude emphasis, she looked past me, out the glass door through which I'd entered moments before. "Unless you've got a companion. It's more for two."

"I don't have a companion," I said, and blushed—it was only when I was telling the truth that I felt as if I were lying. "That guy was just dropping me off."

"It's eighteen dollars for now, then," she replied, "but if a companion joins you, you'll have to pay more."

"A companion won't be joining me," I said evenly. I pulled a twenty-dollar bill from the pocket of my shorts and slid it across the counter to her. She took my money and handed me two dollars and a card to fill out with a pen attached to a bead chain. "I'm on foot, so I can't do the car section," I said, gesturing to the form. I smiled, but she didn't smile back. "Also—I don't really have an address. I'm traveling, so I—"

"Write down the address you'll be returning to," she said.

"See, that's the thing. I'm not sure where I'll live afterwards because—"

"Your folks, then," she barked. "Wherever home is."

"Okay," I said, and wrote Eddie's address, though in truth my connection to Eddie in the four years since my mother died had become so pained and distant I couldn't rightly consider him my stepfather anymore. I had no "home," even though the house we built still stood. Leif and Karen and I were inextricably bound as siblings, but we spoke and saw one another rarely, our lives profoundly different. Paul and I had finalized our divorce the month before, after a harrowing yearlong separation. I had beloved friends whom I sometimes referred to as family, but our commitments to each other were informal and intermittent, more familial in word than in deed. *Blood is thicker than water,* my mother had always said when I was growing up, a sentiment I'd often disputed. But it turned out that it didn't matter whether she was right or wrong. They both flowed out of my cupped palms.

"Here you are," I said to the woman, sliding the form across the counter in her direction, though she didn't turn to me for several moments. She was watching a small television that sat on a table behind the counter. The evening news. Something about the O. J. Simpson trial.

"Do you think he's guilty?" she asked, still looking at the TV.

"It seems like it, but it's too soon to know, I guess. We don't have all the information yet."

"Of course he did it!" she shouted.

When she finally gave me a key, I walked across the parking lot to a door at the far end of the building, unlocked it and went inside, and set my things down and sat on the soft bed. I was in the Mojave Desert, but the room was strangely dank, smelling of wet carpet and Lysol. A vented white metal box in the corner roared to life—a swamp cooler that blew icy air for a few minutes and then turned itself off with a dramatic clatter that only exacerbated my sense of uneasy solitude.

I thought about going out and finding myself a companion. It was such an easy thing to do. The previous years had been a veritable feast of one- and two- and three-night stands. They seemed so ridiculous to me now, all that intimacy with people I didn't love, and yet still I ached for the simple sensation of a body pressed against mine, obliterating everything else. I stood up from the bed to shake off the longing, to stop my mind from its hungry whir: *I could go to a bar. I could let a man buy me a drink. We could be back here in a flash.*

Just behind that longing was the urge to call Paul. He was my ex-husband now, but he was still my best friend. As much as I'd pulled away from him in the years after my mother's death, I'd also leaned hard into him. In the midst of my mostly silent agonizing over our marriage, we'd had good times, been, in oddly real ways, a *happy couple.*

The vented metal box in the corner turned itself on again and I went to stand before it, letting the frigid air blow against my bare legs. I was dressed in the clothes I'd been wearing since I'd left Portland the night before, every last thing brand-new. It was my hiking outfit and in it I felt a bit foreign, like someone I hadn't yet become. Wool socks beneath a pair of leather hiking boots with metal fasts. Navy blue shorts with important-looking pockets that closed with Velcro tabs. Underwear made of a special quick-dry fabric and a plain white T-shirt over a sports bra.

They were among the many things I'd spent the winter and spring saving up my money to buy, working as many shifts as I could get at the restaurant where I waited tables. When I'd purchased them, they hadn't felt foreign to me. In spite of my recent forays into edgy urban life, I was easily someone who could be described as *outdoorsy*. I had, after all, spent my teen years roughing it in the Minnesota northwoods. My family vacations had always involved some form of camping, and so had the trips I'd taken with Paul or alone or with friends. I'd slept in the back of my truck, camped out in parks and national forests more times than I could count. But now, here, having only these clothes at hand, I felt suddenly like a fraud. In the six months since I'd decided to hike the PCT, I'd had at least a dozen conversations in which I explained why this trip was a good idea and how well suited I was to the challenge. But now, alone in my room at White's Motel, I knew there was no denying the fact that I was on shaky ground.

"Perhaps you should try a shorter trip first," Paul had suggested when I told him about my plan during one of our should-we-stay-together-or-get-divorced discussions several months before.

"Why?" I'd asked with irritation. "Don't you think I can hack it?"

"It isn't that," he said. "It's only that you've never gone backpacking, as far as I know."

"I've gone backpacking!" I'd said indignantly, though he was right: I hadn't. In spite of all the things I'd done that struck me as related to backpacking, I'd never actually walked into the wilderness with a backpack on and spent the night. Not even once.

I've never gone backpacking! I thought with a rueful hilarity now. I looked suddenly at my pack and the plastic bags I'd toted with me from Portland that held things I hadn't yet taken from their packaging. My backpack was forest green and trimmed with black, its body composed of three large compartments rimmed by fat pockets of mesh and nylon that sat on either side like big ears. It stood of its own volition, supported by the unique plastic shelf that jutted out along its bottom. That it stood like that instead of slumping over onto its side as other packs did provided me a small, strange comfort. I went to it and touched its top as if I were caressing a child's head. A month ago, I'd been firmly advised to pack my backpack just as I would on my hike and take it on a trial run. I'd meant to do it before I left Minneapolis, and then I'd meant to do it once I got to Portland. But I hadn't. My trial run would be tomorrow—my first day on the trail.

I reached into one of the plastic bags and pulled out an orange whistle, whose packaging proclaimed it to be "the world's loudest." I ripped it open and held the whistle up by its yellow lanyard, then put it around my neck, as if I were a coach. Was I supposed to hike wearing it like this? It seemed silly, but I didn't know. Like so much else, when I'd purchased the world's loudest whistle, I hadn't thought it all the way through. I took it off and tied it to the frame of my pack, so it would dangle over my shoulder when I hiked. There, it would be easy to reach, should I need it.

Would I need it? I wondered meekly, bleakly, flopping down on the bed. It was well past dinnertime, but I was too anxious to feel hungry, my aloneness an uncomfortable *thunk* that filled my gut.

"You finally got what you wanted," Paul had said when we bade each other goodbye in Minneapolis ten days before.

"What's that?" I'd asked.

"To be alone," he replied, and smiled, though I could only nod uncertainly.

It had been what I wanted, though *alone* wasn't quite it. What I had to have when it came to love was beyond explanation, it seemed. The end of my marriage was a great unraveling that began with a letter that arrived a week after my mother's death, though its beginnings went back further than that.

The letter wasn't for me. It was for Paul. Fresh as my grief was, I still dashed excitedly into our bedroom and handed it to him when I saw the return address. It was from the New School in New York City. In another lifetime—only three months before, in the days before I learned my mother had cancer—I'd helped him apply to a PhD program in political philosophy. Back in mid-January, the idea of living in New York City had seemed like the most exciting thing in the world. But now, in late March—as he ripped the letter open and exclaimed that he'd been accepted, as I embraced him and in every way seemed to be celebrating this good news—I felt myself splitting in two. There was the woman I was before my mom died and the one I was now, my old life sitting on the surface of me like a bruise. The real me was beneath that, pulsing under all the things I used to think I knew. How I'd finish my BA in June and a couple of months later, off we'd go. How we'd rent an apartment in the East Village or Park Slope—places I'd only imagined and read about. How I'd wear funky ponchos with adorable knitted hats and cool boots while becoming a writer in the same romantic, down-and-out way that so many of my literary heroes and heroines had.

All of that was impossible now, regardless of what the letter said. My mom was dead. My mom was dead. My mom was dead. Everything I ever imagined about myself had disappeared into the crack of her last breath.

I couldn't leave Minnesota. My family needed me. Who would help Leif finish growing up? Who would be there for Eddie in his loneliness? Who would make Thanksgiving dinner and carry on our family traditions? Someone had to keep what remained of our family together. And that someone had to be me. I owed at least that much to my mother.

"You should go without me," I said to Paul as he held the letter. And I said it again and again as we talked throughout the next weeks, my conviction growing by the day. Part of me was terrified by the idea of him leaving me; another part of me desperately hoped he would. If he left, the door of our marriage would swing shut without my having to kick it. I would be free and nothing would be my fault. I loved him, but I'd been impetuous and nineteen when we'd wed; not remotely ready to commit myself to another person, no matter how dear he was. Though I'd had attractions to other men since shortly after we married, I'd kept them in check. But I couldn't do that anymore. My grief obliterated my ability to hold back. So much had been denied me, I reasoned. Why should I deny myself?

My mom had been dead a week when I kissed another man. And another a week after that. I only made out with them and the others that followed—vowing not to cross a sexual line that held some meaning to me—but still I knew I was wrong to cheat and lie. I felt trapped by my own inability to either leave Paul or stay true, so I waited for him to leave me, to go off to graduate school alone, though of course he refused.

He deferred his admission for a year and we stayed in Minnesota so I could be near my family, though my nearness in the year that followed my mother's death accomplished little. It turned out I wasn't able to keep my family together. I wasn't my mom. It was only after her death that I realized who she was: the apparently magical force at the center of our family who'd kept us all invisibly spinning in the powerful orbit around her. Without her, Eddie slowly became a stranger. Leif and Karen and I drifted into our own lives. Hard as I fought for it to be otherwise, finally I had to admit it too: without my mother, we weren't what we'd been; we were four people floating separately among the flotsam of our grief, connected by only the thinnest rope. I never did make that Thanksgiving dinner. By the time Thanksgiving rolled around eight months after my mom died, my family was something I spoke of in the past tense.

So when Paul and I finally moved to New York City a year after we had originally intended to, I was happy to go. There, I could have a fresh start. I would stop messing around with men. I would stop grieving so fiercely. I would stop raging over the family I used to have. I would be a writer who lived in New York City. I would walk around wearing cool boots and an adorable knitted hat.

It didn't go that way. I was who I was: the same woman who pulsed beneath the bruise of her old life, only now I was somewhere else.

During the day I wrote stories; at night I waited tables and made out with one of the two men I was simultaneously not *crossing the line* with. We'd lived in New York only a month when Paul dropped out of graduate school, deciding he wanted to play guitar instead. Six months later, we left altogether, returning briefly to Minnesota before departing on a months-long working road trip all across the West, making a wide circle that included the Grand Canyon and Death Valley, Big Sur and San Francisco. At trip's end in late spring, we landed in Portland and found restaurant jobs, staying first with my friend Lisa in her tiny apartment and then on a farm ten miles outside the city, where—in exchange for looking after a goat and a cat and a covey of exotic game hens—we got to live rent-free for the summer. We pulled the futon from our truck and slept on it in the living room under a big wide window that looked out over a filbert orchard. We took long walks and picked berries and made love. *I can do this,* I thought. *I can be Paul's wife.*

But again I was wrong. I could only be who it seemed I had to be. Only now more so. I didn't even remember the woman I was before my life had split in two. Living in that little farmhouse on the edge of Portland, a few months past the second anniversary of my mother's death, I wasn't worried about crossing the line anymore. When Paul accepted a job offer in Minneapolis that required him to return to Minnesota midway through our exotic hen-sitting gig, I stayed behind in Oregon and fucked the ex-boyfriend of the woman who owned the exotic hens. I fucked a cook at the restaurant where I'd picked up a job waiting tables. I fucked a massage therapist who gave me a piece of banana cream pie and a free massage. All three of them over the span of five days.

It seemed to me the way it must feel to people who cut themselves on purpose. Not pretty, but clean. Not good, but void of regret. I was trying to heal. Trying to get the bad out of my system so I could be good again. To cure me of myself. At summer's end, when I returned to Minneapolis to live with Paul, I believed I had. I thought I was different, better, *done*. And I was for a time, sailing faithfully through the autumn and into the new year. Then I had another affair. I knew I was at the end of a line. I couldn't bear myself any longer. I had to finally speak the words to Paul that would tear my life apart. Not that I didn't love him. But that I had to be alone, though I didn't know why.

My mom had been dead three years.

When I said all the things I had to say, we both fell onto the floor and sobbed. The next day, Paul moved out. Slowly we told our friends that we were splitting up. We hoped we could work it out, we said. We were not necessarily going to get divorced. First, they were in disbelief—we'd seemed so *happy*, they all said. Next, they were mad—not at us, but at me. One of my dearest friends took the photograph of me she kept in a frame, ripped it in half, and mailed it to me. Another made out with Paul. When I was hurt and jealous about this, I was told by another friend that this was exactly what I deserved: a taste of my own medicine. I couldn't rightfully disagree, but still my heart was broken. I lay alone on our futon feeling myself almost levitate from pain.

Three months into our separation, we were still in a torturous limbo. I wanted neither to get back together with Paul nor to get divorced. I wanted to be two people so I could do both. Paul was dating a smatter-ing of women, but I was suddenly celibate. Now that I'd smashed up my marriage over sex, sex was the furthest thing from my mind.

"You need to get the hell out of Minneapolis," said my friend Lisa during one of our late-night heartbreak conversations. "Come visit me in Portland," she said.

Within the week, I quit my waitressing job, loaded up my truck, and drove west, traveling the same route I'd take exactly one year later on my way to hike the Pacific Crest Trail.

By the time I reached Montana, I knew I'd done the right thing—the wide green land visible for miles outside my windshield, the sky going on even farther. The city of Portland flickered beyond, out of sight. It would be my luscious escape, if only for a brief time. There, I'd leave my troubles behind, I thought.

Instead, I only found more.

3

HUNCHING IN A REMOTELY
UPRIGHT POSITION

When I woke the next morning in my room at White's Motel, I showered and stood naked in front of the mirror, watching myself solemnly brush my teeth. I tried to feel something like excitement but came up only with a morose unease. Every now and then I could see myself—truly see myself—and a sentence would come to me, thundering like a god into my head, and as I saw myself then in front of that tarnished mirror what came was *the woman with the hole in her heart.* That was me. That was why I'd longed for a companion the night before. That was why I was here, naked in a motel, with this preposterous idea of hiking alone for three months on the PCT. I set my toothbrush down, then leaned into the mirror and stared into my own eyes. I could feel myself disintegrating inside myself like a past-bloom flower in the wind. Every time I moved a muscle, another petal of me blew away. *Please,* I thought. *Please.*

I went to the bed and looked at my hiking outfit. I'd laid it out carefully on the bed before I'd gotten into the shower, the way my mom had done for me when I was a child on the first day of school. When I put on my bra and T-shirt, the tiny scabs that still rimmed my new tattoo caught on the shirt's sleeve and I delicately picked at them. It was my only tattoo—a blue horse on my left deltoid. Paul had one to match. We'd had them done together in honor of our divorce, which had become final only the month before. We weren't married anymore, but the tattoos seemed proof to us of our everlasting bond.

I wanted to call Paul even more desperately than I had the previous night, but I couldn't let myself. He knew me too well. He'd hear the sorrow and hesitation in my voice and discern that it was not only that I felt anxious about beginning on the PCT. He'd sense that I had something to tell.

I put my socks on and laced up my boots, went to the window, and pushed the curtain back. The sun was blinding against the white stones of the parking lot. There was a gas station across the way—a good place to hitch a ride to the PCT, I supposed. When I let go of the curtain, the room went dark again. I liked it that way, like a safe cocoon that I'd never have to leave, though I knew I was wrong. It was nine in the morning and already hot outside, the vented white box in the corner come alive with its breezy roar. In spite of everything that implied I was going nowhere, I had someplace to be: it was day 1 on the PCT.

I opened the compartments of my pack and pulled everything out, tossing each item onto the bed. I lifted the plastic bags and emptied them too, then stared at the pile of things. It was everything I had to carry for the next three months.

There was a blue compression sack that held the clothes I wasn't already wearing—a pair of fleece pants, a long-sleeved thermal shirt, a thick fleece anorak with a hood, two pair of wool socks and two pair of underwear, a thin pair of gloves, a sun hat, a fleece hat, and rain pants—and another, sturdier sack called a dry bag, packed to the gills with all the food I'd need over the next fourteen days, before I reached my first resupply stop at a place called Kennedy Meadows. There was a sleeping bag and a camp chair that could be unclipped to use as a sleeping pad and a headlamp like the kind miners wear and five bungee cords. There was a water purifier and a tiny collapsible stove, a tall aluminum canister of gas, and a little pink lighter. There was a small cooking pot nested inside a larger cooking pot and utensils that folded in half and a cheap pair of sports sandals I intended to wear in camp at the end of each day. There was a quick-dry pack towel, a thermometer keychain, a tarp, and an insulated plastic mug with a handle. There was a snakebite kit and a Swiss army knife, a miniature pair of binoculars in a fake leather zip-up case and a coil of fluorescent-colored rope, a compass I hadn't yet learned how to use and a book that would teach me how to use the compass called *Staying Found* that I had intended to read on the plane to LA, but hadn't. There was a first aid kit in a pristine red canvas case that snapped shut and a roll of toilet paper in a ziplock bag and a stainless-steel trowel that had its own black sheath that said U-Dig-It on the front. There was a small bag of toiletries and personal items I thought I'd need along the way—shampoo and conditioner, soap and lotion and deodorant, nail clippers and insect repellent and sunscreen, a hairbrush and a natural menstrual sponge, and a tube of waterproof sunblock lip balm. There was a flashlight and a metal candle lantern with a votive candle inside and an extra candle and a foldable saw—for what, I did not know—and a green nylon bag with my tent inside. There were two 32-ounce plastic water bottles and a dromedary bag capable of holding 2.6 gallons of water and a nylon fist that unfurled into a rain cover for my backpack and a Gore-Tex ball that opened up to become my raincoat. There were things I brought in case the other things I brought failed—extra batteries, a box of waterproof matches, a Mylar blanket, and a bottle of iodine pills. There were two pens and three books in addition to *Staying Found*: *The Pacific Crest Trail, Volume 1: California* (the very guidebook that had set me off on this journey, written by a quartet of authors who spoke in one calm but stern voice about the rigors and rewards of the trail), William Faulkner's *As I Lay Dying,* and Adrienne Rich's *The Dream of a Common Language*. There was an eight-by-eleven two-hundred-page hardback sketchbook that I used as a journal and a ziplock bag with my driver's license inside and a small wad of cash, a sheaf of postage stamps, and a tiny spiral notebook with the addresses of friends scrawled on a few pages. There was a full-sized, professional-quality 35-millimeter Minolta X-700 camera with a separate attachable zoom lens and another separate attachable flash and a tiny collapsible tripod, all of which was packed inside a padded camera case the size of a football.

Not that I was a photographer.

I'd gone to an outdoor store in Minneapolis called REI about a dozen times over the previous months to purchase a good portion of these items. Seldom was this a straightforward affair. To buy even a water bottle without first thoroughly considering the latest water bottle technology was folly, I quickly learned. There were the pros and cons of various materials to take into account, not to mention the research that had been done regarding design. And this was only the smallest, least complex of the purchases I had to make. The rest of the gear I would need was ever more complex, I realized after consulting with the men and women of REI, who inquired hopefully if they could help me whenever they spotted me before displays of ultralight stoves or strolling among the tents. These employees ranged in age and manner and area of wilderness adventure proclivity, but what they had in common was that every last one of them could talk about gear, with interest and nuance, for a length of time that was so dumbfounding that I was ultimately bedazzled by it. They *cared* if my sleeping bag had snag-free zipper guards and a face muff that allowed the hood to be cinched snug without obstructing my breathing. They took *pleasure* in the fact that my water purifier had a pleated glass-fiber element for increased surface area. And their knowledge had a way of rubbing off on me. By the time I made the decision about which backpack to purchase—a top-of-the-line Gregory hybrid external frame that claimed to have the balance and agility of an internal—I felt as if I'd become a backpacking expert.

It was only as I stood gazing at that pile of meticulously chosen gear on the bed in my Mojave motel room that I knew with profound humility that I was not.

I worked my way through the mountain of things, wedging and cramming and forcing them into every available space of my pack until nothing more could possibly fit. I had planned to use the bungee cords to attach my food bag, tent, tarp, clothing sack, and camp chair that doubled as a sleeping pad to the outside of my pack—in the places on the external frame meant for that purpose—but now it was apparent that there were other things that would have to go on the outside too. I pulled the bungee cords around all the things I'd planned to and then looped a few extra things through them as well: the straps of my sandals and the camera case and the handles of the insulated mug and the candle lantern. I clipped the metal trowel in its U-Dig-It sheath to my backpack's belt and attached the keychain that was a thermometer to one of my pack's zippers.

When I was done, I sat on the floor, sweaty from my exertions, and stared peaceably at my pack. And then I remembered one last thing: water.

I'd chosen to begin my hike where I had simply because from there I estimated it would take me about a hundred days to walk to Ashland, Oregon—the place I'd originally planned to end my hike because I'd heard good things about the town and thought I might like to stay there to live. Months ago, I'd traced my finger southward down the map, adding up the miles and the days, and stopped at Tehachapi Pass, where the PCT crosses Highway 58 in the northwest corner of the Mojave Desert, not far from the town of Mojave. What I hadn't realized until a couple of weeks before was that I was beginning my hike on one of the driest sections of the trail, a section where even the fastest, fittest, and most seasoned hikers couldn't always get from one water source to another each day. For me, it would be impossible. It would take me two days to reach the first water source seventeen miles into my hike, I guessed, so I would have to carry enough to get me through.

I filled my 32-ounce bottles in the bathroom sink and put them in my pack's mesh side pockets. I dug out my dromedary bag from the place I'd crammed it in my pack's main compartment and filled up all 2.6 gallons of it. Water, I later learned, weighs 8.3 pounds a gallon. I don't know how much my pack weighed on that first day, but I do know the water alone was 24.5 pounds. And it was an unwieldy 24.5 pounds. The dromedary bag was like a giant flattish water balloon, sloshing and buckling and slipping out of my hands and flipping itself onto the floor as I attempted to secure it to my pack. The bag was rimmed with webbing straps; with great effort I wove the bungee cords through them, next to the camera bag and sandals and the insulated cup and candle lantern, until I grew so frustrated that I pulled out the insulated cup and threw it across the room.

Finally, when everything I was going to carry was in the place that I needed to carry it, a hush came over me. I was ready to begin. I put on my watch, looped my sunglasses around my neck by their pink neoprene holder, donned my hat, and looked at my pack. It was at once enormous and compact, mildly adorable and intimidatingly self-contained. It had an animate quality; in its company, I didn't feel entirely alone. Standing, it came up to my waist. I gripped it and bent to lift it.

It wouldn't budge.

I squatted and grasped its frame more robustly and tried to lift it again. Again it did not move. Not even an inch. I tried to lift it with both hands, with my legs braced beneath me, while attempting to wrap it in a bear hug, with all of my breath and my might and my will, with everything in me. And still it would not come. It was exactly like attempting to lift a Volkswagen Beetle. It looked so cute, so *ready* to be lifted—and yet it was impossible to do.

I sat down on the floor beside it and pondered my situation. How could I carry a backpack more than a thousand miles over rugged mountains and waterless deserts if I couldn't even budge it an inch in an air-conditioned motel room? The notion was preposterous and yet I *had* to lift that pack. It hadn't occurred to me that I wouldn't be able to. I'd simply thought that if I added up all the things I needed in order to go backpacking, it would equal a weight that I could carry. The people at REI, it was true, had mentioned weight rather often in their soliloquies, but I hadn't paid much attention. It seemed there had been more important questions to consider. Like whether a face muff allowed the hood to be cinched snug without obstructing my breathing.

I thought about what I might take out of my pack, but each item struck me as either so obviously needed or so in-case-of-emergency necessary that I didn't dare remove it. I would have to try to carry the pack as it was.

I scooted over the carpet and situated myself on my rump right in front of my pack, wove my arms through the shoulder straps, and clipped the sternum strap across my chest. I took a deep breath and began rocking back and forth to gain momentum, until finally I hurled myself forward with everything in me and got myself onto my hands and knees. My backpack was no longer on the floor. It was officially attached to me. It still seemed like a Volkswagen Beetle, only now it seemed like a Volkswagen Beetle that was parked on my back. I stayed there for a few moments, trying to get my balance. Slowly, I worked my feet beneath me while simultaneously scaling the metal cooling unit with my hands until I was vertical enough that I could do a dead lift. The frame of the pack squeaked as I rose, it too straining from the tremendous weight. By the time I was standing—which is to say, hunching in a remotely upright position—I was holding the vented metal panel that I'd accidentally ripped loose from the cooling unit in my efforts.

I couldn't even begin to reattach it. The place it needed to go was only inches out of my reach, but those inches were entirely out of the question. I propped the panel against the wall, buckled my hip belt, and staggered and swayed around the room, my center of gravity pulled in any direction I so much as leaned. The weight dug painfully into the tops of my shoulders, so I cinched my hip belt tighter and tighter still, trying to balance the burden, squeezing my middle so tightly that my flesh ballooned out on either side. My pack rose up like a mantle behind me, towering several inches above my head, and gripped me like a vise all the way down to my tailbone. It felt pretty awful, and yet perhaps this was how it felt to be a backpacker.

I didn't know.

I only knew that it was time to go, so I opened the door and stepped into the light.

PART TWO

TRACKS

The words are purposes.
The words are maps.

ADRIENNE RICH,
"Diving into the Wreck"

Will you take me as I am?
Will you?

JONI MITCHELL,
"California"

4

THE PACIFIC CREST TRAIL, VOLUME 1: CALIFORNIA

I'd done a lot of dumb and dangerous things in my life, but soliciting a ride with a stranger was not yet one of them. Horrible things happened to hitchhikers, I knew, especially to women hitchhiking alone. They were raped and decapitated. Tortured and left for dead. But as I made my way from White's Motel to the nearby gas station, I could not allow such thoughts to distract me. Unless I wanted to walk twelve miles along the broiling shoulder of the highway to reach the trail, I needed a ride.

Plus, hitchhiking was simply what PCT hikers *did* on occasion. And I was a PCT hiker, right? *Right?*

Right.

The Pacific Crest Trail, Volume 1: California had explained the process with its usual equanimity. On some occasions the PCT would cross a road and miles down that road would be the post office where one would have mailed the box of food and supplies needed on the next section of the trail. Hitchhiking was the only practical solution when it came to fetching those boxes and returning to the trail.

I stood near the soda machines up against the gas station building, watching people come and go, trying to work up the nerve to approach one of them, hoping I'd sense that I was safe from harm when I saw the right person. I watched old desert-grizzled men in cowboy hats and families whose cars were full already and teenagers who pulled up with music blasting out their open windows. Nobody in particular looked like a murderer or rapist, but nobody in particular didn't look like one either. I bought a can of Coke and drank it with a casual air that belied the fact that I could not stand up properly because of the unbelievable weight on my back. Finally, I had to make a move. It was nearly eleven, pitching steadily into the heat of a June day in the desert.

A minivan with Colorado plates pulled up and two men got out. One man was about my age, the other looked to be in his fifties. I approached them and asked for a ride. They hesitated and glanced at each other, their expressions making it apparent that they were united in their silent search for a reason to say no, so I kept talking, explaining in quick bursts about the PCT.

"Sure," the older one said finally, with obvious reluctance.

"Thank you," I trilled girlishly. When I hobbled toward the big door on the side of the van, the younger man rolled it open for me. I gazed inside, realizing suddenly that I had no idea how to get in. I couldn't even attempt to step up into it with my pack on. I'd have to take my pack off, and yet how? If I undid the buckles that held the backpack's straps around my waist and over my shoulders, there would be no way that I could keep it from falling so violently away from me that it might rip my arms off.

"You need a hand?" the young man asked.

"No. I've got it," I said in a falsely unruffled tone. The only thing I could think to do was turn my back to the van and squat to sit on the doorframe while clutching the edge of the sliding door, letting my pack rest on the floor behind me. It was bliss. I unclipped my pack's straps and carefully extricated myself without tipping my pack over and then turned to climb inside the van to sit beside it.

The men were friendlier to me once we were on our way, driving west through an arid landscape of parched-looking bushes and pale mountains stretching off into the distance. They were a father and son from a suburb of Denver, on their way to a graduation ceremony in San Luis Obispo. Before long, a sign announcing Tehachapi Pass appeared and the older man slowed the van and pulled to the side of the road. The younger man got out and slid the big door open for me. I'd hoped to put my pack on the same way I'd taken it off, aided by the height of the van's floor as I squatted in the doorway, but before I could step out, the man pulled out my pack and dropped it heavily in the gravelly dirt by the side of the road. It fell so hard I feared my dromedary bag would burst. I climbed out after it and pulled it back to standing position and dusted it off.

"Are you sure you can lift that?" he asked. "'Cause *I* barely can."

"Of course I can lift it," I said.

He stood there, as if waiting for me to prove it.

"Thanks for the ride," I said, wanting him to leave, so he wouldn't be witness to my humiliating pack-donning routine.

He nodded and slid the van's door shut. "Be safe out there."

"I will," I said, and watched him get back in the van.

I stood by the silent highway after they drove away. Small clouds of dust blew in swirling gusts beneath the glaring noon sun. I was at an elevation of nearly 3,800 feet, surrounded in all directions by beige, barren-looking mountains dotted with clusters of sagebrush, Joshua trees, and waist-high chaparral. I was standing at the western edge of the Mojave Desert and at the southern foot of the Sierra Nevada, the vast mountain range that stretched north for more than four hundred miles to Lassen Volcanic National Park, where it connected with the Cascade Range, which extended from northern California all the way through Oregon and Washington and beyond the Canadian border. Those two mountain ranges would be my world for the next three months; their crest, my home. On a fence post beyond the ditch I spied a palm-sized metal blaze that said PACIFIC CREST TRAIL.

I was here. I could begin at last.

It occurred to me that now would be the perfect time to take a photograph, but to unpack the camera would entail such a series of gear and bungee cord removals that I didn't even want to attempt it. Plus, in order to get myself in the picture, I'd have to find something to prop the camera on so I could set its timer and get into place before it took the shot, and nothing around me looked too promising. Even the fence post that the PCT blaze was attached to seemed too desiccated and frail. Instead, I sat down in the dirt in front of my pack, the same way I'd done in the motel room, wrested it onto my shoulders, and then hurled myself onto my hands and knees and did my dead lift to stand.

Elated, nervous, hunching in a remotely upright position, I buckled and cinched my pack and staggered the first steps down the trail to a brown metal box that was tacked to another fence post. When I lifted the lid, I saw a notebook and pen inside. It was the trail register, which

I'd read about in my guidebook. I wrote my name and the date and read the names and notes from the hikers who'd passed through in the weeks ahead of me, most of them men traveling in pairs, not one of them a woman alone. I lingered a bit longer, feeling a swell of emotion over the occasion, and then I realized there was nothing to do but go, so I did.

The trail headed east, paralleling the highway for a while, dipping down into rocky washes and back up again. *I'm hiking!* I thought. And then, *I am hiking on the Pacific Crest Trail.* It was this very act, of hiking, that had been at the heart of my belief that such a trip was a reasonable endeavor. What is hiking but walking, after all? *I can walk!* I'd argued when Paul had expressed his concern about my never actually having gone backpacking. I walked all the time. I walked for hours on end in my work as a waitress. I walked around the cities I lived in and visited. I walked for pleasure and purpose. All of these things were true. But after about fifteen minutes of walking on the PCT, it was clear that I had never walked into desert mountains in early June with a pack that weighed significantly more than half of what I did strapped onto my back.

Which, it turns out, is not very much like walking at all. Which, in fact, resembles walking less than it does hell.

I began panting and sweating immediately, dust caking my boots and calves as the trail turned north and began to climb rather than undulate. Each step was a toil, as I ascended higher and higher still, interrupted only by the occasional short descent, which was not so much a break in the hell as it was a new kind of hell because I had to brace myself against each step, lest gravity's pull cause me, with my tremendous, uncontrollable weight, to catapult forward and fall. I felt like the pack was not so much attached to me as me to it. Like I was a building with limbs, unmoored from my foundation, careening through the wilderness.

Within forty minutes, the voice inside my head was screaming, *What have I gotten myself into?* I tried to ignore it, to hum as I hiked, though humming proved too difficult to do while also panting and moaning in agony and trying to remain hunched in that remotely upright position while also propelling myself forward when I felt like a building with legs. So then I tried to simply concentrate on what I heard—my feet thudding against the dry and rocky trail, the brittle leaves and branches of the low-lying bushes I passed clattering in the hot wind—but it could not be done. The clamor of *What have I gotten myself into?* was a mighty shout. It could not be drowned out. The only possible distraction was my vigilant search for rattlesnakes. I expected one around every bend, ready to strike. The landscape was made for them, it seemed. And also for mountain lions and wilderness-savvy serial killers.

But I wasn't thinking of them.

It was a deal I'd made with myself months before and the only thing that allowed me to hike alone. I knew that if I allowed fear to overtake me, my journey was doomed. Fear, to a great extent, is born of a story we tell ourselves, and so I chose to tell myself a different story from the one women are told. I decided I was safe. I was strong. I was brave. Nothing could vanquish me. Insisting on this story was a form of mind control, but for the most part, it worked. Every time I heard a sound of unknown origin or felt something horrible cohering in my imagination, I pushed it away. I simply did not let myself become afraid. Fear begets fear. Power begets power. I willed myself to beget power. And it wasn't long before I actually *wasn't* afraid.

I was working too hard to be afraid.

I took one step and then another, moving along at barely more than a crawl. I hadn't thought that hiking the PCT would be easy. I'd known it would take some getting adjusted. But now that I was out here, I was less sure I would adjust. Hiking the PCT was different than I'd imagined. *I* was different than I'd imagined. I couldn't even remember what it was I'd imagined six months ago, back in December, when I'd first decided to do this.

I'd been driving on a stretch of highway east of Sioux Falls, South Dakota, when the idea came to me. I'd driven to Sioux Falls from Minneapolis the day before with my friend Aimee to retrieve my truck, which had been left there the week before when it broke down while a friend was borrowing it.

By the time Aimee and I arrived in Sioux Falls, my truck had been towed from the street. Now it was in a lot surrounded by a chain-link fence and buried in snow from the blizzard that had passed through a couple of days before. It had been for this blizzard that I'd gone to REI the previous day to purchase a shovel. As I waited in line to pay for it, I'd spotted a guidebook about something called the Pacific Crest Trail. I picked it up and studied its cover and read the back before returning it to its place on the shelf.

Once Aimee and I had cleared the snow away from my truck that day in Sioux Falls, I got inside and turned the key. I assumed I'd hear nothing but that dead clicking sound that automobiles make when they've got nothing left to give you, but it started right up. We could've driven back to Minneapolis then, but we decided to check into a motel for the night instead. We went out to a Mexican restaurant for an early dinner, elated with the unexpected ease of our journey. As we ate chips and salsa and drank margaritas, I got a funny feeling in my gut.

"It's like I swallowed the chips whole," I told Aimee, "like the edges are still intact and jabbing me inside." I felt full and tingly down low, like I'd never felt before. "Maybe I'm pregnant," I joked, and then the moment I said it, I realized I wasn't joking.

"Are you?" asked Aimee.

"I could be," I said, suddenly terrified. I'd had sex a few weeks before with a man named Joe. I'd met him the previous summer in Portland, when I'd gone there to visit Lisa and escape my troubles. I'd been there only a few days when he'd walked up to me in a bar and put his hand on my wrist.

"Nice," he said, outlining the sharp edges of my tin bracelet with his fingers.

He had neon punk-rock hair cut close to the scalp and a garish tattoo that covered half his arm, though his face was in precise contradiction to those disguises: tenacious and tender—like a kitten wanting milk. He was twenty-four and I was twenty-five. I hadn't slept with anyone since Paul and I had broken up three months before. That night we had sex on Joe's lumpy futon on the floor and barely slept, talking until the sun rose, mostly about him. He told me about his smart mother and his alcoholic father and the fancy and rigorous school where he'd earned his BA the year before.

"Have you ever tried heroin?" he asked in the morning.

I shook my head and laughed idly. "Should I?"

I could've let it drop. Joe had only just started using it when he met me. It was something he did separate from me, with a group of friends he'd made whom I didn't know. I could've glided right past it, but something compelled me to pause instead. I was intrigued. I was unattached. In my youth and sorrow, I was ready to self-destruct.

So I didn't just say yes to heroin. I pulled it in with both hands.

I was cuddled up with Joe, postsex, on his ratty couch the first time I used it, a week after we'd met. We took turns sucking up the smoke from a burning dab of black tar heroin that sat on a sheet of aluminum foil through a pipe that was made of foil too. Within a few days, I wasn't in Portland to visit Lisa and escape my sorrows anymore. I was in Portland falling into a drug-fueled half love with Joe. I moved into his apartment above an abandoned drugstore, where we spent most of the summer having adventuresome sex and doing heroin. In the beginning, it was a few times a week, then it was every couple of days, then it was every day. First we smoked it, then we snorted it. *But we would never shoot it!* we said. Absolutely not.

Then we shot it.

It was good. It was like something inordinately beautiful and out of this world. Like I'd found an actual planet that I didn't know had been there all along. Planet Heroin. The place where there was no pain, where it was unfortunate but essentially okay that my mother was dead and my biological father was not in my life and my family had collapsed and I couldn't manage to stay married to a man I loved.

At least that's how it felt while I was high.

In the mornings, my pain was magnified by about a thousand. In the mornings there weren't only those sad facts about my life. Now there was also the additional fact that I was a pile of shit. I'd wake in Joe's squalid room implicated by every banal thing: the lamp and the table, the book that had fallen and rested now belly-down and open, its flimsy pages buckled on the floor. In the bathroom, I'd wash my face and sob into my hands for a few fast breaths, getting ready for the waitressing job I'd picked up at a breakfast place. I'd think: *This is not me. This is not the way I am. Stop it. No more.* But in the afternoons I'd return with a wad of cash to buy another bit of heroin and I'd think: *Yes. I get to do this. I get to waste my life. I get to be junk.*

But this was not to be. Lisa called me one day and said she wanted to see me. I'd stayed in touch with her, hanging out for long afternoons at her place, telling her glimmers of what I was up to. As soon as I walked into her house this time, I knew something was up.

"So tell me about heroin," she demanded.

"Heroin?" I replied lightly. What could I possibly say? It was inexplicable, even to me. "I'm not becoming a junkie, if that's what you're worried about," I offered. I was leaning against her kitchen counter, watching her sweep the floor.

"That's what I'm worried about," she said sternly.

"Well, don't," I said. I explained it to her as rationally and playfully as I could. It had been only a couple of months. We would stop soon. Joe and I were simply messing around, doing something fun. "It's summertime!" I exclaimed. "Remember how you suggested that I come here to escape? I'm escaping." I laughed, though she didn't laugh along. I reminded her that I'd never had trouble with drugs before; that I drank alcohol with moderation and reserve. I was an experimentalist, I told her. An artist. The kind of woman who said yes instead of no.

She challenged my every statement, questioned my every rationale. She swept and swept and swept the floor as our talk turned into an argument. She eventually became so furious with me that she swatted me with the broom.

I went back to Joe's and we talked about how Lisa just didn't understand.

Then, two weeks later, Paul called.

He wanted to see me. Right now. Lisa had told him about Joe and about my using heroin, and he'd immediately driven the seventeen hundred miles straight through from Minneapolis to talk to me. I met him within the hour at Lisa's apartment. It was a warm, sunny day in late September. I'd turned twenty-six the week before. Joe hadn't remembered. It was the first birthday of my life when not one person had said happy birthday to me.

"Happy birthday," said Paul when I walked in the door.

"Thank you," I said, too formally.

"I meant to call, but I didn't have your number—I mean, Joe's."

I nodded. It was strange to see him. My husband. A phantom from my actual life. The realest person I knew. We sat at the kitchen table with the branches of a fig tree tapping on the window nearby, the broom with which Lisa had struck me propped against the wall.

He said, "You look different. You seem so . . . How can I say this? You seem like you aren't here."

I knew what he meant. The way he looked at me told me everything I'd refused to hear from Lisa. I *was* different. I wasn't there. Heroin had made me that way. And yet the idea of giving it up seemed impossible. Looking Paul squarely in the face made me realize that I couldn't think straight.

"Just tell me why you're doing this to yourself," he demanded, his eyes gentle, his face so familiar to me. He reached across the table and took my hands, and we held on to each other, locked eye to eye, tears streaming first down my face, then down his. He wanted me to go home with him that afternoon, he said evenly. Not for a reunion with him but to get away. Not from Joe, but from heroin.

I told him I needed to think. I drove back to Joe's apartment and sat in the sun on a lawn chair that Joe kept on the sidewalk outside the building. Heroin had made me dumb and distant from myself. A thought would form and then evaporate. I could not quite get ahold of my mind, even when I wasn't high. As I sat there a man walked up to me and said his name was Tim. He took my hand and shook it and told me that I could trust him. He asked if I could give him three dollars for diapers, then if he could use my phone inside the apartment, and then if I had change for a five-dollar bill, and on and on in a series of twisting questions and sorry stories that confused and compelled me to stand and pull the last ten dollars I had out of my jeans pocket.

When he saw the money, he took a knife out of his shirt. He held it almost politely to my chest and hissed, "Give me that money, sweetheart."

I packed my few things, wrote a note to Joe and taped it to the bathroom mirror, and called Paul. When he pulled up to the corner, I got into his car.

I sat in the passenger seat as we drove across the country, feeling my real life present but unattainable. Paul and I fought and cried and shook the car with our rage. We were monstrous in our cruelty and then we talked kindly afterward, shocked at each other and ourselves. We decided that we would get divorced and then that we would not. I hated him and I loved him. With him I felt trapped, branded, held, and beloved. Like a daughter.

"I didn't ask you to come and get me," I yelled in the course of one of our arguments. "You came for your own reasons. Just so you could be the big hero."

"Maybe," he said.

"Why'd you come all this way to get me?" I asked, panting with sorrow.

"Because," he said, gripping the steering wheel, staring out the windshield into the starry night. "Just because."

I saw Joe several weeks later, when he came to visit me in Minneapolis. We weren't a couple anymore, but we immediately started back up with our old ways—getting high every day for the week he was there, having sex a couple of times. But when he left, I was done. With him and with heroin. I hadn't given it another thought until I was sitting with Aimee in Sioux Falls and I noticed the bizarre being-poked-by-sharp-edges-of-uncrushed-tortilla-chips feeling in my gut.

We left the Mexican restaurant and went to a vast supermarket in search of a pregnancy test. As we walked through the brightly lit store, I silently reasoned with myself that I probably wasn't pregnant. I'd dodged that bullet so many times—fretted and worried uselessly, imagining pregnancy symptoms so convincing that I was stunned when my period arrived. But now I was twenty-six and wizened by sex; I wasn't going to fall for another scare.

Back at the motel I shut the bathroom door behind me and peed onto the test stick while Aimee sat on the bed outside. Within moments, two dark blue lines appeared on the test's tiny pane.

"I'm pregnant," I said when I came out, tears filling my eyes. Aimee and I reclined on the bed talking about it for an hour, though there was nothing much to say. That I would get an abortion was a fact so apparent it seemed silly to discuss anything else.

It takes four hours to drive from Sioux Falls to Minneapolis. Aimee followed me the next morning in her car, in case my truck broke down again. I drove without listening to the radio, thinking about my pregnancy. It was the size of a grain of rice and yet I could feel it in the deepest, strongest part of me, taking me down, shaking me up, reverberating out. Somewhere in the southwestern farmlands of Minnesota, I burst into tears, crying so hard I could barely steer, and not only for the pregnancy I didn't want. I was crying over all of it, over the sick mire I'd made of my life since my mother died; over the stupid existence that had become my own. I was not meant to be this way, to live this way, to fail so darkly.

It was then that I remembered that guidebook I'd plucked from a shelf at REI while waiting to buy the shovel a couple of days before. The thought of the photograph of a boulder-strewn lake surrounded by rocky crags and blue sky on its cover seemed to break me open, frank as a fist to the face. I believed I'd only been killing time when I'd picked up the book while standing in line, but now it seemed like something more—a sign. Not only of what I could do, but of what I had to do.

When Aimee and I reached Minneapolis, I waved her off at her exit, but I didn't go to mine. Instead, I drove to REI and bought *The Pacific Crest Trail, Volume 1: California* and took it back to my apartment and stayed up reading it all night. I read it a dozen times over the next months. I got an abortion and learned how to make dehydrated tuna flakes and turkey jerky and took a refresher course on basic first aid and practiced using my water purifier in my kitchen sink. I had to change. *I had to change* was the thought that drove me in those months of planning. Not into a different person, but back to the person I used to be—strong and responsible, clear-eyed and driven, ethical and good. And the PCT would make me that way. There, I'd walk and think about my entire life. I'd find my strength again, far from everything that had made my life ridiculous.

But here I was, on the PCT, ridiculous again, though in a different way, hunching in an ever-more-remotely upright position on the first day of my hike.

Three hours in, I came to a rare level spot near a gathering of Joshua trees, yuccas, and junipers and stopped to rest. To my monumental relief, there was a large boulder upon which I could sit and remove my pack in the same fashion I had in the van in Mojave. Amazed to be free of its weight, I strolled around and accidentally brushed up against one of the Joshua trees and was bayoneted by its sharp spikes. Blood instantly spurted out of three stab wounds on my arm. The wind blew so fiercely that when I removed my first aid kit from my pack and opened it up, all of my Band-Aids blew away. I chased them uselessly across the flat plain and then they were gone, down the mountain and out of reach. I sat in the dirt and pressed the sleeve of my T-shirt against my arm and took several swigs from my water bottle.

I'd never been so exhausted in all of my life. Part of it was due to my body adjusting to the exertion and the elevation—I was up at about 5,000 feet now, 1,200 feet higher than where I'd begun, on Tehachapi Pass—but most of my exhaustion could be blamed on the outrageous weight of my pack. I looked at it hopelessly. It was my burden to bear, of my very own ludicrous making, and yet I had no idea how I was going to bear it. I retrieved my guidebook and looked through it, holding the fluttering pages against the wind, hoping that the familiar words and maps would dispel my growing unease; that the book would convince me, in its benign four-part harmony, that I could do this, the same way it had in the months that I'd been hatching this plan. There were no photographs of the four authors of *The Pacific Crest Trail, Volume 1: California,* but I could see them each in my mind's eye: Jeffrey P. Schaffer, Thomas Winnett, Ben Schifrin, and Ruby Jenkins. They were sensible and kind, wise and all-knowing. They would guide me through. They had to.

Plenty of people at REI had told me of their own backpacking excursions, but none had ever hiked the PCT and it hadn't occurred to me to attempt to track down someone who had. It was the summer of 1995, the stone ages when it came to the Internet. Now there are dozens of online PCT hiker journals and a deep well of information about the trail, both static and ever changing, but I had none of that. I had only *The Pacific Crest Trail, Volume 1: California.* It was my bible. My lifeline. The only book I'd read about hiking on the PCT, or anywhere else for that matter.

But paging through it for the first time while actually sitting on the trail was less reassuring than I'd hoped. There were things I'd overlooked, I saw now, such as a quote on page 6 by a fellow named Charles Long, with whom the authors of *The Pacific Crest Trail, Volume 1: California* heartily agreed, that said, "How can a book describe the psychological factors a person must prepare for . . . the despair, the alienation, the anxiety and especially the pain, both physical and mental, which slices to the very heart of the hiker's volition, which are the real things that must be planned for? No words can transmit those factors . . ."

I sat pie-eyed, with a lurching knowledge that indeed no words *could* transmit those factors. They didn't have to. I now knew exactly what they were. I'd learned about them by having hiked a little more than three miles in the desert mountains beneath a pack that resembled a Volkswagen Beetle. I read on, noting intimations that it would be wise to improve one's physical fitness before setting out, to train specifically for the hike, perhaps. And, of course, admonishments about backpack weight. Suggestions even to refrain from carrying the entire guidebook itself because it was too heavy to carry all at once and unnecessary anyway—one could photocopy or rip out needed sections and include the necessary bit in the next resupply box. I closed the book.

Why hadn't *I* thought of that? Of ripping the guidebook into sections?

Because I was a big fat idiot and I didn't know what the hell I was doing, that's why. And I was alone in the wilderness with a beast of a load to carry while finding that out.

I wrapped my arms around my legs and pressed my face into the tops of my bare knees and closed my eyes, huddled into the ball of myself, the wind whipping my shoulder-length hair in a frenzy.

When I opened my eyes several minutes later, I saw that I was sitting next to a plant I recognized. This sage was less verdant than the sage my mother had grown in our yard for years, but its shape and scent were the same. I reached over and picked a handful of the leaves and rubbed them between my palms, then put my face in them and inhaled deeply, the way my mother had taught me to do. *It gives you a burst of energy,* she'd always declared, imploring my siblings and me to follow her lead on those long days when we'd been working to build our house and our bodies and spirits had flagged.

Inhaling it now, I didn't so much smell the sharp, earthy scent of the desert sage as I did the potent memory of my mother. I looked up at the blue sky, feeling, in fact, a burst of energy, but mostly feeling my mother's presence, remembering why it was that I'd thought I could hike this trail. Of all the things that convinced me that I should not be afraid while on this journey, of all the things I'd made myself believe so I could hike the PCT, the death of my mother was the thing that made me believe the most deeply in my safety: nothing bad could happen to me, I thought. The worst thing already had.

I stood and let the wind blow the sage leaves from my hands and walked to the edge of the flat area I was occupying. The land beyond gave way to a rocky outcropping below. I could see the mountains that surrounded me for miles, sloping gently down into a wide desert valley. White, angular wind turbines lined the ridges in the distance. My guidebook told me that they generated electricity for the residents of the cities and towns below, but I was far from that now. From cities and towns. From electricity. From California, it even seemed, though I was squarely in the heart of it, of the real California, with its relentless wind and Joshua trees and rattlesnakes lurking in places I had yet to find.

As I stood there, I knew I was done for the day, though when I'd stopped I'd intended to push on. Too tired to light my stove and too exhausted to be hungry in any case, I pitched my tent, though it was only four in the afternoon. I took things from my pack and tossed them into the tent to keep it from blowing away, then pushed the pack in too and crawled in behind it. I was immediately relieved to be inside, even though *inside* meant only a cramped green nylon cave. I set up my little camp chair and sat in the small portal where the tent's ceiling was high enough to accommodate my head. Then I rummaged through my things to find a book: not *The Pacific Crest Trail, Volume 1: California*, which I should have been reading to see what lay ahead the next day, and not *Staying Found*, which I should have read before starting the trail, but Adrienne Rich's book of poems, *The Dream of a Common Language*.

This, I knew, was an unjustifiable weight. I could imagine the disapproving expressions on the faces of the authors of *The Pacific Crest Trail, Volume 1: California*. Even the Faulkner novel had more right to be in my pack, if only because I hadn't yet read it and therefore it could be explained as entertainment. I'd read *The Dream of a Common Language* so often that I'd practically memorized it. In the previous few years, certain lines had become like incantations to me, words I'd chanted to myself through my sorrow and confusion. That book was a consolation, an old friend, and when I held it in my hands on my first night on the trail, I didn't regret carrying it one iota—even though carrying it meant that I could do no more than hunch beneath its weight. It was true that *The Pacific Crest Trail, Volume 1: California* was now my bible, but *The Dream of a Common Language* was my religion.

I opened it up and read the first poem out loud, my voice rising above the sound of the wind battering the walls of my tent. I read it again and again and again.

It was a poem called "Power."

5

TRACKS

I am technically fifteen days older than the Pacific Crest Trail. I was born in 1968, on September 17, and the trail was officially designated by an act of Congress on October 2 of that same year. The trail existed in various forms long before that—sections of it having been forged and pieced together since the 1930s, when a band of hikers and wilderness enthusiasts first took interest in creating a Mexico-to-Canada trail—but it wasn't until 1968 that the PCT was designated and not until 1993 that it was complete. It was officially dedicated almost exactly two years before I woke that first morning among the Joshua trees that had stabbed me. The trail didn't feel two years old to me. It didn't even feel like it was about my age. It felt ancient. Knowing. Utterly and profoundly indifferent to me.

I woke at dawn but couldn't bring myself to so much as sit up for an hour, lingering instead in my sleeping bag while reading my guidebook, still drowsy, though I'd slept for twelve hours—or at least I'd been reclining that long. The wind had awakened me repeatedly throughout the night, smacking against my tent in great bursts, sometimes hard enough so the walls whipped up against my head. It died down a few hours before dawn, but then it was something else that woke me: the silence. The irrefutable proof that I was out here in the great alone.

I crawled out of my tent and stood slowly, my muscles stiff from yesterday's hike, my bare feet tender on the rocky dirt. I still wasn't hungry, but I forced myself to eat breakfast, scooping two spoonfuls of a powdered soy substance called Better Than Milk into one of my pots and stirring water into it before adding granola. It didn't taste better than milk to me. Or worse. It didn't taste like anything. I might as well have been eating grass. My taste buds had seemingly gone numb. I continued to press the spoon into my mouth anyway. I'd need the nutrition for the long day ahead. I drank the last of the water in my bottles and awkwardly refilled them from my dromedary bag, which flopped heavily in my hands. According to *The Pacific Crest Trail, Volume 1: California*, I was thirteen miles away from my first water source: Golden Oak Springs, which, in spite of yesterday's poor showing, I expected to reach by day's end.

I loaded my pack the way I had the day before in the motel, cramming and wedging things in until nothing more would fit, then attaching the rest by bungee cords to the outside. It took me an hour to break camp and set off. Almost immediately I stepped over a small pile of scat on the trail, a few feet from where I'd been sleeping. It was black as tar. A coyote, I hoped. Or was it a mountain lion? I searched the dirt for tracks, but saw none. I scanned the landscape, ready to see a large feline face among the sagebrush and rocks.

I began to walk, feeling experienced in a way I hadn't the day before, less cautious with each step in spite of the scat, stronger beneath my pack. That strength crumbled within fifteen minutes, as I ascended and then ascended some more, pushing into the rocky mountains, walking switchback after switchback. My pack's frame creaked behind me with each step, straining from the weight. The muscles of my upper back and shoulders were bound in tense, hot knots. Every so often, I stopped and bent over to brace my hands against my knees and shift the pack's weight off my shoulders for a moment of relief before staggering on.

By noon I was up over 6,000 feet and the air had cooled, the sun suddenly disappearing behind clouds. Yesterday it had been hot in the desert, but now I shivered as I ate my lunch of a protein bar and dried apricots, my sweat-drenched T-shirt growing cold on my back. I dug the fleece jacket out of my clothing bag and put it on. Afterwards, I lay down on my tarp to rest for a few minutes and, without meaning to, fell asleep.

I woke to raindrops falling on my face and looked at my watch. I'd slept for nearly two hours. I hadn't dreamed of anything, hadn't had any awareness that I'd been sleeping at all, as if instead someone had come up behind me and knocked me unconscious with a rock. When I sat up I saw that I was engulfed in a cloud, the mist so impenetrable I couldn't see beyond a few feet. I cinched on my pack and continued hiking through the light rain, though my whole body felt as if it were pushing through deep water with each step. I bunched up my T-shirt and shorts to cushion the spots on my hips and back and shoulders that were being rubbed raw by my pack, but that only made it worse.

I continued up, into the late afternoon and evening, unable to see anything except what was immediately before me. I wasn't thinking of snakes, as I'd been the day before. I wasn't thinking, *I'm hiking on the Pacific Crest Trail.* I wasn't even thinking, *What have I gotten myself into?* I was thinking only of moving myself forward. My mind was a crystal vase that contained only that one desire. My body was its opposite: a bag of broken glass. Every time I moved, it hurt. I counted my steps to take my mind off the pain, silently ticking the numbers off in my head to one hundred before starting over again. The blocks of numbers made the walk slightly more bearable, as if I only had to go to the end of each one.

As I ascended, I realized I didn't understand what a mountain was, or even if I was hiking up one mountain or a series of them glommed together. I'd not grown up around mountains. I'd walked on a few, but only on well-trod paths on day hikes. They'd seemed to be nothing more than really big hills. But they were not that. They were, I now realized, layered and complex, inexplicable and analogous to nothing. Each time I reached the place that I thought was the top of the mountain or the series of mountains glommed together, I was wrong. There was still more *up* to go, even if first there was a tiny slope that went tantalizingly down. So up I went until I reached what really was the top. I knew it was the top because there was snow. Not on the ground, but falling from the sky, in thin flakes that swirled in mad patterns, pushed by the wind.

I hadn't expected it to rain in the desert, and I certainly hadn't expected it to snow. As with the mountains, there'd been no deserts where I grew up, and though I'd gone on day hikes in a couple of them, I didn't really understand what deserts were. I'd taken them to be dry, hot, and sandy places full of snakes, scorpions, and cactuses. They were not that. They were that and also a bunch of other things. They were layered and complex and inexplicable and analogous to nothing. My new existence was beyond analogy, I realized on that second day on the trail.

I was in entirely new terrain.

What a mountain was and what a desert was were not the only things I had not expected. I hadn't expected the flesh on my tailbone and hips and the fronts of my shoulders to bleed. I hadn't expected to average a bit less than a mile an hour, which is what, by my calculations—made possible by the highly descriptive guidebook—I'd been covering so far, lumping my many breaks in with the time I actually spent walking. Back when my hike on the PCT had been nothing but an idea, I'd planned to average fourteen miles a day over the course of my trip, though most days I'd actually walk farther than that because my anticipated average included the rest days I'd take every week or two, when I wouldn't hike at all. But I hadn't factored in my lack of fitness, nor the genuine rigors of the trail, until I was on it.

I descended in a mild panic until the snow turned back into mist and the mist to clear views of the muted greens and browns of the mountains that surrounded me near and far, their alternately sloping and jagged profiles a stark contrast to the pale sky. As I walked, the only sound was that of my boots crunching against the gravelly trail and the squeaky creak of my pack that was slowly driving me insane. I stopped and took my pack off and swabbed its frame with my lip balm in the place where I thought the squeak might live, but when I hiked on I realized that it had made no difference. I said a few words out loud to distract myself. It had been only a little more than forty-eight hours since I'd said goodbye to the men who'd given me a ride to the trail, but it felt like it had been a week and my voice sounded strange all by itself in the air. It seemed to me that I'd run into another hiker soon. I was surprised I hadn't seen anyone yet, though my solitude came in handy an hour later, when suddenly I had the urge to do what I called in my mind *use the bathroom,* though out here using the bathroom meant maintaining an unsupported squat so I could shit in a hole of my own making. It was for this reason I'd brought the stainless-steel trowel that was looped through my backpack's waistband in its own black nylon sheath with *U-Dig-It* printed on the front.

I didn't dig it, but it was the backpacker way, so there was nothing else to do. I hiked until I found what seemed a reasonable spot to venture a few steps off the trail. I took my pack off, pulled my trowel from its sheath, and darted behind a sage bush to dig. The ground was a rocky, reddish beige and seemingly solid. Digging a hole in it was like attempting to penetrate a granite kitchen counter sprinkled with sand

and pebbles. Only a jackhammer could've done the job. Or a man, I thought furiously, stabbing at the dirt with the tip of my trowel until I thought my wrists would break. I chipped and chipped uselessly, my body shimmering into a crampy cold sweat. I finally had to stand up just so I wouldn't shit my pants. I had no choice but to pull them off—by then I'd abandoned underwear because they only exacerbated my raw hips situation—and simply squat down and go. I was so weak with relief when I was done that I almost toppled over into the pile of my own hot dung.

Afterwards, I limped around gathering rocks and built a small crap cairn, burying the evidence before hiking on.

I believed I was going to Golden Oak Springs, but by seven o'clock it was still nowhere in sight. I didn't care. Too tired to be hungry, I skipped dinner again, thus saving the water I'd have used to make it, and found a spot flat enough to pitch my tent. The tiny thermometer that dangled from the side of my pack said it was 42 degrees. I peeled off my sweaty clothes and draped them over a bush to dry before I crawled into my tent.

In the morning, I had to force them on. Rigid as boards, they'd frozen overnight.

I reached Golden Oak Springs a few hours into my third day on the trail. The sight of the square concrete pool lifted my spirits enormously, not only because at the springs there was water, but also because humans had so clearly constructed it. I put my hands in the water, disturbing a few bugs that swam across its surface. I took out my purifier and placed its intake tube into the water and began to pump the way I'd practiced in my kitchen sink in Minneapolis. It was harder to do than I remembered it being, perhaps because when I'd practiced I'd only pumped a few times. Now it seemed to take more muscle to compress the pump. And when I did manage to pump, the intake tube floated up to the surface, so it took in only air. I pumped and pumped until I couldn't pump anymore and I had to take a break; then I pumped again, finally refilling both my bottles and the dromedary bag. It took me nearly an hour, but it had to be done. My next water source was a daunting nineteen miles away.

I had every intention of hiking on that day, but instead I sat in my camp chair near the spring. It had warmed up at last, the sun shining on my bare arms and legs. I took off my shirt, pulled my shorts down low, and lay with my eyes closed, hoping the sun would soothe the patches of skin on my torso that had been worn raw by my pack. When I opened my eyes, I saw a small lizard on a nearby rock. He seemed to be doing push-ups.

"Hello, lizard," I said, and he stopped his push-ups and held perfectly still before disappearing in a flash.

I needed to make time. I was already behind what I considered my schedule, but I could not force myself to leave the small verdant patch of live oaks that surrounded Golden Oak Springs that day. In addition to the raw patches of flesh, my muscles and bones ached from hiking, and my feet were dotted with an ever-increasing number of blisters. I sat in the dirt examining them, knowing there was little I could do to prevent the blisters from going from bad to worse. I ran my finger delicately over them and then up to the black bruise the size of a silver dollar that bloomed on my ankle—not a PCT injury, but rather evidence of my pre-PCT idiocy.

It was because of this bruise that I'd opted not to call Paul when I'd been so lonely at that motel back in Mojave; this bruise at the center of the story I knew he'd hear hiding in my voice. How I'd intended to stay away from Joe in the two days I spent in Portland before catching my flight to LA, but hadn't. How I'd ended up shooting heroin with him in spite of the fact that I hadn't touched it since that time he'd come to visit me in Minneapolis six months before.

"My turn," I'd said urgently after watching him shoot up back in Portland. The PCT suddenly seeming so far in my future, though it was only forty-eight hours away.

"Give me your ankle," Joe had said when he couldn't find a vein in my arm.

I spent the day at Golden Oak Springs with my compass in hand, reading *Staying Found*. I found north, south, east, and west. I walked jubilantly without my pack down a jeep road that came up to the springs to see what I could see. It was spectacular to walk without my pack on, even in the state my feet were in, sore as my muscles were. I felt not only upright, but lifted, as if two elastic bands were attached to my shoulders from above. Each step was a leap, light as air.

When I reached an overlook, I stopped and gazed across the expanse.

It was only more desert mountains, beautiful and austere, and more rows of white angular wind turbines in the distance. I returned to my camp, set up my stove, and attempted to make myself a hot meal, my first on the trail, but I couldn't get my stove to sustain a flame, no matter what I tried. I pulled the little instruction book out, read the troubleshooting section, and learned that I'd filled the stove's canister with the wrong kind of gas. I'd filled it with unleaded fuel instead of the special white gas that it was meant to have, and now the generator was clogged, its tiny pan blackened with soot by my efforts.

I wasn't hungry anyway. My hunger was a numb finger, barely prodding. I ate a handful of tuna jerky flakes and fell asleep by 6:15.

Before I set out on the fourth day, I doctored my wounds. An REI worker had encouraged me to buy a box of Spenco 2nd Skin—gel patches meant to treat burns that also happened to be great for blisters. I plastered them in all the places my skin was bleeding or blistered or red with rash—on the tips of my toes and the backs of my heels, over my hip bones and across the front of my shoulders and lower back. When I was done, I shook my socks out, trying to soften them before I put them on. I had two pair, but each had become stiff with dirt and dried sweat. It seemed they were made of cardboard rather than cloth, though I switched them out every few hours, wearing one pair while the other air-dried, dangling from the bungee cords on my pack.

After I hiked away from the springs that morning, fully loaded down with 24.5 pounds of water again, I realized I was having a kind of strange, abstract, retrospective fun. In moments among my various agonies, I noticed the beauty that surrounded me, the wonder of things both small and large: the color of a desert flower that brushed against me on the trail or the grand sweep of the sky as the sun faded over the mountains. I was in the midst of such a reverie when I skidded on pebbles and fell, landing on the hard trail facedown with a force that took my breath away. I lay unmoving for a good minute, from both the searing pain in my leg and the colossal weight on my back, which pinned me to the ground. When I crawled out from beneath my pack and assessed the damage, I saw that a gash in my shin was seeping copious blood, a knot the size of a fist already forming beneath the gash. I poured a tiny bit of my precious water over it, flicking the dirt and pebbles out the best I could, then pressed a lump of gauze against it until the bleeding slowed and I limped on.

I walked the rest of the afternoon with my eyes fixed on the trail immediately in front of me, afraid I'd lose my footing again and fall. It was then that I spotted what I'd searched for days before: mountain lion tracks. It had walked along the trail not long before me in the same direction as I was walking—its paw prints clearly legible in the dirt for a quarter mile. I stopped every few minutes to look around. Aside from small patches of green, the landscape was mostly a range of blonds and browns, the same colors as a mountain lion. I walked on, thinking about the newspaper article I'd recently come across about three women in California—each one had been killed by a mountain lion on separate occasions over the past year—and about all those nature shows I'd watched as a kid in which the predators go after the one they judge to be the weakest in the pack. There was no question that was me: the one most likely to be ripped limb from limb. I sang aloud the little songs that came into my head—"Twinkle, Twinkle, Little Star" and "Take Me Home, Country Roads"—hoping that my terrified voice would scare the lion away, while at the same time fearing it would alert her to my presence, as if the blood crusted on my leg and the days-old stench of my body weren't enough to lure her.

As I scrutinized the land, I realized that I'd come far enough by now that the terrain had begun to change. The landscape around me was still arid, dominated by the same chaparral and sagebrush as it had been all along, but now the Joshua trees that defined the Mojave Desert appeared only sporadically. More common were the juniper trees, piñon pines, and scrub oaks. Occasionally, I passed through shady meadows thick with grass. The grass and the reasonably large trees were a comfort to me. They suggested water and life. They intimated that I could do this.

Until, that is, a tree stopped me in my path. It had fallen across the trail, its thick trunk held aloft by branches just low enough that I couldn't pass beneath, yet so high that climbing over it was impossible, especially given the weight of my pack. Walking around it was also out of the question: the trail dropped off too steeply on one side and the brush was too dense on the other. I stood for a long while, trying to map out a way past the tree. I had to do it, no matter how impossible it seemed. It was either that or turn around and go back to the motel in Mojave. I thought of my little eighteen-dollar room with a deep swooning desire, the yearning to return to it flooding my body. I backed up to the tree, unbuckled my pack, and pushed it up and over its rough trunk, doing my best to drop it over the other side without letting it fall so hard on the ground that my dromedary bag would pop from the impact. Then I climbed over the tree after it, scraping my hands that were already tender from my fall. In the next mile I encountered three other blown-down trees. By the time I made it past them all, the scab on my shin had torn open and was bleeding anew.

On the afternoon of the fifth day, as I made my way along a narrow and steep stretch of trail, I looked up to see an enormous brown horned animal charging at me.

"Moose!" I hollered, though I knew that it wasn't a moose. In the panic of the moment, my mind couldn't wrap around what I was seeing and a moose was the closest thing to it. "Moose!" I hollered more desperately as it neared. I scrambled into the manzanitas and scrub oaks that bordered the trail, pulling myself into their sharp branches as best I could, stymied by the weight of my pack.

As I did this, the species of the beast came to me and I understood that I was about to be mauled by a Texas longhorn bull.

"Mooooose!" I shouted louder as I grabbed for the yellow cord tied to the frame of my pack that held the world's loudest whistle. I found it, brought it to my lips, closed my eyes, and blew with all my might, until I had to stop to get a breath of air.

When I opened my eyes, the bull was gone.

So was all the skin on the top of my right index finger, scraped off on the manzanitas' jagged branches in my frenzy.

The thing about hiking the Pacific Crest Trail, the thing that was so profound to me that summer—and yet also, like most things, so very simple—was how few choices I had and how often I had to do the thing I least wanted to do. How there was no escape or denial. No numbing it down with a martini or covering it up with a roll in the hay. As I clung to the chaparral that day, attempting to patch up my bleeding finger, terrified by every sound that the bull was coming back, I considered my options. There were only two and they were essentially the same. I could go back in the direction I had come from, or I could go forward in the direction I intended to go. The bull, I acknowledged grimly, could be in either direction, since I hadn't seen where he'd run once I closed my eyes. I could only choose between the bull that would take me back and the bull that would take me forward.

And so I walked on.

It took all I had to cover nine miles a day. To cover nine miles a day was a physical achievement far beyond anything I'd ever done. Every part of my body hurt. Except my heart. I saw no one, but, strange as it was, I missed no one. I longed for nothing but food and water and to be able to put my backpack down. I kept carrying my backpack anyway. Up and down and around the dry mountains, where Jeffrey pines and black oaks lined the trail, crossing jeep roads that bore the tracks of big trucks, though none were in sight.

On the morning of the eighth day I got hungry and dumped all my food out on the ground to assess the situation, my desire for a hot meal suddenly fierce. Even in my exhausted, appetite-suppressed state, by then I'd eaten most of what I didn't have to cook—my granola and nuts, my dried fruit and turkey and tuna jerky, my protein bars and chocolate and Better Than Milk powder. Most of the food I had left needed to be cooked and I had no working stove. I didn't have a resupply box waiting for me until I reached Kennedy Meadows, 135 trail miles into my journey. A well-seasoned hiker would have traversed those 135 miles in the time I'd been on the trail. At the rate I was moving, I wasn't even halfway there. And even if I did make it through to Kennedy Meadows on the food I had, I still needed to have my stove repaired and filled with the proper fuel—and Kennedy Meadows, being more of a high-elevation base for hunters and hikers and fishers than a town, was no place to do it. As I sat in the dirt, ziplock bags of dehydrated food that I couldn't cook scattered all around me, I decided to veer off the trail. Not far from where I sat, the PCT crossed a network of jeep roads that ran in various directions.

I began walking down one, reasoning that I'd eventually find civilization in the form of a highway that paralleled the trail approximately twenty miles to the east. I walked not knowing exactly what road I was on, going only on faith that I would find something, walking and walking in the bright hot sun. I could smell myself as I moved. I'd packed deodorant and each morning I'd swabbed it under my arms, but it made no difference anymore. I hadn't bathed in over a week. My body was covered with dirt and blood, my hair, dense with dust and dried sweat, plastered to my head underneath my hat. I could feel the muscles in my body growing stronger by the day and at the same time, in equal measure, my tendons and joints breaking down. My feet hurt both inside and out, their flesh rubbed raw with blisters, their bones and muscles fatigued from the miles. The road was blissfully level or gently descending, a welcome break from the relentless up and down of the trail, but still I suffered. For long stretches I tried to imagine that I didn't actually have feet, that instead my legs ended in two impervious stumps that could endure anything.

After four hours I began to regret my decision. I might starve to death out there or be killed by marauding longhorn bulls, but on the PCT at least I knew where I was. I reread my guidebook, uncertain by now that I was even on one of the roads they'd described in a cursory way. I took out my map and compass every hour to assess and reassess my position. I pulled out *Staying Found* to read again how exactly to use a map and compass. I studied the sun. I passed a small herd of cows that were unbound by a fence and my heart leapt at the sight of them, though none moved in my direction. They only stopped eating to lift their heads and watch me pass while I delicately chanted to them, "Cow, cow, cow."

The land through which the road passed was surprisingly green in places, dry and rocky in others, and twice I passed tractors parked silent and eerie by the side of the road. I walked in a state of wonder at the beauty and the silence, but by late afternoon, apprehension rose in my throat.

I was on a road, but I had not seen a human being in eight days. This was civilization and yet, aside from the free-range cows and the two abandoned tractors, and the road itself, there was no sign of it. I felt as if I were starring in a science fiction movie, as if I were the only person left on the planet, and for the first time in my journey, I felt like I might cry. I took a deep breath to push away my tears and took off my pack and set it in the dirt to regroup. There was a bend in the road ahead and I walked around it without my pack to see what I could.

What I saw were three men sitting in the cab of a yellow pickup truck. One was white. One was black. One was Latino.

It took perhaps sixty seconds for me to reach them on foot. They watched me with the same expression on their faces as I'd had when I saw the longhorn bull the day before. As if any moment they might yell "Moose!" My relief at the sight of them was enormous. Yet as I strode toward them my whole body tingled with the complicated knowledge that I was no longer the sole star in a film about a planet devoid of people. Now I was in a different kind of movie entirely: I was the sole woman with three men of unknown intent, character, and origin watching me from the shade of a yellow truck.

When I explained my situation to them through the open driver's-side window, they gazed at me silently, their eyes shifting from startled to stunned to scoffing until they all burst out laughing.

"Do you know what you walked into, honey?" the white man asked me when he'd recovered, and I shook my head. He and the black man looked to be in their sixties, the Latino barely out of his teens.

"You see this here mountain?" he asked. He pointed straight ahead through the windshield from his position behind the wheel. "We're getting ready to blow that mountain up." He explained to me that a mining operation had bought rights to this patch of land and they were mining for decorative rock that people use in their yards. "My name's Frank," he said, tapping the brim of his cowboy hat. "And technically you're trespassing, young lady, but we won't hold that against you." He looked at me and winked. "We're just miners. We don't own the land or else we'd have to shoot you."

He laughed again and then gestured to the Latino in the middle and told me his name was Carlos.

"I'm Walter," said the black man sitting by the passenger window.

They were the first people I'd seen since the two guys in the minivan with the Colorado plates who'd dropped me by the side of the road more than a week before. When I spoke, my voice sounded funny to me, seemed to be higher and faster than I'd remembered, as if it were something I couldn't quite catch and hold on to, as if every word were a small bird fluttering away. They told me to get in the back of the truck, and we drove the short distance around the bend to retrieve my pack. Frank stopped and they all got out. Walter picked up my pack and was shocked by the weight.

"I was in Korea," he said, hoisting it onto the truck's metal bed with considerable effort. "And we ain't never carried a pack that heavy. Or maybe once I carried one that heavy, but that was when I was being punished."

Quickly, without my being much involved, it was decided I'd go home with Frank, where his wife would feed me dinner and I could bathe and sleep in a bed. In the morning, he'd help me get someplace where I could have my stove repaired.

"Now explain all this to me again?" Frank asked a few times, and each time all three of them listened with confused and rapt attention. They lived perhaps twenty miles from the Pacific Crest Trail and yet none of them had ever heard of it. None could fathom what business a woman had hiking it by herself, and Frank and Walter told me so, in jovial, gentlemanly terms.

"I think it's kind of cool," said Carlos after a while. He was eighteen, he told me, about to join the military.

"Maybe you should do this instead," I suggested.

"Nah," he said.

The men got into the truck again and I rode in the back for a couple of miles by myself, until we reached the spot where Walter had parked his truck. He and Carlos drove off in it and left me alone with Frank, who had another hour of work to do.

I sat in the cab of the yellow truck watching Frank go back and forth on a tractor, grading the road. Each time he passed, he waved to me, and as he rode away I surreptitiously explored the contents of his truck. In the glove compartment there was a silver flask of whiskey. I took a shallow swig, and quickly put it back, my lips on fire. I reached under the seat and pulled out a slim black case and opened it up and saw a gun as silver as the whiskey flask and shut it again and shoved it beneath the seat. The keys to the truck dangled from the ignition, and I thought idly about what would happen if I started it up and drove away. I took off my boots and massaged my feet. The little bruise on my ankle that I'd gotten from shooting heroin in Portland was still there, but faded to a faint morose yellow now. I ran my finger over it, over the bump of the tiny track mark still detectable at its core, amazed at my own ludicrousness, and then put my socks back on so I wouldn't have to see it anymore.

"What kind of woman are you?" Frank asked when he was done with his work and he'd climbed into the truck beside me.

"What kind?" I asked. Our eyes locked and something in his unveiled itself, and I looked away.

"Are you like Jane? Like the kind of woman Tarzan would like?"

"I guess so," I said, and laughed, though I felt a creeping anxiety, wishing that Frank would start the truck and drive. He was a big man, rangy and chiseled and tan. A miner who looked to me like a cowboy. His hands reminded me of all the hands of the men I'd known growing up, men who worked their bodies for a living, men whose hands would never get clean no matter how hard they scrubbed. As I sat there with him, I felt the way I always do when alone in certain circumstances with certain men—that anything could happen. That he could go about his business, mannerly and kind, or he could grab me and change the course of things entirely in an instant. With Frank in his truck, I watched his hands, his every move, each cell in my body on high alert, though I appeared as relaxed as if I'd just woken from a nap.

"I've got a little something for us," he said, reaching into the glove compartment to remove the flask of whiskey. "It's my reward for a hard day's work." He unscrewed the cap and handed it to me. "Ladies first."

I took it from him and held it to my lips and let the whiskey wash into my mouth.

"Yep. That's the kind of woman you are. That's what I'm going to call you: Jane." He took the flask from me and had a long drink.

"You know I'm not actually out here completely alone," I blurted, making up the lie as I spoke. "My husband—his name is Paul—he's also hiking. He started at Kennedy Meadows. Do you know where that is? We each wanted the experience of hiking alone, so he's hiking south and I'm hiking north and we're meeting in the middle, and then we'll go the rest of the summer together."

Frank nodded and took another sip from the flask. "Well, then he's crazier than you," he said, after thinking about it for a while. "It's one thing to be a woman crazy enough to do what you're doing. Another thing to be a man letting his own wife go off and do this."

"Yeah," I said, as if I agreed with him. "So anyway. We'll be reunited in a few days." I said it with such conviction that I felt convinced of it myself—that Paul that very minute was making his way toward me. That in fact we hadn't filed for divorce two months before, on a snowy day in April. That he was coming for me. Or that he would know if I didn't make it any further down the trail. That my disappearance would be noted in a matter of days.

But the opposite was true. The people in my life were like the Band-Aids that had blown away in the desert wind that first day on the trail. They scattered and then they were gone. No one expected me to even so much as call when I reached my first stop. Or the second or third.

Frank leaned back against his seat and adjusted his big metal belt buckle. "There's something else I like to reward myself with after a hard day's work," he said.

"What's that?" I asked, with a tentative smile, my heart hammering in my chest. My hands on my lap felt tingly. I was acutely aware of my backpack, too far away in the bed of the truck. In a flash, I decided I'd leave it behind if I had to push the truck door open and run.

Frank reached under the seat, where the gun resided in its little black case.

He came up with a clear plastic bag. Inside, there were long thin ropes of red licorice, each bunch wound like a lasso. He held the bag out to me and asked, "You want some, Miss Jane?"

6

A BULL IN BOTH DIRECTIONS

I devoured a good six feet of Frank's red licorice as he drove, and I'd have eaten a good six feet more if it had been available.

"You wait here," he told me once we pulled up in the little dirt driveway that ran alongside his house—a trailer in a small encampment of trailers in the desert brush. "I'll go in and tell Annette who you are."

A few minutes later they emerged together. Annette was plump and gray-haired, the expression on her face unwelcoming and suspicious. "Is that all you got?" she grouched as Frank pulled my pack from his truck. I followed them inside, where Frank immediately disappeared into the bathroom.

"Make yourself at home," said Annette, which I took to mean that I should sit at the dining table that bordered the kitchen while she made me a plate of food. A small blaring television sat on the far corner of the table, the volume so loud it was almost hard to hear. Another story about the O. J. Simpson trial. I watched it until Annette came and set the plate down before me, then turned off the TV.

"It's all you hear about. O.J. this and O.J. that," she said. "You wouldn't think there were children starving in Africa. You go on and start," she said, gesturing to my food.

"I'll wait," I said in a casual tone that belied the desperation I felt. I gazed down at my plate. It was piled high with barbecued ribs, canned corn, and potato salad. I thought to rise and wash my hands, but I feared doing so might delay dinner. It didn't matter. The notion of whether it was necessary to wash one's hands before eating was now as distant to me as the news report on the TV.

"Eat!" Annette commanded, setting a plastic cup of cherry Kool-Aid before me.

I lifted a forkful of potato salad to my mouth. It was so good I almost fell out of my chair.

"You a college girl?"

"Yes," I said, oddly flattered that I appeared that way to her, in spite of my filth and stench. "Or I used to be. I graduated four years ago," I said, and then took another bite of food, realizing it was technically a lie. Though I'd promised my mother in the last days of her life that I would finish my BA, I hadn't. My mother had died on the Monday of our spring break and I'd returned to school the following Monday. I'd staggered my way through a full load of classes that last quarter, half blind with grief, but I did not receive my degree because I'd failed to do one thing. I had not written a five-page paper for an intermediate-level English class. It should have been a breeze, but when I tried to start writing, I could only stare at my blank computer screen. I walked across the stage in a cap and gown and accepted the little document baton that was handed to me, but when I unrolled it, it said what I knew it would: that until I finished that paper, I would not have my bachelor's degree. I had only my college loans, which, by my calculations, I'd be paying off until I was forty-three.

The next morning Frank left me at a convenience store on the highway after instructing me to catch a ride to a town called Ridgecrest. I sat on the front porch of the store until a guy who distributed chips came along and said yes when I asked him for a ride, in spite of the fact that it was against company rules to pick up a hitchhiker. His name was Troy, he told me once I'd climbed into his big truck. He drove around southern California five days a week, delivering bags of chips of all varieties. He'd been married to his high school sweetheart for seventeen years, since he was seventeen.

"Seventeen years out of the cage, and seventeen years in," he joked, though his voice was raw with regret. "I'd do anything to trade places with you," he said as we drove. "I'm a free spirit who never had the balls to be free."

He left me at Todd's Outdoor Supply Store, where Mr. Todd himself dismantled my stove, cleaned it, installed a new filter, sold me the correct gas, and then led me through a stove-lighting trial run just to be sure. I bought more duct tape and 2nd Skin for my wounded flesh and went to a restaurant and ordered a chocolate malt and a cheeseburger with fries, feeling as I had at dinner the evening before: shattered by each delicious bite. Afterwards, I walked through town as cars whizzed by, the faces of the drivers and passengers turning to look at me with cold curiosity. I passed fast-food joints and car dealerships, unsure of whether I should stick out my thumb for a ride or spend a night in Ridgecrest and head back to the PCT the next day. As I stood near an intersection, trying to figure out which direction to go, a scruffy-looking man rode up beside me on a bicycle. He held a wrinkled paper bag.

"You heading out of town?" he asked.

"Maybe," I said. His bike was too small for him—made for a boy instead of a man—with garish flames painted along the sides.

"Which direction you headed?" he asked. His body odor was so strong I almost coughed, though I guessed I smelled almost as bad as he did. In spite of the bath I'd taken the night before at Frank and Annette's after dinner, I was still dressed in my dirty clothes.

"I might stay in a motel for the night," I told him.

"Don't do that!" he bellowed. "I did that and they put me in jail."

I nodded, realizing that he thought that I was like him. A drifter. An outlaw. Not a so-called college girl, or even a former one. I didn't even try to explain about the PCT.

"You can have this," he said, holding the paper bag out to me. "It's bread and bologna. You can make sandwiches."

"No, thanks," I said, both repulsed and touched by his offer.

"Where you from?" he asked, reluctant to ride away.

"Minnesota."

"Hey!" he cried, a smile spreading across his grubby face. "You're my sister. I'm from Illinois. Illinois and Minnesota are like neighbors."

"Well, *almost* neighbors—there's Wisconsin in between," I said, and instantly regretted it, not wanting to hurt his feelings.

"But that's still neighbors," he said, and held his open palm down low so I would give him five.

I gave him five.

"Good luck," I said to him as he pedaled away.

I walked to a grocery store and wandered up and down the aisles before touching anything, dazzled by the mountains of food. I bought a few things to replace the food I'd eaten when I hadn't been able to make my dehydrated dinners and walked along a busy thruway until I found what looked like the cheapest motel in town.

"My name's Bud," the man behind the counter said when I asked for a room. He had a hangdog expression and a smoker's cough. Tan jowls hung off the sides of his wrinkled face. When I told him about hiking the PCT, he insisted on washing my clothes. "I can just throw them in with the sheets and towels, darling. It ain't nothing at all," he said when I protested.

I went to my room, stripped, and put on my rainpants and raincoat, though it was a hot June day; then I walked back to the office and handed my little pile of dirty clothes shyly over to Bud, thanking him again.

"It's 'cause I like your bracelet. That's why I offered," said Bud. I pulled up the sleeve of my raincoat and we looked at it. It was a faded silver cuff, a POW/MIA bracelet my friend Aimee had clamped onto my wrist as we said goodbye on a street in Minneapolis weeks before.

"Let me see who you got there." He reached across the counter and took my wrist and turned it so he could read the words. "William J. Crockett," he said, and let go. Aimee had done some research and told me who William J. Crockett was: an air force pilot who'd been two months shy of his twenty-sixth birthday when his plane was shot down in Vietnam. She'd worn the bracelet for years without ever taking it off. Since the moment she'd given it to me, neither had I. "I'm a Vietnam vet myself, so I keep my eyes out for that sort of thing. That's also why I gave you the only room we got that has a tub," said Bud. "I was there in '63, when I was barely eighteen. But now I'm against war. All kinds of war. One hundred percent against it. Except in certain cases." There was a cigarette burning in a plastic ashtray nearby that Bud picked up but didn't bring to his lips. "So I'm gonna assume you know there's a lot of snow up there on the Sierra Nevada this year."

"Snow?" I asked.

"It's been a record year. Entirely socked in. There's a BLM office here in town if you want to call them and ask about conditions," he said, and took a drag. "I'll have your clothes ready in an hour or two."

I returned to my room and took a shower and then a bath. Afterwards, I pulled back the bedspread and lay on the bedsheets. My room didn't have an air conditioner, but I felt cool anyway. I felt better than I'd ever felt in all of my life, now that the trail had taught me how horrible I could feel. I got up, rummaged through my pack, then reclined on the bed and read *As I Lay Dying* while Bud's words about the snow thrummed through me.

I knew snow. I had grown up in Minnesota, after all. I'd shoveled it, driven in it, and balled it up in my hands to throw. I'd watched it through windows for days as it fell into piles that stayed frozen for months on the ground. But this snow was different. It was snow that covered the Sierra Nevada so indomitably that the mountains had been named for it—in Spanish, Sierra Nevada means "the snowy range."

It seemed absurd to me that I'd been hiking in that snowy range all along—that the arid mountains I'd traversed since the moment I set foot on the PCT were technically part of the Sierra Nevada. But they weren't the High Sierras—the formidable range of granite peaks and cliffs beyond Kennedy Meadows that mountaineer and writer John Muir had famously explored and adored more than a hundred years before. I hadn't read Muir's books about the Sierra Nevada before I hiked the PCT, but I knew he was the founder of the Sierra Club. Saving the Sierra Nevada from sheepherders, mining operations, tourist development, and other encroachments of the modern age had been his lifelong passion. It's thanks to him and those who supported his cause that most of the Sierra Nevada is still wilderness today. Wilderness that was now apparently snowbound.

I wasn't entirely taken by surprise. The authors of my guidebook had warned me about the snow I might encounter in the High Sierras, and I'd come prepared. Or at least the version of prepared I'd believed was sufficient before I began hiking the PCT: I'd purchased an ice ax and mailed it to myself in the box I would collect at Kennedy Meadows. It had been my assumption when I purchased the ice ax that I'd need it only occasionally, for the highest stretches of trail. The guidebook assured me that in a regular year most of the snow would be melted by the time I hiked the High Sierras in late June and July. It hadn't occurred to me to investigate whether this had been a regular year.

I found a phone book in the bedside table and paged through it, then dialed the number for the local office of the Bureau of Land Management.

"Oh, yes, there's lots of snow up there," said the woman who answered. She didn't know the specifics, she told me, but she knew for certain it had been a record year for snowfall in the Sierras. When I told her I was hiking the PCT, she offered to give me a ride to the trail. I hung up the phone feeling more relieved that I didn't have to hitchhike than worried about the snow. It simply seemed so far away, so impossible.

The kind woman from the BLM brought me back to the trail at a place called Walker Pass the next afternoon. As I watched her drive away, I felt both chastened and slightly more confident than I had nine days before when I'd begun my hike. In the previous days, I'd been charged by a Texas longhorn bull, torn and bruised by falls and mishaps, and had navigated my way down a remote road past a mountain that was soon to be blown up. I'd made it through miles of desert, ascended and descended countless mountains, and gone days without seeing another person. I'd worn my feet raw, chafed my body until it bled, and carried not only myself over miles of rugged wilderness, but also a pack that weighed more than half of what I did. And I'd done it alone.

That was worth something, right? I thought as I walked through the rustic campground near Walker Pass and found a place to camp. It was late but still light, June in the last week of spring. I pitched my tent and cooked my first hot meal on the trail on my newly functioning stove—dried beans and rice—and watched the sky's light fade in a brilliant show of colors over the mountains, feeling like the luckiest person alive. It was fifty-two miles to Kennedy Meadows, sixteen to my first water on the trail.

In the morning, I loaded my pack with another full supply of water and crossed Highway 178. The next road that crossed the Sierra Nevada was 150 as-the-crow-flies miles north, near Tuolumne Meadows. I followed the PCT along its rocky, ascendant course in the hot morning sun, catching views of the mountains in all directions, distant and close—the Scodies to the near south, the El Paso Mountains far off to the east, the Dome Land Wilderness to the northwest, which I'd reach in a few days. They all looked the same to me, though each was subtly different. I'd become used to having mountains constantly in sight; my vision had changed over the past week. I'd adjusted to the endless miles-long panoramas; become familiar with the perception that I was walking on the land in the very place where it met the sky. The crest.

But mostly I didn't look up. Step by step, my eyes were on the sandy and pebbly trail, my feet sometimes slipping beneath me as I climbed up and switched back. My pack squeaked annoyingly with each step, the sound still emanating from that spot only a few inches from my ear.

As I hiked, I tried to force myself not to think about the things that hurt—my shoulders and upper back, my feet and hips—but I succeeded for only short bursts of time. As I traversed the eastern flank of Mount Jenkins, I paused several times to take in vast views of the desert that spread east below me to the vanishing point. By afternoon I had come to a rockslide and stopped. I looked up the mountain and followed the slide with my eyes all the way down. There was a great river of angular fist-sized metamorphic rocks—in place of the once-flat two-foot-wide trail that any human could walk through. And I wasn't even a normal human. I was a human with a god-awful load on my back and without even a trekking pole to balance myself. Why I had neglected to bring a trekking pole, while not failing to bring a foldable saw, I did not know. Finding a stick was impossible—the sparse low and scraggly trees around me were of no use. There was nothing to do but to push on.

My legs trembled as I stepped onto the rockslide in a half squat, fearful that my usual hunching in a remotely upright position would upset the rocks and cause them to slide en masse farther down the mountain, carrying me with them. I fell once, landing hard on my knee, and then I rose to pick my way even more tediously across, the water in the giant dromedary bag on my back sloshing with each step. When I reached the other side of the slide, I was so relieved it didn't matter that my knee was pulsing in pain and bleeding. *That's behind me,* I thought with gratitude, but I was mistaken.

I had to cross three more rockslides that afternoon.

I camped that night on a high saddle between Mount Jenkins and Mount Owens, my body traumatized by what it had taken to get there, though I'd covered only 8.5 miles. I had silently lambasted myself for not hiking more quickly, but now, as I sat in my camp chair catatonically spooning my dinner into my mouth from the hot pot that sat in the dirt between my feet, I was only thankful that I'd made it this far. I was at an elevation of 7,000 feet, the sky everywhere around me. To the west I could see the sun fading over the undulating land in a display of ten shades of orange and pink; to the east the seemingly endless desert valley stretched out of sight.

The Sierra Nevada is a single uptilted block of the earth's crust. Its western slope comprises 90 percent of the range, the peaks gradually descending to the fertile valleys that eventually give way to the California coast—which parallels the PCT roughly two hundred miles to the west for most of the way. The eastern slope of the Sierra Nevada is entirely different: a sharp escarpment that drops abruptly down to a great flat plain of desert that runs all the way to the Great Basin in Nevada. I'd seen the Sierra Nevada only once before, when I'd come west with Paul a few months after we left New York. We'd camped in Death Valley and the next day drove for hours across a landscape so desolate it seemed not of this earth. By midday the Sierra Nevada appeared on the western horizon, a great white impenetrable wall rising from the land. It was nearly impossible for me to conjure that image now as I sat on the high mountain saddle. I wasn't standing back from that wall anymore. I was on its spine. I stared out over the land in a demolished rapture, too tired to even rise and walk to my tent, watching the sky darken. Above me, the moon rose bright, and below me, far in the distance, the lights in the towns of Inyokern and Ridgecrest twinkled on. The silence was tremendous. The absence felt like a weight. This is what I came for, I thought. This is what I got.

When at last I stood and readied my camp for bed, I realized that for the first time on the trail, I hadn't put on my fleece anorak as the sun went down. I hadn't even put on a long-sleeved shirt. There wasn't the slightest chill in the air, even 7,000 feet up. That night I was grateful for the soft warm air on my bare arms, but by ten the next morning my gratitude was gone.

It was seared off of me by the relentless, magnificent heat.

By noon the heat was so merciless and the trail so exposed to the sun I wondered honestly if I would survive. It was so hot the only way I could keep going was by stopping every ten minutes to rest for five, when I would chug water from my bottle that was hot as tea. As I hiked, I moaned again and again, as if that would provide some cooling relief, but nothing changed. The sun still stared ruthlessly down on me, not caring one iota whether I lived or died. The parched scrub and scraggly trees still stood indifferently resolute, as they always had and always would.

I was a pebble. I was a leaf. I was the jagged branch of a tree. I was nothing to them and they were everything to me.

I rested in what shade I could find, fantasizing in intricate detail about cold water. The heat was so intense that my memory of it is not so much a sensation as a sound, a whine that rose to a dissonant keen with my head at its very center. Despite the things I'd endured so far on the trail, I'd never once considered quitting. But now, only ten days out, I was done. I wanted off.

I staggered north toward Kennedy Meadows, furious with myself for having come up with this inane idea. Elsewhere, people were having barbecues and days of ease, lounging by lakes and taking naps. They had access to ice cubes and lemonade and rooms whose temperature was 70 degrees. I knew those people. I loved those people. I hated them too, for how far away they were from me, near death on a trail few had ever even heard of. I was going to quit. *Quit, quit, quit,* I chanted to myself as I moaned and hiked and rested (ten, five, ten, five). I was going to get to Kennedy Meadows, retrieve my resupply box, eat every candy bar I'd packed into it, and then hitch a ride to whatever town the driver who picked me up was going to. I would get myself to a bus station and from there go anywhere.

Alaska, I decided instantly. Because in Alaska there was most definitely ice.

As the notion of quitting settled in, I came up with another reason to bolster my belief that this whole PCT hike had been an outlandishly stupid idea. I'd set out to hike the trail so that I could reflect upon my life, to think about everything that had broken me and make myself whole again. But the truth was, at least so far, I was consumed only with my most immediate and physical suffering. Since I'd begun hiking, the struggles of my life had only fluttered occasionally through my mind. Why, oh why, had my good mother died and how is it I could live and flourish without her? How could my family, once so close and strong, have fallen apart so swiftly and soundly in the wake of her death? What had I done when I'd squandered my marriage with Paul—the solid, sweet husband who'd loved me so steadfastly? Why had I gotten myself in a sad tangle with heroin and Joe and sex with men I hardly knew?

These were the questions I'd held like stones all through the winter and spring, as I prepared to hike the Pacific Crest Trail. The ones I'd wept over and wailed over, excavated in excruciating detail in my journal. I'd planned to put them all to rest while hiking the PCT. I'd imagined endless meditations upon sunsets or while staring out across pristine mountain lakes. I'd thought I'd weep tears of cathartic sorrow and restorative joy each day of my journey. Instead, I only moaned, and not because my heart ached. It was because my feet did and my back did and so did the still-open wounds all around my hips. And also, during that second week on the trail—when spring was on the very cusp of turning officially to summer—because I was so hot I thought my head would explode.

When I wasn't internally grumbling about my physical state, I found my mind playing and replaying scraps of songs and jingles in an eternal, nonsensical loop, as if there were a mix-tape radio station in my head. Up against the silence, my brain answered back with fragmented lines from tunes I'd heard over the course of my life—bits from songs I loved and clear renditions of jingles from commercials that almost drove me mad. I spent hours trying to push ads for Doublemint Gum and Burger King out of my head, an afternoon trying to recall the next line to an Uncle Tupelo song that went "Falling out the window. Tripping on a wrinkle in the rug. . . ." An entire day was spent trying to piece together all the words of Lucinda Williams's "Something About What Happens When We Talk."

My feet on fire, my flesh rubbed raw, my muscles and joints aching, the finger that had been denuded of its skin when the bull charged me throbbing with a mild infection, my head broiling and abuzz with random bits of music, at the end of the blistering tenth day of my hike I practically crawled into a shady grove of cottonwoods and willows that my guidebook identified as Spanish Needle Creek. Unlike many of the places my guidebook listed that had falsely promising names that included the word *creek,* Spanish Needle Creek truly was one, or at least it was good enough for me—a few inches of water shimmered over the rocks on the creek's shaded bed. Immediately, I shed my pack and my boots and my clothes and sat naked in the cool, shallow water, splashing it over my face and head. In my ten days on the trail, I'd yet to see another human, so I lounged without concern for anyone coming along, dizzy with ecstasy as I laboriously pumped the cold water through my water purifier and guzzled bottle after bottle.

When I woke the next morning to the soft sound of Spanish Needle Creek, I dallied in my tent, watching the sky brighten through the mesh ceiling. I ate a granola bar and read my guidebook, bracing myself for the trail ahead. I rose finally and went to the creek and bathed in it one last time, savoring the luxury. It was only nine in the morning, but it was hot already, and I dreaded leaving the shady patch along the creek.

As I soaked in the four-inch-deep water, I decided I wasn't going to hike to Kennedy Meadows. Even that was too far at the rate I was going. My guidebook listed a road the trail would cross in twelve miles. On it, I'd do what I'd done before: walk down it until I found a ride. Only this time I wasn't going to come back.

As I prepared to depart, I heard a noise to the south. I turned and saw a bearded man wearing a backpack coming up the trail. His trekking pole made a sharp clicking sound against the packed dirt with each step.

"Hello!" he called out to me with a smile. "You must be Cheryl Strayed."

"Yes," I said in a faltering voice, every bit as stunned to see another human being as I was to hear him speak my name.

"I saw you on the trail register," he explained when he saw my expression. "I've been following your tracks for days." I'd soon become used to people approaching me in the wilderness with such familiarity; the trail register served as a kind of social newsletter all summer long. "I'm Greg," he said, shaking my hand before he gestured to my pack: "Are you actually carrying that thing?"

We sat in the shade talking about where we were going and where we'd been. He was forty, an accountant from Tacoma, Washington, with a straitlaced, methodical accountant's air. He'd been on the PCT since early May, having started where the trail begins at the Mexican border, and he planned to hike all the way to Canada. He was the first person I'd met who was doing essentially what I was doing, though he was hiking much farther. He didn't need me to explain what I was doing out here. He understood.

As we spoke, I felt both elated to be in his company and flattened by my growing awareness that he was an entirely different breed: as thoroughly prepared as I was not; versed in trail matters I didn't even know existed. He'd been planning his hike for years, gathering information by corresponding with others who'd hiked the PCT in summers before, and attending what he referred to as "long-trail" hiking conferences. He rattled off distances and elevations and talked in great detail about the pros and cons of internal versus external pack frames. He repeatedly mentioned a man I'd never heard of named Ray Jardine—a legendary long-distance hiker, Greg told me in a reverent tone. Jardine was an expert and indisputable guru on all things PCT, especially on how to hike it without carrying a heavy load. He asked me about my water purifier, my daily protein intake, and the brand of the socks I was wearing. He wanted to know how I treated my blisters and how many miles I was averaging a day. Greg was averaging twenty-two. That very morning he'd hiked the seven miles I had agonized over the entire previous day.

"It's been harder than I thought it would be," I confessed, my heart heavy with the knowledge that I was even more of a big fat idiot than I'd initially reckoned. "It's all I can do to cover eleven or twelve," I lied, as if I'd even done that.

"Oh, sure," Greg said, unsurprised. "That's how it was for me at the beginning too, Cheryl. Don't worry about it. I'd go fourteen or fifteen miles if I was lucky and then I'd be beat. And that was with me training ahead of time, taking weekend trips with my pack fully loaded and so on. Being out here is different. It takes your body a couple of weeks to get conditioned enough to do the big miles."

I nodded, feeling enormously consoled, less by his answer than by his very presence. Despite his clear superiority, he was my kin. I wasn't sure if he felt the same way about me. "What have you been doing with your food at night?" I asked meekly, afraid of his answer.

"Usually I sleep with it."

"Me too," I gushed with relief. Before my trip I'd had notions of diligently hanging my food from trees each night, as every good backpacker is advised to do. So far I'd been too exhausted to even consider it. Instead, I'd kept my food bag inside my tent with me—the very place one is warned not to put it—using it as a pillow upon which to prop my swollen feet.

"I pull it right into my tent," said Greg, and a little something inside of me flared to life. "That's what the backcountry rangers do. They just don't tell anyone about it, because they'd catch hell if some bear came along and mauled someone because of it. I'll be hanging my food in the more touristy parts of the trail, where the bears have become habituated, but until then I wouldn't worry about it."

I nodded confidently, hoping to communicate the false notion that I knew how to correctly hang a food bag from a tree in such a way that would thwart a bear.

"But then of course we might not even make it up into those areas," said Greg.

"We might not make it?" I said, blushing with the irrational thought that he'd somehow divined my plan to quit.

"Because of the snow."

"Right. The snow. I heard there was some snow." In the heat I'd forgotten about it entirely. Bud and the woman from the BLM and Mr. Todd and the man who tried to give me the bag of bread and bologna seemed like nothing now but a far-off dream.

"The Sierra's completely socked in," Greg said, echoing Bud's words. "Lots of hikers have given up entirely because there was a record snowpack this year. It's going to be tough to get through."

"Wow," I said, feeling a mix of both terror and relief—now I'd have both an excuse and the language for quitting. *I wanted to hike the PCT, but I couldn't! It was socked in!*

"In Kennedy Meadows we're going to have to make a plan," Greg said. "I'll be laying over there a few days to regroup, so I'll be there when you arrive and we can figure it out."

"Great," I said lightly, not quite willing to tell him that by the time he got to Kennedy Meadows I would be on a bus to Anchorage.

"We'll hit snow just north of there and then the trail's buried for several hundred miles." He stood and swung his pack on with ease. His hairy legs were like the poles of a dock on a Minnesota lake. "We picked the wrong year to hike the PCT."

"I guess so," I said as I attempted to lift my pack and lace my arms casually through its straps, the way Greg had just done, as if by sheer desire to avoid humiliation I'd suddenly sprout muscles twice the strength of the ones I had, but my pack was too heavy and I still couldn't get it an inch off the ground.

He stepped forward to help me lift it on. "That's one heavy pack," he said as we struggled it onto my back. "Much heavier than mine."

"It's so good to see you," I said once I had it on, attempting to not seem to be hunching in a remotely upright position because I had to, but rather leaning forward with purpose and intention. "I haven't seen anyone on the trail so far. I thought there'd be more—hikers."

"Not many people hike the PCT. And certainly not this year, with the record snow. A lot of people saw that and postponed their trips until next year."

"I wonder if that's what we should do?" I asked, hoping he'd say he thought that was a great idea, coming back next year.

"You're the only solo woman I've met so far out here and the only one I've seen on the register too. It's kind of neat."

I replied with a tiny whimper of a smile.

"You all ready to go?" he asked.

"Ready!" I said, with more vigor than I had. I followed him up the trail, walking as fast as I could to keep up, matching my steps with the click of his trekking pole. When we reached a set of switchbacks fifteen minutes later, I paused to take a sip of water.

"Greg," I called to him as he continued on. "Nice to meet you."

He stopped and turned. "Only about thirty miles to Kennedy Meadows."

"Yeah," I said, giving him a weak nod. He'd be there the next morning. If I continued on, it would take me three days.

"It'll be cooler up there," Greg said. "It's a thousand feet higher than this."

"Good," I replied wanly.

"You're doing fine, Cheryl," he said. "Don't worry about it too much. You're green, but you're tough. And tough is what matters the most out here. Not just anyone could do what you're doing."

"Thanks," I said, so buoyed by his words that my throat constricted with emotion.

"I'll see you up in Kennedy Meadows," he said, and began to hike away.

"Kennedy Meadows," I called after him with more clarity than I felt.

"We'll make a plan about the snow," he said before disappearing from sight.

I hiked in the heat of that day with a new determination. Inspired by Greg's faith in me, I didn't give quitting another thought. As I hiked, I pondered the ice ax that would be in my resupply box. The ice ax that allegedly belonged to me. It was black and silver and dangerous-looking, an approximately two-foot-long metal dagger with a shorter, sharper dagger that ran crosswise at the end. I bought it, brought it home, and placed it in the box labeled *Kennedy Meadows*, assuming that by the time I actually reached Kennedy Meadows I would know how to use it—having by then been inexplicably transformed into an expert mountaineer.

By now, I knew better. The trail had humbled me. Without some kind of ice ax training, there wasn't any question that I was far more likely to impale myself with it than I was to use it to prevent myself from sliding off the side of a mountain. On my trailside breaks that day, in the hundred-plus-degree heat, I flipped through the pages of my guidebook to see if it said anything about how to use an ice ax. It did not. But of hiking over snow-covered ground it said that both crampons and an ice ax were necessary, as well as a firm grasp of how to use a compass, "an informed respect for avalanches," and "a lot of mountaineering sense."

I slammed the book shut and hiked on through the heat into the Dome Land Wilderness, heading toward what I hoped would be an ice ax crash course taught by Greg in Kennedy Meadows. I hardly knew him and yet he had become a beacon for me, my guiding star to the north. If he could do this, I could, I thought furiously. He wasn't tougher than me. No one was, I told myself, without believing it. I made it the mantra of those days; when I paused before yet another series of switchbacks or skidded down knee-jarring slopes, when patches of flesh peeled off my feet along with my socks, when I lay alone and lonely in my tent at night I asked, often out loud: *Who is tougher than me?*

The answer was always the same, and even when I knew absolutely there was no way on this earth it was true, I said it anyway: *No one.*

As I hiked, the terrain slowly shifted from desert to forest, the trees grew taller and more lush, the shallow streambeds more likely to have a seep of water, the meadows dense with wildflowers. There had been flowers in the desert too, but they'd been less abundant, more exotic, preciously and grandiosely festooned. The wildflowers I encountered now were a more common bunch, growing as they did in bright blankets or rimming the shaded edges of the trail. Many of them were familiar to me, being the same species as or close cousins to those that prospered in Minnesota summers. As I passed them, I felt the presence of my mother so acutely that I had the sensation that she was there; once I even paused to look around for her before I could go on.

On the afternoon of the day I met Greg, I saw my first bear on the trail, though technically I heard it first, an unmistakably muscular snort that stopped me in my tracks. When I looked up, I saw an animal as big as a refrigerator standing on all fours on the trail twenty feet away from me. The instant our eyes met, the same startled expression swept across both of our faces.

"BEAR!" I yelped, and reached for my whistle the moment after he turned and ran, his thick rump rippling in the sun as my whistle peeped its murderously loud peep.

It took me a few minutes to work up the courage to continue on. In addition to the reality that I now had to walk in the very direction in which the bear had run, my mind was reeling with the fact that he didn't seem to be a black bear. I'd seen lots of black bears before; the woods of northern Minnesota were thick with them. Often, I'd startled them in this very manner while walking or running on the gravel road I grew up on. But those black bears were different from the one I'd just seen. They were black. Black as tar. Black as planting soil you bought in big bags from the garden store. This bear hadn't been like any of them. Its coat was cinnamon brown, almost blond in places.

I began to walk tentatively, attempting to make myself believe that surely the bear was not a grizzly or a brown bear—the black bear's more predatory ursine cousins. Of course it was not. I knew it could not be. Those bears didn't live in California any longer; they'd all been killed off years ago. And yet why was the bear I'd seen so very, very, indisputably . . . *not black*?

I held my whistle for an hour, preparing to blow it while also singing songs so as not to take the refrigerator-sized whatever sort of bear it was by surprise should I come upon him again. I belted out my old fallback tunes—the ones I'd used when I'd become convinced the week before that a mountain lion was stalking me—singing *Twinkle, twinkle, little star* . . . and *Country roads, take me home* . . . in artificially brave tones, then letting the mix-tape radio station in my head take over so I simply sang fragments of songs I longed to hear. "A mulatto, an albino, a mosquito, my libido. YEAHH!"

It was because of this very singing that I almost stepped on a rattlesnake, having failed to absorb that the insistent rattling that increased in volume was actually a rattle. And not just any old rattle, but one attached to the tail end of a serpent as thick as my forearm.

"AH!" I shrieked when my eyes landed on the snake coiled up a few feet away from me. If I'd been able to jump, I would have. I jumped but my feet didn't leave the trail. Instead, I scrambled away from the snake's small blunt head, yowling in terror. It was a good ten minutes before I could work up the courage to step around it in a wide arc, my entire body quaking.

The rest of the day was a slow march, my eyes scanning both the ground and the horizon, terrified at every sound, while also chanting to myself: *I am not afraid.* Shaken as I was, I couldn't help but feel grateful to glimpse a couple of the animals that shared this place that had begun to feel a tiny bit like mine. I realized that in spite of my hardships, as I approached the end of the first leg of my journey, I'd begun to feel a blooming affection for the PCT. My backpack, heavy as it was, had come to feel like my almost animate companion. No longer was it the absurd Volkswagen Beetle I'd painfully hoisted on in that motel room in Mojave a couple of weeks before. Now my backpack had a name: Monster.

I meant it in the nicest possible way. I was amazed that what I needed to survive could be carried on my back. And, most surprising of all, that I could carry it. That I could bear the unbearable. These realizations about my physical, material life couldn't help but spill over into the emotional and spiritual realm. That my complicated life could be made so simple was astounding. It had begun to occur to me that perhaps it was okay that I hadn't spent my days on the trail pondering the sorrows of my life, that perhaps by being forced to focus on my physical suffering some of my emotional suffering would fade away. By the end of that second week, I realized that since I'd begun my hike, I hadn't shed a single tear.

I hiked the final miles to the narrow flat where I made camp the night before I reached Kennedy Meadows in the familiar agony that had been my constant companion. I was relieved to see that a wide fallen tree bordered my campsite. It was long dead, its trunk worn gray and smooth, shorn of its bark ages ago. It formed a high smooth bench, where I sat and removed my pack with ease. As soon as I got my pack off, I lay on the tree as if it were a couch—a sweet respite from the ground. The tree was just wide enough that if I lay still, I could rest without rolling off either side. It felt spectacular. I was hot, thirsty, hungry, and tired, but all of those things were nothing in comparison to the burning pain that emanated from the knots in my upper back. I closed my eyes, sighing with relief.

A few minutes later, I felt something on my leg. I looked down and saw that I was covered with black ants, an entire army of them, making a conga line from a hole in the tree and swarming my body. I shot off the log, shouting louder than I had when I'd seen the bear and the rattlesnake, batting at the harmless ants, breathless with an unreasonable fear. And not just of the ants, but of everything. Of the fact that I wasn't of this world, even if I insisted I was.

I cooked my dinner and retreated into my tent as soon as I could, well before dark, simply so I could be inside, even if inside only meant being surrounded by a thin sheet of nylon. Before I began hiking the PCT, I'd imagined that I'd sleep inside my tent only when it threatened to rain, that most nights I'd lay my sleeping bag on top of my tarp and sleep beneath the stars, but about this, like so much else, I'd been wrong. Each evening, I ached for the shelter of my tent, for the smallest sense that something was shielding me from the entire rest of the world, keeping me safe not from danger, but from vastness itself. I loved the dim, clammy dark of my tent, the cozy familiarity of the way I arranged my few belongings all around me each night.

I pulled out *As I Lay Dying,* put on my headlamp, and positioned my food bag beneath my calves while saying a little prayer that the bear I saw earlier in the day—the black bear, I emphasized—wouldn't bust through my tent to steal it from me.

When I woke at eleven to the yipping of coyotes, the light from my headlamp had grown dim; the Faulkner novel was still open on my chest.

In the morning, I could barely stand up. It wasn't just that morning, day 14. It had been happening for the past week, an ever-increasing array of problems and pains that made it impossible for me to stand or walk like a regular person when I first emerged from my tent. It was as if I were suddenly a very old woman, limping into the day. I'd managed to carry Monster more than a hundred miles over rough and sometimes steep terrain by then, but as each new day began, I couldn't even tolerate my own weight; my feet tender and swollen from the previous day's exertions; my knees too stiff to do what a normal gait required of them.

I'd finished ambling barefoot around my camp and was packed up and ready to go when two men appeared on the trail from the south. Like Greg, they greeted me by name before I'd even spoken a word. They were Albert and Matt, a father-and-son team from Georgia, hiking the entire trail. Albert was fifty-two; Matt, twenty-four. Both had been Eagle Scouts and they looked it. They had a clean-cut sincerity and a military precision that belied their grizzled beards, their dust-caked calves, and the five-foot stench cloud that surrounded their every move.

"Jiminy Cricket," Albert drawled when he saw Monster. "What you got in there, girly-o? Looks like everything but the kitchen sink."

"Just backpacking things," I said, reddening with shame. Each of their packs was about half the size of mine.

"I'm just teasing you," Albert said kindly. We chatted about the scorching trail behind us and the frozen one ahead. As we spoke, I felt just as I had when I'd met Greg: giddy to be with them, though being with them only underscored how insufficiently I'd prepared for my hike. I could feel their eyes on me, read them as they shifted from one thought to the next, as they registered my preposterous pack and my dubious grasp of the business at hand, while also acknowledging the moxie it had taken to make it this far on my own. Matt was a big lug of a guy, built like a linebacker, his reddish-brown hair curling softly over his ears and glinting golden on his gargantuan legs. He was only a couple of years younger than me, but so shy he struck me as a kid, letting his dad do most of the talking while he stood off to the side.

"Pardon my question," asked Albert, "but how many times are you urinating a day in this heat?"

"Um . . . I haven't been keeping track. Should I be?" I asked, feeling exposed yet again for the wilderness fraud that I was. I hoped they hadn't been camped near enough to hear me shrieking about the ants the evening before.

"Ideally, it's seven," said Albert crisply. "That's the old Boy Scout rule, though with this heat and the waterless conditions on the trail, combined with the extreme level of exertion, we've been lucky if it's three."

"Yeah. Me too," I said, though in fact there'd been one twenty-four-hour period—in the midst of the most ferocious heat—that I hadn't gone even once. "I saw a bear south of here," I said to change the subject. "A brown bear, which was a black bear, of course. But it looked brown. In color, I mean, the black bear."

"They're just cinnamon-colored down in these parts," said Albert. "Bleached by the California sun, I suppose." He tapped the brim of his hat. "We'll be seeing you up in Kennedy Meadows, miss. Pleasure to meet you."

"There's another guy up ahead named Greg," I said. "I met him a couple of days ago and he said he'd still be there." My insides leapt when I spoke Greg's name, for no other reason than he was the only person I knew on the trail.

"We've been following him for a good stretch, so it'll be nice to finally meet him," said Albert. "There's another couple a fellas behind us. Most likely they'll be along any time," he said, and turned to look down the trail in the direction that we'd come from. "Two kids named Doug and

Tom, about the same age as y'all. They started not long before you did, a touch south."

I waved Albert and Matt off and sat for a few minutes pondering the existence of Doug and Tom, and then I rose and spent the next several hours hiking harder than ever, with the single-minded goal that they would not catch up to me before I reached Kennedy Meadows. I was dying to meet them, of course—but I wanted to meet them as the woman who'd left them in her dust instead of the woman they'd overtaken. Like Greg, Albert and Matt had started hiking at the Mexican border and were by now well seasoned, logging twenty-some miles each day. But Doug and Tom were different. Like me, they'd started only recently on the PCT—*not long before you did,* Albert had said, and just *a touch south.* His words replayed themselves in my mind, as if replaying them would wring more meaning and specificity from them. As if by them I could discern how fast or slow I was traveling in comparison to Doug and Tom. As if the answer to that question held the key to my success or failure at this—the hardest thing I'd ever done.

I stopped in my tracks when that thought came into my mind, that hiking the PCT was the hardest thing I'd ever done. Immediately, I amended the thought. Watching my mother die and having to live without her, that was the hardest thing I'd ever done. Leaving Paul and destroying our marriage and life as I knew it for the simple and inexplicable reason that I felt I had to—that had been hard as well. But hiking the PCT was hard in a different way. In a way that made the other hardest things the tiniest bit less hard. It was strange but true. And perhaps I'd known it in some way from the very beginning. Perhaps the impulse to purchase the PCT guidebook months before had been a primal grab for a cure, for the thread of my life that had been severed.

I could feel it unspooling behind me—the old thread I'd lost, the new one I was spinning—while I hiked that morning, the snowy peaks of the High Sierras coming into occasional view. As I walked, I didn't think of those snowy peaks. Instead, I thought of what I would do once I arrived at the Kennedy Meadows General Store that afternoon, imagining in fantastic detail the things I would purchase to eat and drink—cold lemonade and candy bars and junk food I seldom ate in my regular life. I pictured the moment when I would lay hands on my first resupply box, which felt to me like a monumental milestone, the palpable proof that I'd made it at least that far. *Hello,* I said to myself in anticipation of what

I'd say once I arrived at the store, *I'm a PCT hiker here to pick up my box. My name is Cheryl Strayed.*

Cheryl Strayed, Cheryl Strayed, Cheryl Strayed—those two words together still rolled somewhat hesitantly off my tongue. Cheryl had been my name forever, but Strayed was a new addition—only officially my name since April, when Paul and I had filed for divorce. Paul and I had taken on each other's last names when we married, and our two names became one long four-syllable name, connected by a hyphen. I never liked it. It was too complicated and cumbersome. Seldom did anyone manage to get it right, and even I stumbled over it a good portion of the time. *Cheryl Hyphen-Hyphen,* an old grumpy man I briefly worked for called me, flummoxed by my actual name, and I couldn't help but see his point.

In that uncertain period when Paul and I had been separated for several months but were not yet sure we wanted to get divorced, we sat down together to scan a set of no-fault, do-it-yourself divorce documents we'd ordered over the phone, as if holding them in our hands would help us decide what to do. As we paged through the documents, we came across a question that asked the name we'd each have after the divorce. The line beneath the question was perfectly blank. On it, to my amazement, we could write anything. Be anyone. We laughed about it at the time, making up incongruous new names for ourselves—names of movie stars and cartoon characters and strange combinations of words that weren't rightly names at all.

But later, alone in my apartment, that blank line stuck in my heart. There was no question that if I divorced Paul, I'd choose a new name for myself. I couldn't continue to be Cheryl Hyphen-Hyphen, nor could I go back to having the name I had had in high school and be the girl I used to be. So in the months that Paul and I hung in marital limbo, unsure of which direction we'd move in, I pondered the question of my last name, mentally scanning words that sounded good with Cheryl and making lists of characters from novels I admired. Nothing fit until one day when the word *strayed* came into my mind. Immediately, I looked it up in the dictionary and knew it was mine. Its layered definitions spoke directly to my life and also struck a poetic chord: *to wander from the proper path, to deviate from the direct course, to be lost, to become wild, to be without a mother or father, to be without a home, to move about aimlessly in search of something, to diverge or digress.*

I had diverged, digressed, wandered, and become wild. I didn't embrace the word as my new name because it defined negative aspects of my circumstances or life, but because even in my darkest days—those very days in which I was naming myself—I saw the power of the darkness. Saw that, in fact, I *had* strayed and that I *was* a stray and that from the wild places my straying had brought me, I knew things I couldn't have known before.

Cheryl Strayed I wrote repeatedly down a whole page of my journal, like a girl with a crush on a boy she hoped to marry. Only the boy didn't exist. I was my own boy, planting a root in the very center of my rootlessness. Still, I had my doubts. To pick a word out of the dictionary and proclaim it mine felt a bit fraudulent to me, a bit childish or foolish, not to mention a touch hypocritical. For years I'd privately mocked the peers in my hippy, artsy, lefty circles who'd taken on names they'd invented for themselves. Jennifers and Michelles who became Sequoias and Lunas; Mikes and Jasons who became Oaks and Thistles. I pressed on anyway, confiding in a few friends about my decision, asking them to begin calling me by my new name to help me test it out. I took a road trip and each time I happened across a guest book I signed it *Cheryl Strayed,* my hand trembling slightly, feeling vaguely guilty, as if I were forging a check.

By the time Paul and I decided to file our divorce papers, I'd broken in my new name enough that I wrote it without hesitation on the blank line. It was the other lines that gave me pause, the endless lines demanding signatures that would dissolve our marriage. Those were the ones I completed with far more trepidation. I didn't exactly want to get divorced. I didn't exactly not want to. I believed in almost equal measure both that divorcing Paul was the right thing to do and that by doing so I was destroying the best thing I had. By then my marriage had become like the trail in that moment when I realized there was a bull in both directions. I simply made a leap of faith and pushed on in the direction where I'd never been.

The day we signed our divorce papers, it was April in Minneapolis and snowing, the flakes coming down in thick swirls, enchanting the city. We sat across a table from a woman named Val who was an acquaintance of ours and also, as it happened, licensed as a notary public. We watched the snow from a wide window in her office downtown, making little jokes when we could. I'd met Val only a few times before; I knew glimmers of things about her that jumbled together in my mind. She was cute, blunt, and impossibly tiny; at least a decade older than us. Her hair was an inch long and bleached blonde except for a longer hank of it that was dyed pink and swooped down like a little wing over her eyes. Silver earrings rimmed her ears and a throng of multicolored tattoos etched her arms like sleeves.

This, and yet she had an actual job in an actual office downtown with a big wide window and a notary public license to boot. We chose her to officiate our divorce because we wanted it to be easy. We wanted it to be cool. We wanted to believe that we were still gentle, good people in the world. That everything we'd said to each other six years before had been true. *What was it we said?* we'd asked each other a few weeks before, half drunk in my apartment, where we'd decided once and for all that we were going through with this.

"Here it is," I'd yelled after riffling through some papers and finding the wedding vows we'd written ourselves, three faded pages stapled together. We'd given them a title: *The Day the Daisies Bloomed*. "The Day the Daisies Bloomed!" I hooted, and we laughed so hard at ourselves, at the people we used to be. And then I set the vows back on top of the pile where I'd found them, unable to read on.

We'd married so young, so uncharacteristically, even our parents asked why we couldn't just live together. We couldn't just live together, even though I was only nineteen and he twenty-one. We were too wildly in love and we believed we had to do something wild to demonstrate that, so we did the wildest thing we could think of and got married. But even married, we didn't think of ourselves as *married people*—we were monogamous, but we had no intention of settling down. We packed our bicycles into boxes and flew with them to Ireland, where a month later, I turned twenty. We rented a flat in Galway and then changed our minds and moved to Dublin and got a matching pair of restaurant jobs—he in a pizza place, me in a vegetarian café. Four months later, we moved to London and walked the streets so destitute we searched for coins on the sidewalk. Eventually, we returned home, and not long after that my mother died and we did all the things that we did that led us here, to Val's office.

Paul and I had clutched each other's hands beneath the table, watching Val as she methodically examined our do-it-yourself no-fault divorce documents. She inspected one page and then the next, and on and on through fifty or sixty, making sure we'd gotten everything right. I felt a kind of loyalty rear up in me as she did this, unified with Paul against whatever contrary claim she might make, as if we were applying to be together for the rest of our lives instead of the opposite.

"It all looks good," she said at last, giving us a reticent smile. And then she went back through the pages again, at a brisker clip this time, pressing her giant notary public stamp against some and sliding dozens of others across the table for us to sign.

"I love him," I blurted when we were nearly through, my eyes filling with tears. I thought about pulling up my sleeve and showing her the square of gauze that covered my brand-new horse tattoo, as proof, but I only stammered on. "I mean, this is not for lack of love, just so you know. I love him and he loves me . . ." I looked at Paul, waiting for him to interject and agree and declare his love too, but he remained silent. "Just so you know," I repeated. "So you won't get the wrong idea."

"I know," Val said, and pushed the pink hank of her hair aside so I could see her eyes fluttering nervously from the papers up to me and then down to the papers again.

"And it's all my fault," I said, my voice swelling and shaking. "He didn't do anything. I'm the one. I broke my own heart."

Paul reached for me and squeezed my leg, consoling me. I couldn't look at him. If I looked at him I would cry. We'd agreed to this together, but I knew that if I turned to him and proposed we forget about divorcing and get back together instead, he would agree. I didn't turn. Something inside of me whirred like a machine that I had started but could not stop. I put my hand down and placed it on top of Paul's hand on my leg.

Sometimes we wondered together if things would have turned out differently if one thing that was true hadn't been true. If my mother hadn't died, for example, would I still have cheated on him? Or if I hadn't cheated on him, would he have cheated on me? And what if nothing had happened—no mother dying, no cheating on anyone—would we still be getting divorced anyway, having simply married too young? We couldn't know, but we were open to knowing. As close as we'd been when we were together, we were closer in our unraveling, telling each other everything at last, words that seemed to us might never have been spoken between two human beings before, so deep we went, saying everything that was beautiful and ugly and true.

"Now that we've been through all this, we should stay together," I half joked in the tender wake of our last heartrending, soul-baring discussion—the one we'd had to decide at last whether or not to get divorced. We were sitting on the couch in the dark of my apartment, having talked through the afternoon and into the evening, both of us too shattered by the time the sun set to get up and switch on a light.

"I hope you can do that someday with someone else," I said when he didn't reply, though the very thought of that someone else pierced my heart.

"I hope you can too," he said.

I sat in the darkness beside him, wanting to believe that I was capable of finding the kind of love I had with him again, only without wrecking it the next time around. It felt impossible to me. I thought of my mother. Thought of how in the last days of her life so many horrible things had happened. Small, horrible things. My mother's whimsical, delirious babblings. The blood pooling to blacken the backs of her bedridden arms. The way she begged for something that wasn't even mercy. For whatever it is that is less than mercy; for what we don't even have a word for. Those were the worst days, I believed at the time, and yet the moment she died I'd have given anything to have them back. One small, horrible, glorious day after the other. Maybe it would be that way with Paul as well, I thought, sitting beside him on the night we decided to divorce. Maybe once they were over, I'd want these horrible days back too.

"What are you thinking?" he asked, but I didn't answer. I only leaned over and switched on the light.

It was up to us to mail the notarized divorce documents. Together Paul and I walked out of the building and into the snow and down the sidewalk until we found a mailbox. Afterwards, we leaned against the cold bricks of a building and kissed, crying and murmuring regrets, our tears mixing together on our faces.

"What are we doing?" Paul asked after a while.

"Saying goodbye," I said. I thought of asking him to go back to my apartment with me, as we'd done a few times over the course of our year-long separation, falling into bed together for a night or an afternoon, but I didn't have the heart.

"Goodbye," he said.

"Bye," I said.

We stood close together, face-to-face, my hands gripping the front of his coat. I could feel the dumb ferocity of the building on one side of me; the gray sky and the white streets like a giant slumbering beast on the other; and us between them, alone together in a tunnel. Snowflakes were melting onto his hair and I wanted to reach up and touch them, but I didn't. We stood there without saying anything, looking into each other's eyes as if it would be the last time.

"Cheryl Strayed," he said after a long while, my new name so strange on his tongue.

I nodded and let go of his coat.

7

THE ONLY GIRL IN THE WOODS

"Cheryl Strayed?" the woman at the Kennedy Meadows General Store asked without a smile. When I nodded exuberantly, she turned and disappeared into the back without another word.

I looked around, drunk with the sight of the packaged food and drinks, feeling a combination of anticipation over the things I'd consume in the coming hours and relief over the fact that my pack was no longer attached to my body, but resting now on the porch of the store.

I was here. I had made it to my first stop. It seemed like a miracle. I'd half expected to see Greg, Matt, and Albert at the store, but they were nowhere in sight. My guidebook explained that the campground was another three miles farther on and I assumed that's where I'd find them, along with Doug and Tom eventually. Thanks to my exertions, they hadn't managed to catch up with me. Kennedy Meadows was a pretty expanse of piney woods and sage and grass meadows at an elevation of 6,200 feet on the South Fork Kern River. It wasn't a town but rather an outpost of civilization spread out over a few miles, consisting of a general store, a restaurant called Grumpie's, and a primitive campground.

"Here you go," the woman said, returning with my box and setting it on the counter. "It's the only one that's got a girl's name on it. That's how I knew." She reached across the counter to me. "This came too."

In her hand was a postcard. I took it and read it: *I hope you made it this far*, it said in a familiar scrawl. *I want to be your clean boyfriend someday.*

I love you. Joe. On the other side was a photograph of the Sylvia Beach Hotel on the Oregon coast, where we'd stayed together once. I stared at the photograph for several moments, a series of feelings washing over me in waves: grateful for a word from someone I knew, nostalgic for Joe, disappointed that only one person had written to me, and heartbroken, unreasonable as it was, that the one person who had wasn't Paul.

I bought two bottles of Snapple lemonade, a king-sized Butterfinger, and a bag of Doritos and went outside and sat on the front steps, devouring the things I'd purchased while reading the postcard over and over again. After a while, I noticed a box in the corner of the porch stuffed full with mostly packaged backpacker food. Above it there was a handwritten sign that said:

PCT hiker FREE box!!!
Leave what you don't want!
Take what you do!

A ski pole was propped behind the box, precisely the thing I needed. It was a ski pole fit for a princess: white, with a bubble-gum-pink nylon wrist strap. I tested it out for a few steps. It was the perfect height. It would help me across not only the snow, but also the many stream fords and rockslides that no doubt lay ahead.

I walked with it an hour later as I made my way along the dirt road that went in a loop around the campground, looking for Greg, Matt, and Albert. It was a Sunday afternoon in June, but the place was mostly empty. I passed by a man preparing his fishing gear and a couple with a cooler of beer and a boom box and eventually came to a campsite where a shirtless gray-haired man with a big tan belly sat at a picnic table reading a book. He looked up as I approached.

"You must be the famous Cheryl of the enormous backpack," he called to me.

I laughed in agreement.

"I'm Ed." He walked toward me to shake my hand. "Your friends are here. They all just caught a ride up to the store—you must have missed them as you were coming—but they asked me to watch for you. You can set up your tent right over there if you'd like. They're all camped here—Greg and Albert and his son." He gestured to the tents around him. "We were taking bets who'd arrive first. You or the two boys from back east coming up behind you."

"Who won?" I asked.

Ed thought for a moment. "No one," he said, and boomed with laughter. "None of us bet on you."

I rested Monster on the picnic table, took it off, and left it there, so when I had to put it on again I wouldn't have to perform my pathetic dead lift from the ground.

"Welcome to my humble abode," Ed said, gesturing to a little pop-up trailer that had a tarp roof extending out its side with a makeshift camp kitchen beneath it. "You hungry?"

There were no showers at the campground, so while Ed made lunch for me, I walked to the river to wash as best as I could with my clothes still on. The river felt like a shock after all that dry territory I'd crossed. And the South Fork Kern River wasn't just any river. It was violent and self-possessed, ice-cold and raging, its might clear evidence of the heavy snows higher up the mountains. The current was too fast to go in even ankle-deep, so I walked down the bank until I found an eddying pool near the river's edge and waded in. My feet ached from the cold water and eventually went numb. I crouched and wetted down my filthy hair and splashed handfuls of water beneath my clothes to wash my body. I felt electric with sugar and the victory of arriving; filled with anticipation of the conversations I'd have over the next couple of days.

When I was done, I walked up the bank and then across a wide meadow, wet and cool. I could see Ed from a distance, and as I approached I watched him move from his camp kitchen to the picnic table with plates of food in his hands, bottles of ketchup and mustard and cans of Coke. I'd known him only a few minutes and yet, like the other men I'd met, he felt instantly familiar to me, as if I could trust him with close to anything. We sat across from each other and ate while he told me about himself. He was fifty, an amateur poet and seasonal vagabond, childless and divorced. I tried to eat at his leisurely pace, taking bites when he did, the same way I'd attempted to match my steps to Greg's a few days before, but I couldn't do it. I was ravenous. I devoured two hot dogs and a mountain of baked beans and another mountain of potato chips in a flash and then sat hungrily wishing for more. Meanwhile, Ed worked his way languidly through his lunch, pausing to open his journal to read aloud poems that he'd composed the day before. He lived in San Diego most of the year, he explained, but each summer he set up camp in Kennedy Meadows in order to greet the PCT hikers as they passed through. He was what's referred to in PCT hiker vernacular as a *trail angel,* but I didn't know that then. Didn't know, even, that there was a PCT hiker vernacular.

"Look here, fellas, we all lost the bet," Ed hollered to the men when they returned from the store.

"I didn't lose!" Greg protested as he came close to squeeze my shoulder. "I put my money on you, Cheryl," he insisted, though the others disputed his claim.

We sat around the picnic table, talking about the trail, and after a while, they all dispersed to take naps—Ed to his trailer; Greg, Albert, and Matt to their tents. I stayed at the picnic table, too excited to sleep, pawing through the contents of the box I'd packed weeks before. The things inside smelled like a world far-off, like the one I'd occupied in what seemed another lifetime, scented with the Nag Champa incense that had permeated my apartment. The ziplock bags and packaging on the food were still shiny and unscathed. The fresh T-shirt smelled of the lavender detergent I bought in bulk at the co-op I belonged to in Minneapolis. The flowery cover of *The Complete Stories* by Flannery O'Connor was unbent.

The same could not be said of Faulkner's *As I Lay Dying,* or rather the thin portion of the book I still had in my pack. I'd torn off the cover and all the pages I'd read the night before and burned them in the little aluminum pie pan I'd brought to place beneath my stove to safeguard against errant sparks. I'd watched Faulkner's name disappear into flames feeling a bit like it was a sacrilege—never had I dreamed I'd be burning books—but I was desperate to lighten my load. I'd done the same with the section from *The Pacific Crest Trail, Volume 1: California* that I'd already hiked.

It hurt to do it, but it had to be done. I'd loved books in my regular, pre-PCT life, but on the trail, they'd taken on even greater meaning. They were the world I could lose myself in when the one I was actually in became too lonely or harsh or difficult to bear. When I made camp in the evenings, I rushed through the tasks of pitching my tent and filtering water and cooking dinner so I could sit afterwards inside the shelter of my tent in my chair with my pot of hot food gripped between my knees. I ate with my spoon in one hand and a book in the other, reading by the light of my headlamp when the sky darkened. In the first week of my hike, I was often too exhausted to read more than a page or two before I fell asleep, but as I grew stronger I was reading more, eager to escape the tedium of my days. And each morning, I burned whatever I'd read the night before.

As I held my unspoiled copy of O'Connor's short stories, Albert emerged from his tent. "Looks to me like you could stand to lose a few things," he said. "Want some help?"

"Actually," I said, smiling ruefully at him, "yes."

"All right, then. Here's what I want you to do: pack up that thing just like you're about to hike out of here for this next stretch of trail and we'll go from there." He walked toward the river with the nub of a toothbrush in hand—the end of which he'd thought to break off to save weight, of course.

I went to work, integrating the new with the old, feeling as if I were taking a test that I was bound to fail. When I was done, Albert returned and methodically unpacked my pack. He placed each item in one of two piles—one to go back into my pack, another to go into the now-empty resupply box that I could either mail home or leave in the PCT hiker free box on the porch of the Kennedy Meadows General Store for others to plunder. Into the box went the foldable saw and miniature binoculars and the megawatt flash for the camera I had yet to use. As I looked on, Albert chucked aside the deodorant whose powers I'd overestimated and the disposable razor I'd brought with some vague notion about shaving my legs and under my arms and—much to my embarrassment—the fat roll of condoms I'd slipped into my first aid kit.

"Do you really need these?" Albert asked, holding the condoms. Albert the Georgia Daddy Eagle Scout, whose wedding band glinted in the sun, who cut off the handle of his own toothbrush, but no doubt carried a pocket-sized Bible in his pack. He looked at me stone-faced as a soldier, while the white plastic wrappers of a dozen ultrathin nonlubricated Trojan condoms made a clickety-clack sound as they unfurled like a party streamer from his hand.

"No," I said, feeling as if I was going to die of shame. The idea of having sex seemed absurd to me now, though when I'd packed my supplies it had struck me as a reasonable prospect, back before I had a clue of what hiking the Pacific Crest Trail would do to my body. I'd not seen myself since I was at the motel in Ridgecrest, but after the men had gone off to nap, I'd taken the opportunity to gaze at my face in the mirror attached to the side of Ed's truck. I looked tan and dirty, despite my recent dunk in the river. I'd become remotely leaner and my dark blonde hair a tad lighter, alternately flattened and sprung alive by a combination of dried sweat, river water, and dust.

I didn't look like a woman who might need twelve condoms.

But Albert didn't pause to ponder such things—whether I'd get laid or not, whether I was pretty. He pushed on, pillaging my pack, inquiring sternly each time before tossing another item I'd previously deemed necessary into the get-rid-of pile. I nodded almost every time he held an item up, agreeing it should go, though I held the line on both *The Complete Stories* and my beloved, intact copy of *The Dream of a Common Language*. I held the line on my journal, in which I recorded everything I did that summer. And when Albert wasn't looking, I tore one condom off the end of the fat roll of condoms he'd tossed aside and slid it discreetly into the back pocket of my shorts.

"So what brought you out here?" Albert asked when his work was done. He sat on the bench of the picnic table, his broad hands folded in front of him.

"To hike the PCT?" I asked.

He nodded and watched as I pushed the various items we'd agreed I could keep back into my pack. "I'll tell you why I'm doing it," he said quickly, before I could answer. "It's been a lifelong dream for me. When I heard about the trail I thought, 'Now there's something I'd like to do before I go to meet the Lord.'" He rapped his fist gently on the table. "So how about you, girly-o? I've got a theory that most folks have a reason. Something that drove 'em out here."

"I don't know," I demurred. I wasn't about to tell a fifty-something Christian Georgia Eagle Scout why I decided to walk alone in the woods for three solid months, no matter how kindly his eyes twinkled when he smiled. The things that compelled me to hike this trail would sound scandalous to him and dubious to me; to both of us, they'd only reveal just how shaky this whole endeavor was.

"Mainly," I said, "I thought it would be something fun."

"You call this fun?" he asked, and we both laughed.

I turned and leaned into Monster, threading my arms into the straps. "So let's see if it made a difference," I said, and buckled it on. When I lifted it from the table, I was amazed at how light it felt, even fully loaded with my new ice ax and a fresh supply of eleven days' worth of food. I beamed at Albert. "Thank you."

He chuckled in response, shaking his head.

Jubilant, I walked away to take my pack on a trial run on the dirt road that made a loop around the campground. Mine was still the biggest pack of the bunch—hiking solo, I had to carry things that those who hiked in pairs could divvy up, and I didn't have the ultralight confidence or skills that Greg did—but in comparison to how my pack had been before Albert helped me purge it, it was so light I felt I could leap into the air. Halfway around the loop I paused and leapt.

I made it only an inch off the ground, but at least it could be done.

"Cheryl?" a voice called out just then. I looked up and saw a handsome young man wearing a backpack walking toward me.

"Doug?" I asked, guessing right. In response he waved his arms and gave out a joyous hoot, and then he walked straight up to me and pulled me in for a hug.

"We read your entry in the register and we've been trying to catch up to you."

"And here I am," I stammered, taken aback by his enthusiasm and good looks. "We're all camped over there." I gestured behind me. "There's a bunch of us. Where's your friend?"

"He'll be coming up soon," Doug said, and hooted again, apropos of nothing. He reminded me of all the golden boys I'd known in my life— classically handsome and charmingly sure of his place at the very top of the heap, confident that the world was his and that he was safe in it, without ever having considered otherwise. As I stood next to him, I had the feeling that any moment he'd reach for my hand and together we'd parachute off a cliff, laughing as we wafted gently down.

"Tom!" Doug bellowed when he saw a figure appear down the road. Together we walked toward him. I could tell even from a distance that Tom was Doug's physical and spiritual opposite—bony, pale, bespectacled. The smile that crept onto his face as we approached was cautious and mildly unconvinced.

"Hello," he said to me when we got close enough, reaching to shake my hand.

In the few short minutes it took for us to reach Ed's camp, we exchanged a flurry of information about who we were and where we were from. Tom was twenty-four; Doug, twenty-one. *New England blue bloods,* my mother would have called them, I knew almost before they told me a thing—which meant to her only that they were basically rich and from somewhere east of Ohio and north of D.C. Over the course of

the coming days, I'd learn all about them. How their parents were sur-
geons and mayors and financial executives. How they'd both attended a
tony boarding school whose fame was so great even I knew it by name.
How they'd vacationed on Nantucket and on private islands off the coast
of Maine and spent their spring breaks in Vail. But I didn't know any of
that yet, how in so many ways their lives were unfathomable to me and
mine to them. I knew only that in some very particular ways they were
my closest kin. They weren't gearheads or backpacking experts or PCT
know-it-alls. They hadn't hiked all the way from Mexico, nor had they
been planning the trip for a decade. And even better, the miles they'd
traversed so far had left them nearly as shattered as they'd left me. They
hadn't, by virtue of their togetherness, gone days without seeing another
human being. Their packs looked of a size reasonable enough that I
doubted they were carrying a foldable saw. But I could tell the instant
I locked eyes with Doug that, despite all his confidence and ease, he
had *been through something*. And when Tom took my hand to shake it,
I could read precisely the expression on his face. It said: *I'VE GOT TO
GET THESE FUCKING BOOTS OFF MY FEET.*

Moments later, he did, sitting on the bench of Ed's picnic table, after
we arrived at our camp and the men gathered around to introduce themselves. I watched as Tom carefully peeled off his filthy socks, clumps
of worn-out moleskin and his own flesh coming off with them. His
feet looked like mine: white as fish and pocked with bloody, oozing
wounds overlaid with flaps of skin that had been rubbed away and now
dangled, still painfully attached to the patches of flesh that had yet to die
a slow, PCT-induced death. I took off my pack and unzipped a pocket
to remove my first aid kit.

"Have you ever tried these?" I asked Tom, holding out a sheet of 2nd
Skin—thankfully, I had packed more into my resupply box. "These have
saved me," I explained. "I don't know if I could go on without them,
actually."

Tom only looked up at me in despair and nodded without elaborat-
ing. I set a couple of sheets of 2nd Skin beside him on the bench.

"You're welcome to these, if you'd like," I said. Seeing them in their
translucent blue wrappers brought to mind the condom in my back
pocket. I wondered if Tom had packed any; if Doug had; if my bringing them had been such a dumb idea after all. Being in Tom and Doug's
presence made it seem slightly less so.

"We thought we'd all go up to Grumpie's at six," Ed said, looking at his watch. "We've got a couple hours. I'll drive us all up in my truck." He looked at Tom and Doug. "Meanwhile, I'd be happy to get you boys a snack."

The men sat at the picnic table, eating Ed's potato chips and cold baked beans, talking about why they chose the pack they chose and the pros and cons of each. Someone brought out a deck of cards, and a game of poker started up. Greg paged through his guidebook at the end of the table near me, where I stood beside my pack, still marveling at its transformation. Pockets that had been bursting full now had tiny cushions of room.

"You're practically a Jardi-Nazi now," said Albert, in a teasing tone, seeing me gazing at my pack. "Those are the disciples of Ray Jardine, if you don't know. They take a highly particular view about pack weight."

"It's the guy I was telling you about," added Greg.

I nodded coolly, trying to conceal my ignorance. "I'm going to get ready for dinner," I said, and ambled to the edge of our campsite. I pitched my tent and then crawled inside, spread out my sleeping bag, and lay on top of it, staring at the green nylon ceiling, while listening to the murmur of the men's conversation and occasional bursts of laughter. I was going out to a restaurant with six men, and I had nothing to wear but what I was already wearing, I realized glumly: a T-shirt over a sports bra and a pair of shorts with nothing underneath. I remembered my fresh T-shirt from my resupply box and sat up and put it on. The entire back of the shirt I'd been wearing since Mojave was now stained a brownish yellow from the endless bath of sweat it had endured. I wadded it up in a ball and put it at the corner of my tent. I'd throw it away at the store later. The only other clothes I had were those I brought for cold weather. I remembered the necklace I'd been wearing until it got so hot that I couldn't bear to have it on; I found it in the ziplock bag in which I kept my driver's license and money and put it on. It was a small turquoise-and-silver earring that used to belong to my mother. I'd lost the other one, so I'd taken a pair of needle-nose pliers to the one that remained and turned it into a pendant on a delicate silver chain. I'd brought it along because it had been my mother's; having it with me felt meaningful, but now I was glad to have it simply because I felt prettier with it on. I ran my fingers through my hair, attempting to shape it into an attractive formation, aided by my tiny comb, but eventually I gave up and pushed it behind my ears.

It was just as well, I knew, that I simply let myself look and feel and smell the way I did. I was, after all, what Ed referred to somewhat inaccurately as *the only girl in the woods,* alone with a gang of men. By necessity, out here on the trail, I felt I had to sexually neutralize the men I met by being, to the extent that was possible, one of them.

I'd never been that way in my life, interacting with men in the even-keeled indifference that being one of the guys entails. It didn't feel like an easy thing to endure, as I sat in my tent while the men played cards. I'd been a girl forever, after all, familiar with and reliant upon the powers my very girlness granted me. Suppressing those powers gave me a gloomy twinge in the gut. Being one of the guys meant I could not go on being the woman I'd become expert at being among men. It was a version of myself I'd first tasted way back when I was a child of eleven and I'd felt that prickly rush of power when grown men would turn their heads to look at me or whistle or say *Hey pretty baby* just loudly enough that I could hear. The one I'd banked on all through high school, starving myself thin, playing cute and dumb so I'd be popular and loved. The one I'd fostered all through my young adult years while trying on different costumes—earth girl, punk girl, cowgirl, riot girl, ballsy girl. The one for whom behind every hot pair of boots or sexy little skirt or flourish of the hair there was a trapdoor that led to the least true version of me.

Now there was only one version. On the PCT I had no choice but to inhabit it entirely, to show my grubby face to the whole wide world. Which, at least for now, consisted of only six men.

"Cherylllll," Doug's voice called softly from a few feet away. "You in there?"

"Yeah," I replied.

"We're going down to the river. Come hang with us."

"Okay," I said, feeling flattered in spite of myself. When I sat up, the condom made a crinkling sound in my back pocket. I took it out and slid it into my first aid kit, crawled out of my tent, and walked toward the river.

Doug, Tom, and Greg were wading in the shallow spot where I'd cleaned up a few hours before. Beyond them, the water raged in torrents, rushing over boulders as big as my tent. I thought of the snow I'd soon be encountering if I continued on with the ice ax I didn't yet know how to use and the white ski pole with its cute little pink wrist strap that had come to me only by chance. I hadn't yet begun to think about what was next on the trail. I'd only listened and nodded when Ed told me that most of the PCT hikers who'd come through Kennedy Meadows in the three weeks he'd been camped here had opted to get off the trail at this point because of the record snowpack that made the trail essentially unpassable for most of the next four or five hundred miles. They caught rides and buses to rejoin the PCT farther north, at lower elevations, he told me. Some intended to loop back later in the summer to hike the section they'd missed; others to skip it. He said that a few had ended their hikes altogether, just as Greg had told me earlier, deciding to hike the PCT another, less record-breaking year. And fewer still had forged ahead, determined to make it through the snow.

Grateful for my cheap camp sandals, I picked my way over the rocks that lined the riverbed toward the men, the water so cold my bones hurt.

"I got something for you," said Doug when I reached him. He held his hand out to me. In it was a shiny feather, about a foot long, so black it shone blue in the sun.

"For what?" I asked, taking it from him.

"For luck," he said, and touched my arm.

When he took his hand away, the place where it had been felt like a burn—I could feel how little I'd been touched in the past fourteen days, how alone I'd been.

"So I was thinking about the snow," I said, holding the feather, my voice raised over the rush of the river. "The people who bypassed? They were all here a week or two before us. A lot more snow has melted by now, so maybe it'll be okay." I looked at Greg and then at the black feather, stroking it.

"The snow depth at Bighorn Plateau on June first was more than double what it was the same day last year," he said, tossing a stone. "A week isn't going to make much of a difference in that regard."

I nodded, as if I knew where Bighorn Plateau was, or what it meant for the snowpack to be double what it was a year ago. I felt like a fraud even having this discussion, like a mascot among players, as if they were the real PCT hikers and I was just happening through. As if somehow, because of my inexperience, my failure to read even a single page written by Ray Jardine, my laughably slow pace, and my belief that it had been reasonable to pack a foldable saw, I had not actually hiked to Kennedy Meadows from Tehachapi Pass, but instead had been carried along.

But I had walked here, and I wasn't ready to give up on seeing the

High Sierra just yet. It had been the section of the trail I'd most anticipated, its untouched beauty extolled by the authors of *The Pacific Crest Trail, Volume 1: California* and immortalized by the naturalist John Muir in the books he'd written a century before. It was the section of mountains he'd dubbed the "Range of Light." The High Sierra and its 13,000- and 14,000-foot-high peaks, its cold, clear lakes and deep canyons were the *point* of hiking the PCT in California, it seemed. Plus, bypassing it would be a logistical mess. If I had to skip the High Sierra, I'd end up in Ashland more than a month before I intended to.

"I'd like to push on, if there's a way," I said, waving the feather with a flourish. My feet didn't hurt anymore. They'd gone blissfully numb in the icy water.

"Well, we do have about forty miles to play with before the going gets seriously rough—from here up to Trail Pass," said Doug. "There's a trail there that intersects the PCT and goes down to a campground. We can hike at least that far and see how it goes—see how much snow there is— and then bail out there if we want to."

"What do you think of that, Greg?" I asked. Whatever he would do was what I'd do.

He nodded. "I think that's a good plan."

"That's what I'm going to do," I said. "I'll be okay. I have my ice ax now."

Greg looked at me. "You know how to use it?"

The next morning he gave me a tutorial.

"This is the shaft," he said, running his hand up the length of the ax. "And this is the spike," he added, touching a finger to the sharp end. "And on the other end there's the head."

The shaft? The head? The spike? I tried not to crack up like an eighth grader in sex ed class, but I couldn't help myself.

"What?" asked Greg, his hand around the shaft of his ax, but I only shook my head. "You've got two edges," he continued. "The blunt edge is the adze. That's what you use to chop your steps. And the other edge is the pick. That's what you use to save your ass when you're sliding off the side of the mountain." He spoke in a tone that assumed I knew this already, as if he were just reviewing the basics before we got started.

"Yep. The shaft, the head, the spike, the pick, the ad," I said.

"The *adze*," he corrected. "There's a *z*." We were standing on a steep bank along the river, the closest thing we could find to simulate an icy slope. "Now let's say you're falling," said Greg, throwing himself down the incline to demonstrate. As he fell, he jammed the pick into the mud. "You want to dig that pick in as hard as you can, while holding on to the shaft with one hand and the head with the other. Like this. And once you're anchored in, you try to get your footing."

I looked at him. "What if you can't get your footing?"

"Well, then you hold on here," he answered, moving his hands on the ax.

"What if I can't hold on that long? I mean, I'll have my pack and everything and, actually, I'm not strong enough to do a single pull-up."

"You hold on," he said dispassionately. "Unless you'd rather slide off the side of the mountain."

I got to work. Again and again I threw myself against the increasingly muddy slope, pretending that I was slipping on ice, and again and again I planted the pick of my ice ax into the soil while Greg watched, coaching and critiquing my technique.

Doug and Tom sat nearby pretending they weren't paying attention. Albert and Matt were lying on a tarp we'd spread out for them beneath the shade of a tree near Ed's truck, too ill to move anywhere but to the outhouse several times an hour. They'd both woken in the middle of the night sick with what we were all beginning to believe was giardia— a waterborne parasite that causes crippling diarrhea and nausea, requires prescription medication to cure, and almost always means a week or more off the trail. It was the reason PCT hikers spent so much time talking about water purifiers and water sources, for fear they'd make one wrong move and have to pay. I didn't know where Matt and Albert had picked up whatever they had, but I prayed I hadn't picked it up too. By late afternoon we all stood over them as they lay pale and limp on their tarp, convincing them it was time they got to the hospital in Ridgecrest. Too sick to resist, they watched as we packed their things and loaded their packs into the back of Ed's truck.

"Thank you for all your help with lightening my pack," I said to Albert when we had a moment alone before he departed. He looked wanly up at me from his bed on the tarp. "I couldn't have done it myself."

He gave me a weak smile and nodded.

"By the way," I said, "I wanted to tell you—about why I decided to hike the PCT? I got divorced. I was married and not long ago I got divorced, and also about four years ago my mom died—she was only forty-five and she got cancer suddenly and died. It's been a hard time in my life and I've sort of gotten offtrack. So I . . ." He opened his eyes wider, looking at me. "I thought it would help me find my center, to come out here." I made a crumpled gesture with my hands, out of words, a bit surprised that I'd let so many tumble out.

"Well, you've got your bearings now, haven't you?" he said, and sat up, his face lighting up despite his nausea. He rose and walked slowly to Ed's truck and got in beside his son. I clambered into the back with their backpacks and the box of things I no longer needed and rode with them as far as the general store. When we reached it, Ed stopped for a few moments; I jumped out with my box and waved to Albert and Matt, hollering *good luck*.

I felt a stinging rush of affection as I watched them drive away. Ed would return in a few hours, but most likely I'd never see Albert and Matt again. I would be hiking into the High Sierra with Doug and Tom the next day, and in the morning I'd have to say goodbye to Ed and Greg too—Greg was laying over in Kennedy Meadows another day, and though he would certainly catch up to me, it would likely be a fleeting visit, and then he too would pass out of my life.

I walked to the porch of the general store and put everything but the foldable saw, the special high-tech flash for my camera, and the miniature binoculars into the PCT hiker free box. Those I packed into my old resupply box and addressed it to Lisa in Portland. As I sealed my box with a roll of tape Ed had loaned me, I kept having the feeling that something was missing.

Later, as I walked the road back to the campground, I realized what it was: the fat roll of condoms.

Every last one was gone.

RANGE OF LIGHT

We are now in the mountains
and they are in us . . .

JOHN MUIR,
My First Summer in the Sierra

If your Nerve, deny you –
Go above your Nerve –

EMILY DICKINSON

8

CORVIDOLOGY

Kennedy Meadows is called the gateway to the High Sierra, and early the next morning I walked through that gate. Doug and Tom accompanied me for the first quarter mile, but then I stopped, telling them to go on ahead because I had to get something from my pack. We embraced and wished one another well, saying goodbye forever or for fifteen minutes, we didn't know. I leaned against a boulder to lift some of Monster's weight from my back, watching them go.

Their leaving made me melancholy, though I also felt something like relief when they disappeared into the dark trees. I hadn't needed to get anything from my pack; I'd only wanted to be alone. Alone had always felt like an actual place to me, as if it weren't a state of being, but rather a room where I could retreat to be who I really was. The radical aloneness of the PCT had altered that sense. Alone wasn't a room anymore, but the whole wide world, and now I was alone in that world, occupying it in a way I never had before. Living at large like this, without even a roof over my head, made the world feel both bigger and smaller to me. Until now, I hadn't truly understood the world's vastness—hadn't even understood how vast a mile could be—until each mile was beheld at walking speed. And yet there was also its opposite, the strange intimacy I'd come to have with the trail, the way the piñon pines and monkey flowers I passed that morning, the shallow streams I crossed, felt familiar and known, though I'd never passed them or crossed them before.

I walked in the cool of the morning to the rhythm of my new white ski pole clicking against the trail, feeling the lightened-but-still-ridiculously-heavy weight of Monster shift and settle in. When I'd set off that morning, I thought that it would feel different to be on the trail, that the hiking would be easier. My pack was lighter, after all, not only thanks to Albert's purge but because I no longer needed to carry more than a couple of bottles of water at a time, now that I'd reached a less arid stretch of the trail. But an hour and a half into the day I stopped for a break, feeling the familiar aches and pains. At the same time, I could ever so slightly feel my body toughening up, just as Greg had promised would happen.

It was day 1 of week 3, officially summer—the last week of June—and I was not only in a different season now, but in different country too, ascending higher in the South Sierra Wilderness. In the forty miles between Kennedy Meadows and Trail Pass, I'd climb from an elevation of just over 6,100 feet to nearly 11,000. Even in the heat of that first afternoon back on the trail, I could feel an edge of cool in the air that would no doubt envelop me at night. There was no question I was in the Sierra now—Muir's beloved Range of Light. I walked beneath great dark trees that put the smaller plants beneath in almost complete shadow and past wide grassy meadows of wildflowers; I scrambled over snowmelt streams by stepping from one unsteady rock to another, aided by my ski pole. At foot speed, the Sierra Nevada seemed just barely surmountable. I could always take another step. It was only when I rounded a bend and glimpsed the white peaks ahead that I doubted my abilities, only when I thought how far I had yet to go that I lost faith that I would get there.

Doug's and Tom's tracks periodically appeared on the alternately muddy and dusty trail, and by midafternoon I came upon them as they sat near a stream, their faces registering surprise when I walked up. I sat next to them and pumped water and we chatted for a while.

"You should camp with us tonight if you catch up with us," said Tom before they hiked on.

"I already have caught up to you," I replied, and we laughed.

That evening I strolled into the small clearing where they'd pitched their tents. After dinner, they shared the two beers they'd brought from Kennedy Meadows, giving me swigs as we sat in the dirt bundled in our clothes. As we drank, I wondered which one of them had taken the eleven ultrathin nonlubricated Trojan condoms I'd purchased in Portland a few weeks before. It seemed it had to be one of them.

The next day when I was hiking alone I came to a wide swath of snow on a steep incline, a giant ice-crusted sheath that obliterated the trail. It was like the rockslide, only scarier, a river of ice instead of stones. If I slipped while attempting to cross it, I would slide down the side of the mountain and crash into the boulders far below, or worse, fall farther into who knew what. Air, it seemed, from my vantage point. If I didn't attempt to cross it, I'd have to go back to Kennedy Meadows. That didn't seem like an altogether bad idea. And yet here I was.

Hell, I thought. Bloody hell. I took out my ice ax and studied my course, which really only meant standing there for several minutes working up the nerve. I could see that Doug and Tom had made it across, their tracks a series of potholes in the snow. I held my ice ax the way Greg had taught me and stepped into one of the potholes. Its existence made my life both harder and easier. I didn't have to chip my own steps, but those of the men were awkwardly placed and slippery and sometimes so deep that my boot got trapped inside and I'd lose my balance and fall, my ice ax so unwieldy it felt more like a burden than an aid. *Arrest,* I kept thinking, imagining what I'd do with the ax if I started to slide down the slope. The snow was different from the snow in Minnesota. In some places it was more ice than flake, so densely packed it reminded me of the hard layer of ice in a freezer that needs defrosting. In other places it gave way, slushier than it first appeared.

I didn't look at the bank of boulders below until I'd reached the other side of the snow and was standing on the muddy trail, trembling but glad. I knew that little jaunt was only a sample of what lay ahead. If I didn't opt to get off the trail at Trail Pass to bypass the snow, I'd soon reach Forester Pass, at 13,160 feet the highest point on the PCT. And if I didn't slip off the side of the mountain while going over that pass, I'd spend the next several weeks crossing nothing but snow. It would be snow far more treacherous than the patch I'd just crossed, but having crossed even this much made what lay ahead more real to me. It told me that I had no choice but to bypass. I wasn't rightly prepared to be on the PCT in a regular year, let alone a year in which the snow depth measurements were double and triple what they'd been the year before. There hadn't been a winter as snowy as the previous one since 1983, and there wouldn't be another for more than a dozen years.

Plus, there wasn't only the snow to consider. There were also the things related to the snow: the dangerously high rivers and streams I'd need to ford alone, the temperatures that would put me at risk of hypothermia, the reality that I'd have to rely exclusively on my map and compass for long stretches when the trail was concealed by the snow—all of those made more grave by the fact that I was alone. I didn't have the gear I needed; I didn't have the knowledge and experience. And because I was solo, I didn't have a margin for error either. By bailing out like most of the other PCT hikers had, I'd miss the glory of the High Sierra. But if I stayed on the trail, I'd risk my life.

"I'm getting off at Trail Pass," I told Doug and Tom as we ate dinner that night. I'd hiked all day alone—logging my second fifteen-plus-mile day—but caught up with them again as they made camp. "I'm going to go up to Sierra City and get back on the trail there."

"We decided to push on," said Doug.

"We talked about it and we think you should join us," said Tom.

"Join you?" I asked, peering out from the tunnel of my dark fleece hood. I was wearing all the clothes I'd brought, the temperature down near freezing. Patches of snow surrounded us beneath the trees in spots shaded from the sun.

"It's not safe for you to go alone," Doug said.

"Neither one of *us* would go alone," said Tom.

"But it's not safe for any of us to go into the snow. Together or alone," I said.

"We want to try it," said Tom.

"Thank you," I said. "I'm touched you'd offer, but I can't."

"Why can't you?" Doug asked.

"Because the point of my trip is that I'm out here to do it alone."

We were silent for a while then, eating our dinners, each of us cradling a warm pot full of rice or beans or noodles in our gloved hands. I felt sad to say no. Not only because I knew it meant I was opting to bypass the High Sierra, but because as much as I said I wanted to do this trip alone, I was soothed by their company. Being near Tom and Doug at night kept me from having to say to myself *I am not afraid* whenever I heard a branch snap in the dark or the wind shook so fiercely it seemed something bad was bound to happen. But I wasn't out here to keep myself from having to say *I am not afraid.* I'd come, I realized, to stare that fear down, to stare everything down, really—all that I'd done to myself and all that had been done to me. I couldn't do that while tagging along with someone else.

After dinner, I lay in my tent with Flannery O'Connor's *Complete*

Stories on my chest, too exhausted to hold the book aloft. It wasn't only that I was cold and tired from the day's hike: at this elevation, the air was thinner. And yet I couldn't exactly fall asleep. In what seemed a fugue state, I thought about what it meant to bypass the High Sierra. It basically ruined everything. All the planning I'd done, the way I'd mapped out the whole summer down to each box and meal. Now I'd be leapfrogging over 450 miles of the trail I'd intended to hike. I'd reach Ashland in early August instead of the middle of September.

"Doug?" I called into the darkness, his tent only an arm's length from mine.

"Yeah?"

"I was thinking, if I bypass, I could hike all of Oregon instead." I rolled onto my side to face in the direction of his tent, half wishing he would come lie next to me in mine—that anyone would. It was that same hungry, empty feeling I'd had back in that Mojave motel when I'd wished I had a companion. Not someone to love. Just someone to press my body against. "Do you happen to know how long the trail is in Oregon?"

"About five hundred miles," he answered.

"That's perfect," I said, my heartbeat quickening with the idea before I closed my eyes and fell into a deep sleep.

The next afternoon Greg caught up to me just before I reached Trail Pass Trail, my route off the PCT.

"I'm bypassing," I said to him reluctantly.

"I am too," he said.

"You are?" I asked with relief and delight.

"It's way too socked-in up here," he said, and we looked around at the wind-twisted foxtail pines among the trailside boulders; the mountains and ridges visible miles away under the pure blue sky. The highest point of the trail was only thirty-five trail miles farther on. The summit of Mount Whitney, the highest peak in the contiguous United States, was closer still, a short detour off the PCT.

Together we descended Trail Pass Trail two miles down to a picnic area and campground at Horseshoe Meadows, where we met up with Doug and Tom and hitched a ride into Lone Pine. I hadn't planned to go there. Some PCT hikers had resupply boxes sent to Lone Pine, but I'd planned to push through to the town of Independence, another fifty trail miles to the north. I still had a few days' worth of food in my bag, but when we reached town I went immediately to a grocery store to replenish my stock. I needed enough to last for the ninety-six-mile section I'd be hiking once I made the bypass, from Sierra City to Belden Town. Afterwards, I found a pay phone and called Lisa and left a message on her answering machine, explaining my new plan as quickly as I could, asking her to send my box addressed to Belden Town immediately and hold all the others until I gave her the details of my new itinerary.

I felt dislocated and melancholy when I hung up the phone, less excited about being in town than I thought I'd be. I walked along the main street until I found the men.

"We're heading back up," said Doug, his eyes meeting mine. My chest felt tight as I hugged him and Tom goodbye. I'd come to feel a sort of love for them, but on top of that, I was worried.

"Are you sure you want to go up into the snow?" I asked.

"Are you sure you don't?" Tom replied.

"You still have your good luck charm," said Doug, pointing to the black feather he'd given me back in Kennedy Meadows. I'd wedged it into Monster's frame, up over my right shoulder.

"Something to remember you by," I said, and we laughed.

After they left, I walked with Greg to the convenience store that doubled as the town's Greyhound bus station. We passed bars that billed themselves as Old West saloons and shops that had cowboy hats and framed paintings of men astride bucking broncos displayed in their front windows.

"You ever see *High Sierra* with Humphrey Bogart?" Greg asked.

I shook my head.

"That was made here. Plus lots of other movies. Westerns."

I nodded, unsurprised. The landscape did in fact look straight out of Hollywood—a high sage-covered flat that was more barren than not, rocky and treeless with a view that went on for miles. The white peaks of the Sierra Nevada to the west cut so dramatically up into the blue sky that they seemed almost unreal to me, a gorgeous façade.

"There's our ride," Greg said, pointing to a big Greyhound bus in a parking lot of the store as we approached.

But he was wrong. There were no buses that went all the way to Sierra City, we learned. We'd have to catch a bus that evening and ride seven hours to Reno, Nevada, then take another one for an hour to Truckee, California. From there we'd have no option but to hitchhike the final forty-five miles to Sierra City. We bought two one-way tickets and an armful of snacks and sat on the warm pavement at the edge of the convenience store parking lot waiting for the bus to come. We polished off whole bags of chips and cans of soda while talking. We ran through the Pacific Crest Trail as a conversational topic, through backpacking gear and the record snowpack one more time, through the "ultralight" theories and practices of Ray Jardine and of his followers—who may or may not have misinterpreted the spirit behind those theories and practices—and finally arrived at ourselves. I asked him about his job and life in Tacoma. He had no pets and no kids and a girlfriend he'd been dating a year. She was an avid backpacker too. His life, it was clear, was an ordered and considered thing. It seemed both boring and astounding to me. I didn't know what mine seemed like to him.

The bus to Reno was nearly empty when we got on at last. I followed Greg to the middle, where we took pairs of seats directly opposite each other across the aisle.

"I'm going to get some sleep," he said once the bus lurched onto the highway.

"Me too," I said, though I knew it wasn't true. Even when I was exhausted, I could never sleep in moving vehicles of any sort, and I wasn't exhausted. I was lit up by being back in the world. I stared out the window while Greg slept. Nobody who'd known me for more than a week had any idea where I was. *I am en route to Reno, Nevada,* I thought with a kind of wonder. I'd never been to Reno. It seemed the most preposterous place for me to be going, dressed as I was and dirty as a dog, my hair dense as a burlap bag. I pulled all the money from my pockets and counted the bills and coins, using my headlamp to see. I had forty-four dollars and seventy-five cents. My heart sank at the paltry sight of it. I'd spent far more money than I'd imagined I would have by now. I hadn't anticipated stops in Ridgecrest and Lone Pine, nor the bus ticket to Truckee. I wasn't going to get more money until I reached my next resupply box in Belden Town more than a week from now, and even then it would be only twenty bucks. Greg and I had agreed we'd get rooms in a motel in Sierra City to rest up for a night after our long travels, but I had the sickening feeling I'd have to find a place to camp instead.

There was nothing I could do about it. I didn't have a credit card. I'd simply have to get through on what I had. I cursed myself for not having put more money in my boxes at the same time that I acknowledged I couldn't have. I'd put into my boxes all the money I'd had. I'd saved up my tips all winter and spring and sold a good portion of my possessions, and with that money I'd purchased all the food in my boxes and all the gear that had been on that bed in the Mojave motel, and I wrote a check to Lisa to cover postage for the boxes and another check to cover four months of payments on the student loans for the degree I didn't have that I'd be paying for until I was forty-three. The amount I had left over was the amount I could spend on the PCT.

I put my money back in my pocket, turned my headlamp off, and stared out my window to the west, feeling a sad unease. I was homesick, but I didn't know if it was for the life I used to have or for the PCT. I could just barely make out the dark silhouette of the Sierra Nevada against the moonlit sky. It looked like that impenetrable wall again, the way it had to me a few years before when I'd first seen it while driving with Paul, but it didn't feel impenetrable anymore. I could imagine myself on it, in it, part of it. I knew the way it felt to navigate it one step at a time. I would be back on it again as soon as I hiked away from Sierra City. I was bypassing the High Sierra—missing Sequoia and Kings Canyon and Yosemite national parks, Tuolumne Meadows and the John Muir and Desolation wildernesses and so much more—but I'd still be hiking another hundred miles in the Sierra Nevada beyond that, before heading into the Cascade Range.

By the time the bus pulled into the station in Reno at 4 a.m., I hadn't slept a minute. Greg and I had an hour to kill before the next bus would depart for Truckee, so we wandered blearily through the small casino that adjoined the bus station, our packs strapped to our backs. I was tired but wired, sipping hot Lipton tea from a Styrofoam cup. Greg played blackjack and won three dollars. I fished three quarters out of my pocket, played all three in a slot machine, and lost everything.

Greg gave me a dry, I-told-you-so smile, as if he'd seen that coming.

"Hey, you never know," I said. "I was in Vegas once—just passing through a couple of years ago—and I put a nickel in a slot machine and won sixty bucks."

He looked unimpressed.

I went into the women's restroom. As I brushed my teeth before a fluorescently lit mirror above a bank of sinks, a woman said, "I like your feather," and pointed to it on my pack.

"Thanks," I said, our eyes meeting in the mirror. She was pale and brown-eyed with a bumpy nose and a long braid down her back; dressed in a tie-dyed T-shirt and a pair of patched-up cutoff jeans and Birkenstock sandals. "My friend gave it to me," I mumbled as toothpaste dribbled out of my mouth. It seemed like forever since I'd talked to a woman.

"It's got to be a corvid," she said, reaching over to touch it delicately with one finger. "It's either a raven or a crow, a symbol of the void," she added, in a mystical tone.

"The void?" I'd asked, crestfallen.

"It's a good thing," she said. "It's the place where things are *born*, where they *begin*. Think about how a black hole absorbs energy and then releases it as something new and alive." She paused, looking meaningfully into my eyes. "My ex-partner is an ornithologist," she explained in a less ethereal tone. "His area of research is corvidology. His thesis was on ravens and because I have a master's in English I had to read the fucking thing like ten times, so I know more than I need to about them." She turned to the mirror and smoothed back her hair. "You on your way to the Rainbow Gathering, by chance?"

"No. I'm—"

"You should come. It's really cool. The gathering's up in the Shasta-Trinity National Forest this year, at Toad Lake."

"I went to the Rainbow Gathering last year, when it was in Wyoming," I said.

"Right on," she said in that particular slow-motion way that people say *right on*. "Happy trails," she said, and reached over and squeezed my arm. "Corvidology!" she cheered as she headed for the door, giving me and my feather a thumbs-up as she went.

By eight Greg and I were in Truckee. By eleven we were still standing on the hot side of the road trying to hitch a ride to Sierra City.

"HEY!" I yelled maniacally at a VW bus as it whizzed past. We'd been snubbed by at least six of them over the past couple of hours. Not being picked up by those who drove VW buses made me particularly indignant. "Fucking hippies," I said to Greg.

"I thought you were a hippy," he said.

"I am. Kind of. But only a little bit." I sat down on the gravel on the road's shoulder and retied the lace of my boot, but when I was done I didn't stand back up. I was dizzy with exhaustion. I hadn't slept for a day and a half.

"You should walk ahead of me and stand by yourself," said Greg. "I'd understand. If you were alone you'd have gotten a ride a long time ago."

"No," I said, though I knew he was right—a single woman is less threatening than a man-woman pair. People want to help a woman alone. Or try to get in her pants. But we were together for now, so together we stayed until, an hour later, a car stopped and we clambered in and rode to Sierra City. It was a scenic village of less than a dozen wooden buildings perched at an elevation of 4,200 feet. The town was wedged in between the North Yuba River and the towering Sierra Buttes that rose brown against the clear blue sky to the north.

Our ride dropped us at the general store in the town's center, a quaint old-timey place where tourists sat eating ice-cream cones on the painted front porch, which was abuzz with a pre–Fourth of July weekend crowd.

"You getting a cone?" asked Greg, pulling out a couple of dollars.

"Nah. Maybe later," I said, keeping my voice light to hide my desperation. I wanted a cone, of course. It was that I didn't dare purchase one, for fear of not being able to afford a room. When we stepped into the small crowded store, I tried not to look at the food. I stood near the cash register instead, scanning tourist brochures while Greg shopped.

"This entire town was wiped out by an avalanche in 1852," I told him when he returned, fanning myself with the glossy brochure. "The snow from the Buttes gave way." He nodded as if he knew this already, licking his chocolate cone. I turned away, the sight of it a small torture to me. "I hope you don't mind, but I need to find someplace cheap. For tonight, I mean." The truth was, I needed to find someplace free, but I was too tired to contemplate camping. The last time I'd slept, I'd been on the PCT in the High Sierra.

"How about this," said Greg, pointing to an old wooden building across the street.

The downstairs was a bar and restaurant; the upstairs had rooms for rent with shared bathrooms. It was only 1:30, but the woman in the bar allowed us to check in early. After I paid for my room I had thirteen dollars left.

"You want to have dinner together downstairs tonight?" Greg asked when we reached our rooms, standing before our side-by-side doors.

"Sure," I said, blushing lightly. I wasn't attracted to him, and yet I couldn't help hoping he was attracted to me, which I knew was absurd.

Perhaps he'd been the one who'd taken my condoms. The idea of that sent a thrill through my body.

"You can go first if you'd like," he said, gesturing down the hall to the bathroom we shared with all of the inhabitants of our floor. We seemed to be the only two occupants so far.

"Thanks," I said, and unlocked the door to my room and stepped inside. A worn-out antique wooden dresser with a round mirror sat against one wall and a double bed against the other with a rickety nightstand and chair nearby. A bare lightbulb dangled from the ceiling in the center of the room. I set Monster down and sat on the bed. It squealed and sank and wobbled precariously beneath my weight, but it felt excellent anyway. My body almost hurt with pleasure to merely sit on the bed, as if I were being the opposite of burned. The camp chair that doubled as my sleeping pad didn't offer much cushioning, it turned out. I'd slept deeply most nights on the PCT, but not because I was comfortable: I was simply too spent to care.

I wanted to sleep, but my legs and arms were streaked with dirt; my stench was magnificent. To get into the bed in such a state seemed almost criminal. I hadn't properly bathed since I'd been at the motel in Ridgecrest nearly two weeks before. I walked down the hall to the bathroom. There wasn't a shower, only a big porcelain tub with claw feet and a shelf piled high with folded towels. I picked up one of the towels and inhaled its detergent-scented splendor, then took off my clothes and looked at myself in the full-length mirror.

I was a startling sight.

I did not so much look like a woman who had spent the past three weeks backpacking in the wilderness as I did like a woman who had been the victim of a violent and bizarre crime. Bruises that ranged in color from yellow to black lined my arms and legs, my back and rump, as if I'd been beaten with sticks. My hips and shoulders were covered with blisters and rashes, inflamed welts and dark scabs where my skin had broken open from being chafed by my pack. Beneath the bruises and wounds and dirt I could see new ridges of muscle, my flesh taut in places that had recently been soft.

I filled the tub with water and got in and scrubbed myself with a washcloth and soap. Within a few minutes, the water became so dark with the dirt and blood that washed off my body that I drained it and filled it up again.

In the second bath of water I reclined, feeling more grateful than perhaps I ever had for anything. After a while, I examined my feet. They were blistered and battered, a couple of my toenails entirely blackened by now. I touched one and saw that it had come almost entirely loose from my toe. That toe had been excruciating for days, growing ever more swollen, as if my toenail would simply pop off, but now it only hurt a little. When I tugged on the nail, it came off in my hand with one sharp shot of pain. In its place there was a layer of something over my toe that wasn't quite skin or nail. It was translucent and slightly shiny, like a tiny piece of Saran Wrap.

"I lost a toenail," I said to Greg at dinner.

"You're losing toenails?" he asked.

"Only one," I said glumly, aware that in fact I'd likely lose more and that this was further evidence of my big fat idiocy.

"It probably means your boots are too small," he said as the waitress approached with two plates of spaghetti and a basket of garlic bread.

I'd planned to order with reserve, especially since I'd spent another fifty cents that afternoon doing laundry, going in together with Greg. But once we sat down I hadn't been able to keep myself from matching Greg's every move—ordering a rum and Coke along with dinner, saying yes to the garlic bread. I tried not to let on that I was adding up the bill in my head as we ate. Greg already knew how unprepared I'd been to hike the PCT. He didn't need to know that there was yet another front on which I was an absolute fool.

But a fool I was. After we got our bill, tacked on a tip, and split it down the middle, I had sixty-five cents.

Back in my room after dinner, I opened *The Pacific Crest Trail, Volume 1: California* to read about the next section of the trail. My next stop was a place called Belden Town, where my resupply box with a twenty-dollar bill inside would be waiting. I could get through to Belden on sixty-five cents, couldn't I? I'd be in the wilderness, after all, and I wouldn't have anywhere to spend my money anyway, I reasoned, though still I felt anxious. I wrote Lisa a letter, asking her to purchase and send me a PCT guidebook for the Oregon section of the trail using the bit of money I'd left with her, and reordering the boxes she'd be mailing me for the rest of California. I went over the list again and again, making sure I had it all correct, lining up the miles with the dates and the places.

When I turned off my light and lay on my creaky bed to sleep, I could hear Greg on the other side of the wall shifting around on his creaky bed too, his closeness as palpable as his distance. Hearing him there made me feel so lonely I would've howled with pain if I'd let myself. I didn't know exactly why. I didn't want anything from him and yet also I wanted everything. What would he do if I knocked on his door? What would I do if he let me in?

I knew what I would do. I'd done it so many times.

"I'm like a guy, sexually," I'd told a therapist I'd seen a couple of times the year before—a man named Vince who volunteered at a community clinic in downtown Minneapolis where people like me could go to talk to people like him for ten bucks a pop.

"What's a guy like?" he'd asked.

"Detached," I said. "Or many of them are, anyway. I'm like that too. Capable of being detached when it comes to sex." I looked at Vince. He was fortyish with dark hair parted in the middle and feathered like two tidy black wings along the sides of his face. I had nothing for him, but if he'd risen and come across the room and kissed me, I'd have kissed him back. I'd have done anything.

But he didn't rise. He only nodded without saying anything, his silence conveying both skepticism and faith. "Who detached from you?" he asked finally.

"I don't know," I said, smiling the way I did when I was uncomfortable. I wasn't exactly looking at him. Instead, I was looking at the framed poster that hung behind him, a black rectangle with a whirl of white that was meant to be the Milky Way. An arrow pointed into its center, above which were written the words YOU ARE HERE. This image had become ubiquitous on T-shirts as well as posters and I always felt mildly irritated by it, unsure of how to take it, whether it was meant to be comical or grave, to indicate the largeness of our lives or the insignificance.

"Nobody's ever broken up with me, if that's what you're asking," I said. "I've always been the one to end relationships." My face felt suddenly hot. I realized I was sitting with my arms wound around each other and my legs wrapped around each other too—in a yogic eagle pose, hopelessly twisted. I tried to relax and sit normally, but it was impossible. Reluctantly, I met his eyes. "Is this the part where I tell you about my father?" I asked, laughing falsely.

It had always been my mother at the center of me, but in that room with Vince I suddenly felt my father like a stake in my heart. *I hate him,* I'd said during my teens. I didn't know what I felt for him now.

He was like a home movie that played in my head, one whose narrative was broken and sketchy. There were big dramatic scenes and inexplicable moments floating free from time, perhaps because most of what I remember about him happened in the first six years of my life. There was my father smashing our dinner plates full of food against the wall in a rage. There was my father choking my mother while straddling her chest and banging her head against the wall. There was my father scooping my sister and me out of bed in the middle of the night when I was five to ask if we would leave forever with him, while my mother stood by, bloodied and clutching my sleeping baby brother to her chest, begging him to stop. When we cried instead of answered, he collapsed onto his knees and pressed his forehead to the floor and screamed so desperately I was sure we were all going to die right then and there.

Once, in the midst of one of his tirades, he threatened to throw my mother and her children naked onto the street, as if we weren't his children too. We lived in Minnesota then. It was winter when he made the threat. I was at an age when everything was literal. It seemed precisely like a thing that he would do. I had an image of the four of us, naked and shrieking, running through the icy snow. He shut Leif, Karen, and me out of our house a couple of times when we lived in Pennsylvania, when my mother was at work and he was left to care for us and he wanted a break. He ordered us into the back yard and locked the doors, my sister and me holding our barely walking baby brother by his gummy hands. We wandered through the grass weeping and then forgot about being upset and played house and rodeo queen. Later, enraged and bored, we approached the back door and pounded and hollered. I remember the door distinctly and also the three concrete stairs that led up to it, the way I had to stand on tiptoes to see through the window in the upper half.

The good things aren't a movie. There isn't enough to make a reel. The good things are a poem, barely longer than a haiku. There is his love of Johnny Cash and the Everly Brothers. There are the chocolate bars he brought home from his job in a grocery store. There are all the grand things he wanted to be, a longing so naked and sorry I sensed it and grieved it even as a young child. There is him singing that Charlie Rich song that goes "Hey, did you happen to see the most beautiful girl in the world?" and saying it was about me and my sister and our mother, that we were the most beautiful girls in the world. But even that is marred. He said this only when he was trying to woo my mother back, when he was claiming that things would be different now, when he was promising her that he would never again do what he'd done before.

He always did it again. He was a liar and a charmer, a heartbreak and a brute.

My mother packed us up and left him and came back, left him and came back. We never went far. There was nowhere for us to go. We didn't have family nearby, and my mother was too proud to involve her friends. The first battered women's shelter in the United States didn't open until 1974, the year my mother finally left my father for good. Instead, we would drive all night long, my sister and me in the back seat, sleeping and waking to the alien green lights of the dashboard, Leif up front with our mom.

The morning would find us home again, our father sober and scrambling eggs, singing that Charlie Rich song before long.

When my mother finally called it quits with him, when I was six, a year after we'd all moved from Pennsylvania to Minnesota, I wept and begged her not to do it. Divorce seemed to me to be the very worst thing that could happen. In spite of everything, I loved my dad and I knew if my mom divorced him I'd lose him, and I was right. After they broke up the last time, we stayed in Minnesota and he returned to Pennsylvania and only intermittently got in touch. Once or twice a year a letter would arrive, addressed to Karen, Leif, and me, and we'd rip it open, filled with glee. But inside would be a diatribe about our mother, about what a whore she was, what a stupid, mooching welfare bitch. Someday he'd get us all, he promised. Someday we'd pay.

"But we didn't pay," I'd said to Vince in our second and final session together. The next time I saw him, he'd explain that he was leaving his position; he'd give me the name and number of another therapist. "After my parents divorced, I realized that my father's absence from my life was, sadly, a *good* thing. There weren't any more violent scenes," I said. "I mean, imagine my life if I'd been raised by my father."

"Imagine your life if you'd had a father who loved you as a father should," Vince countered.

I tried to imagine such a thing, but my mind could not be forced to do it. I couldn't break it down into a list. I couldn't land on love or security, confidence or a sense of belonging. A father who loved you as a father should was greater than his parts. He was like the whirl of white on the YOU ARE HERE poster behind Vince's head. He was one giant inexplicable thing that contained a million other things, and because I'd never had one, I feared I'd never find myself inside that great white swirl.

"What about your stepfather?" Vince asked. He glanced at the notebook on his lap, reading words he'd scrawled, presumably about me.

"Eddie. He detached too," I said lightly, as if it were nothing to me at all, as if it were almost amusing. "It's a long story," I said in the direction of the clock that hung near the YOU ARE THERE poster. "And time's almost up."

"Saved by the bell," Vince said, and we laughed.

I could see the outline of Monster by the dim streetlights that filtered into my room in Sierra City, the feather Doug had given me sticking up from the place where I'd wedged it into my pack's frame. I thought about corvidology. I wondered if the feather was really a symbol or if it was simply something I hauled along the way. I was a terrible believer in things, but I was also a terrible nonbeliever in things. I was as searching as I was skeptical. I didn't know where to put my faith, or if there was such a place, or even precisely what the word *faith* meant, in all of its complexity. Everything seemed to be possibly potent and possibly fake. "You're a seeker," my mother had said to me when she was in her last week, lying in bed in the hospital, "like me." But I didn't know what my mother sought, exactly. Did she? It was the one question I hadn't asked, but even if she'd told me, I'd have doubted her, pressing her to explain the spiritual realm, asking her how it could be proved. I even doubted things whose truth was verifiable. *You should see a therapist,* everyone had told me after my mother died, and ultimately—in the depths of my darkest moments the year before the hike—I had. But I didn't keep the faith. I never did call the other therapist Vince had recommended. I had problems a therapist couldn't solve; grief that no man in a room could ameliorate.

I got out of bed, wrapped a towel around my naked body, and, stepping barefoot into the hall, walked past Greg's door. In the bathroom, I shut the door behind me, turned on the tub's faucet, and got in. The hot water was like magic, the thunder of it filling the room until I shut it off and there was a silence that seemed more silent than it had before. I lay back against the perfectly angled porcelain and stared at the wall until I heard a knock on the door.

"Yes?" I said, but there was no reply, only the sound of footsteps retreating down the hallway. "Someone's in here," I called, though that was obvious. Someone was in here. It was me. I was here. I felt it in a way I hadn't in ages: the me inside of me, occupying my spot in the fathomless Milky Way.

I reached for a washcloth on the shelf near the tub and scrubbed myself with it, though I was already clean. I scrubbed my face and my neck and my throat and my chest and my belly and my back and my rump and my arms and my legs and my feet.

"The first thing I did when each of you was born was kiss every part of you," my mother used to say to my siblings and me. "I'd count every finger and toe and eyelash," she'd say. "I'd trace the lines on your hands."

I didn't remember it, and yet I'd never forgotten it. It was as much a part of me as my father saying he'd throw me out the window. More.

I lay back and closed my eyes and let my head sink into the water until it covered my face. I got the feeling I used to get as a child when I'd done this very thing: as if the known world of the bathroom had disappeared and become, through the simple act of submersion, a foreign and mysterious place. Its ordinary sounds and sensations turned muted, distant, abstract, while other sounds and sensations not normally heard or registered emerged.

I had only just begun. I was three weeks into my hike, but everything in me felt altered. I lay in the water as long as I could without breathing, alone in a strange new land, while the actual world all around me hummed on.

9

STAYING FOUND

I'd bypassed. Passed by. I was out of danger now. I'd leapfrogged over the snow. It was clear sailing through the rest of California, I supposed. Then through Oregon to Washington. My new destination was a bridge that crossed the Columbia River, which formed the border between the two states. The Bridge of the Gods. It was 1,008 trail miles away; I'd hiked only 170 so far, but my pace was picking up.

In the morning, Greg and I walked out of Sierra City for a mile and a half along the shoulder of the road until we reached the place where it intersected the PCT, then walked together for a few minutes on the trail before pausing to say goodbye.

"That's called mountain misery," I said, pointing at the low green bushes that edged the trail. "Or at least that's what the guidebook says. Let's hope it's not literal."

"I think it might be," Greg said, and he was right: the trail would rise nearly three thousand feet over the eight miles ahead. I was braced for the day, Monster loaded down with a week's worth of food. "Good luck," he said, his brown eyes meeting mine.

"Good luck to you too." I pulled him into a hard embrace.

"Stay with it, Cheryl," he said as he turned to go.

"You too," I called after him, as if he wouldn't.

Within ten minutes he was out of sight.

I was excited to be back on the trail, 450 PCT miles north of where I'd been. The snowy peaks and high granite cliffs of the High Sierra were no longer in view, but the trail felt the same to me. In many ways, it looked the same too. For all the endless mountain and desert panoramas I'd seen, it was the sight of the two-foot-wide swath of the trail that was the most familiar, the thing upon which my eyes were almost always trained, looking for roots and branches, snakes and stones. Sometimes the trail was sandy, other times rocky or muddy or pebbly or cushioned with layers upon layers of pine needles. It could be black or brown or gray or blond as butterscotch, but it was always the PCT. Home base.

I walked beneath a forest of pine, oak, and incense cedar, then passed through a stand of Douglas firs as the trail switchbacked up and up, seeing no one all that sunny morning as I ascended, though I could feel Greg's invisible presence. With each mile that feeling waned, as I imagined him getting farther and farther ahead of me, hiking at his customary blazing pace. The trail passed from the shady forest to an exposed ridge, where I could see the canyon below me for miles, the rocky buttes overhead. By midday I was up above seven thousand feet and the trail grew muddy, though it hadn't rained in days, and finally, when I rounded a bend, I came upon a field of snow. Or rather, what I took to be a field, which implied there was an end to it. I stood at its edge and searched for Greg's footprints, but saw none. The snow wasn't on a slope, just a flat among a sparse forest, which was a good thing, since I didn't have my ice ax any longer. I'd left it that morning in the PCT hiker free box at the Sierra City post office as Greg and I strolled out of town. I didn't have the money to mail it back to Lisa's, much to my regret, given its expense, but I wasn't willing to carry it either, believing I'd have no use for it from here on out.

I jabbed my ski pole into the snow, skidded onto its icy surface, and began to walk, a feat I achieved only intermittently. In some places I skittered over the top of it; in others, my feet crashed through, sometimes forming potholes halfway up to my knees. Before long, the snow was packed into the ankles of my boots, my lower legs so snowburned it felt as if the flesh had been scraped away with a dull knife.

That worried me less than the fact that I couldn't see the trail because it was buried beneath the snow. The route seemed apparent enough, I assured myself, holding the pages from my guidebook as I walked, pausing to study each word as I went. After an hour, I stopped, suddenly scared. Was I on the PCT? All the while, I'd been searching for the small metal diamond-shaped PCT markers that were occasionally tacked to trees, but I hadn't seen any. This wasn't necessarily reason for alarm. I'd learned that the PCT markers were not to be relied upon. On some stretches they appeared every few miles; on others, I'd hike for days without spotting one.

I pulled the topographical map of this area out of my shorts pocket. When I did, the nickel in my pocket came with it and fell into the snow. I reached for it, bending over unsteadily beneath my pack, but the moment my fingers grazed it, the nickel sank deeper and disappeared. I clawed through the snow looking for it, but it was gone.

Now I only had sixty cents.

I remembered the nickel in Vegas, the one with which I'd played the slots and won sixty dollars. I laughed out loud thinking about it, feeling as if these two nickels were connected, though I couldn't explain why other than to say the daffy thought came to me as I stood there in the snow that day. Maybe losing the nickel was good luck the same way that the black feather that symbolized the void actually meant something positive. Maybe I wasn't really in the very midst of the thing I'd just worked so hard to avoid. Maybe around the next bend I'd be in the clear.

I was shivering by now, standing in the snow in my shorts and sweat-drenched T-shirt, but I didn't dare continue on until I got my bearings. I unfolded the guidebook pages and read what the authors of *The Pacific Crest Trail, Volume 1: California* had to say about this portion of the trail. "From the trailside ridge, you confront a steady, bush-lined ascent," it said to describe the place I thought I might have been. "Eventually your trail levels off at an open-forested flat . . ." I turned in a slow circle, getting a 360-degree view. Was this the open-forested flat? It would seem that the answer would be clear, but it was not. It was only clear that everything was buried in snow.

I reached for my compass, which hung from a cord on the side of my pack near the world's loudest whistle. I hadn't used it since the day I was hiking on that road after my first hard week on the trail. I studied it in conjunction with the map and made my best guess about where I might be and walked on, inching forward uncertainly on the snow, alternately skidding across the top or breaking through the surface, my shins and calves growing ever more chafed each time. An hour later I saw a metal diamond that said PACIFIC CREST TRAIL tacked to a snowbound tree, and my body flooded with relief. I still didn't know precisely where I was, but at least I knew I was on the PCT.

By late afternoon I came to a ridgeline from which I could see down into a deep snow-filled bowl.

"Greg!" I called, to test if he was near. I hadn't seen a sign of him all day long, but I kept expecting him to appear, hoping the snow would slow him enough that I'd catch him and we could navigate through it together. I heard faint shouts and saw a trio of skiers on an adjoining ridge on the other side of the snowy bowl, close enough to hear, but impossible to reach. They waved their arms in big motions to me and I waved back. They were far enough away and dressed in enough ski gear that I couldn't make out whether they were male or female.

"Where are we?" I yelled across the snowy expanse.

"What?" I barely heard them yell back.

I repeated the words over and over again—*Where are we, Where are we*—until my throat grew raw. I knew approximately where I believed myself to be, but I wanted to hear what they'd say, just to be sure. I asked and asked without getting through, so I tried one last time, putting everything I had into it, practically hurling myself off the side of the mountain with the effort, "*WHERE ARE WE?*"

There was a pause, which told me they'd finally registered my question, and then in unison they yelled back, "*CALIFORNIA!*"

By the way they fell against one another, I knew they were laughing.

"Thanks," I called out sarcastically, though my tone was lost in the wind.

They called something back to me that I couldn't quite make out. They repeated it again and again, but it got muddled each time until finally they shouted out the words one by one and I heard them.

"*ARE*"

"*YOU*"

"*LOST?*"

I thought about it for a moment. If I said yes, they'd rescue me and I'd be done with this godforsaken trail.

"*NO,*" I roared. I wasn't lost.

I was screwed.

I looked around at the trees, the waning light slanting through them. It would be evening soon and I'd have to find a place to camp. I would pitch my tent in the snow and wake in the snow and continue on in the snow. This, in spite of everything I'd done to avoid it.

I walked on and eventually found what passed for a fairly cozy spot to pitch a tent when you have no choice but to allow a frozen sheaf of snow beneath a tree to be cozy. When I crawled into my sleeping bag, wearing my rain gear over all my clothes, I was chilly but okay, my water bottles wedged in close beside me so they wouldn't freeze.

In the morning, the walls of my tent were covered with swirls of frost, condensation from my breath that had frozen in the night. I lay quiet but awake for a while, not ready to confront the snow yet, listening to the songs of birds I couldn't name. I only knew that the sound of them had become familiar to me. When I sat up and unzipped the door and looked out, I watched the birds flitter from tree to tree, elegant and plain and indifferent to me.

I got my pot and poured water and Better Than Milk into it and stirred, then added some granola and sat eating it near the open door of my tent, hoping that I was still on the PCT. I stood and washed out my pot with a handful of snow and scanned the landscape. I was surrounded by rocks and trees that jutted out from the icy snow. I felt both uneasy about my situation and astounded by the vast lonesome beauty. Should I continue on or turn back? I wondered, though I knew my answer. I could feel it lodged in my gut: of course I was continuing on. I'd worked too hard to get here to do otherwise. Turning back made logical sense. I could retrace my steps to Sierra City and catch another ride farther north still, clear of the snow. It was safe. It was reasonable. It was probably the right thing to do. But nothing in me would do it.

I walked all day, falling and skidding and trudging along, bracing so hard with my ski pole that my hand blistered. I switched to the other hand and it blistered too. Around every bend and over every ridge and on the other side of every meadow I hoped there would be no more snow. But there was always more snow amid the occasional patches where the ground was visible. *Is that the PCT?* I'd wonder when I saw the actual ground. I could never be certain. Only time would tell.

I sweated as I hiked, the whole backside of me wet where my pack covered my body, regardless of the temperature or what clothing I wore. When I stopped, I began shivering within minutes, my wet clothes suddenly icy cold. My muscles had at last begun to adjust to the demands of long-distance hiking, but now new demands were placed on them, and not only to brace myself in the constant effort to stay upright. If the ground upon which I was walking was on a slope, I had to chop out each step in order to get my footing, lest I slip down the mountain and crash into the rocks and bushes and trees below, or worse, go sailing over the edge. Methodically, I kicked into the snow's icy crust, making footholds step by step. I remembered Greg teaching me how to do this very thing with my ice ax back in Kennedy Meadows. Now I wished for that ice ax with an almost pathological fervor, picturing it sitting uselessly in the PCT hiker free box in Sierra City. With all the kicking and bracing, my feet blistered in new places as well as in all the old places that had blistered back in my first days of hiking, the flesh on my hips and shoulders still rubbed raw by Monster's straps.

I walked on, a penitent to the trail, my progress distressingly slow. I'd generally been covering two miles an hour as I hiked most days, but everything was different in the snow: slower, less certain. I thought it would take me six days to reach Belden Town, but when I'd packed my food bag with six days' worth of food, I didn't have any idea what I'd encounter. Six days in these conditions were out of the question, and not only for the physical challenge of moving through the snow. Each step was also a calculated effort to stay approximately on what I hoped was the PCT. With my map and compass in hand, I tried to remember all I could from *Staying Found,* which I'd burned long ago. Many of the techniques—triangulating and cross bearing and bracketing—had perplexed me even when I'd been holding the book in my hand. Now they were impossible to do with any confidence. I'd never had a mind for math. I simply couldn't hold the formulas and numbers in my head. It was a logic that made little sense to me. In my perception, the world wasn't a graph or formula or an equation. It was a story. So mostly I relied on the narrative descriptions in my guidebook, reading them over and over, matching them up with my maps, attempting to divine the intent and nuance of every word and phrase. It was like being inside a giant standardized test question: *If Cheryl climbs north along a ridge for an hour at a rate of 1.5 miles per hour, then west to a saddle from which she can see two oblong lakes to the east, is she standing on the south flank of Peak 7503?*

I guessed and guessed again, measuring, reading, pausing, calculating, and counting before ultimately putting my faith in whatever I believed to be true. Fortunately, this stretch of the trail held plenty of clues, riddled with peaks and cliffs, lakes and ponds that were often visible from the trail. I still had the same feeling as I had from the start, when I'd begun walking the Sierra Nevada from its southern beginning—as if I were perched above the whole world, looking down on so much. I pushed from ridge to ridge, feeling relieved when I spotted bare ground in the patches where the sun had melted the snow clean away; quivering with joy when I identified a body of water or a particular rock formation that matched what the map reflected or the guidebook described. In those moments, I felt strong and calm, and then a moment later, when I paused yet again to take stock, I became certain that I'd done a very, very stupid thing in opting to continue on. I passed trees that seemed disconcertingly familiar, as if I'd surely passed them an hour before. I gazed across vast stretches of mountains that struck me as not so different from the vast stretch I'd seen earlier. I scanned the ground for footprints, hoping to be reassured by even the slightest sign of another human being, but saw none. I saw only animal tracks—the soft zigzags of rabbits or the scampering triangles of what I supposed were porcupines or raccoons. The air came alive with the sound of the wind whipping the trees at times and at other times it was profoundly hushed by the endless silencing snow. Everything but me seemed utterly certain of itself. The sky didn't wonder where it was.

"HELLO!" I bellowed periodically, knowing each time that no one would answer, but needing to hear a voice anyway, even if it was only my own. My voice would guard me against it, I believed, *it* being the possibility that I could be lost in this snowy wilderness forever.

As I hiked, the fragments of songs pushed their way into the mix-tape radio station in my head, interrupted occasionally by Paul's voice, telling me how foolish I'd been to trek into the snow like this alone. He would be the one who would do whatever had to be done if indeed I didn't return. In spite of our divorce, he was still my closest kin, or at least the one organized enough to take on such a responsibility. I remembered him lambasting me as we drove from Portland to Minneapolis, when he'd plucked me out of the grips of heroin and Joe the autumn before. "Do you know you could die?" he'd said with disgust, as if he half wished I had so he could prove his point. "Every time you do heroin it's like you're playing Russian roulette. You're putting a gun to your head and pulling the trigger. You don't know which time the bullet's going to be in the chamber."

I'd had nothing to say in my defense. He was right, though it hadn't seemed that way at the time.

But walking along a path I carved myself—one I hoped was the PCT—was the opposite of using heroin. The trigger I'd pulled in stepping into the snow made me more alive to my senses than ever. Uncertain as I was as I pushed forward, I felt right in my pushing, as if the effort itself meant something. That perhaps being amidst the undesecrated beauty of the wilderness meant I too could be undesecrated, regardless of what I'd lost or what had been taken from me, regardless of the regrettable things I'd done to others or myself or the regrettable things that had been done to me. Of all the things I'd been skeptical about, I didn't feel skeptical about this: the wilderness had a clarity that included me.

Somber and elated, I walked in the cool air, the sun glimmering through the trees, bright against the snow, even though I had my sunglasses on. As omnipresent as the snow was, I also sensed its waning, melting imperceptibly by the minute all around me. It seemed as alive in its dying as a hive of bees was in its life. Sometimes I passed by places where I heard a gurgling, as if a stream ran beneath the snow, impossible to see. Other times it fell in great wet heaps from the branches of the trees.

On my third day out from Sierra City, as I sat hunched near the open door of my tent doctoring my blistered feet, I realized the day before had been the Fourth of July. The fact that I could so clearly imagine what not only my friends but also a good portion of the residents of the United States had done without me made me feel all the more far away. No doubt they'd had parties and parades, acquired sunburns and lit firecrackers, while I was here, alone in the cold. In a flash, I could see myself from far above, a speck on the great mass of green and white, no more or less significant than a single one of the nameless birds in the trees. Here it could be the fourth of July or the tenth of December. These mountains didn't count the days.

The next morning I walked through the snow for hours until I came to a clearing where there was a large fallen tree, its trunk bare of both snow and branches. I took my pack off and climbed up on top of it, its bark rough beneath me. I pulled a few strips of beef jerky out of my pack and sat eating it and swigging my water. Soon I saw a streak of red to my right: a fox walking into the clearing, his paws landing soundlessly on top of the snow. He gazed straight ahead without looking at me, not even seeming to know I was there, though that seemed impossible. When the fox was directly in front of me, perhaps ten feet away, he stopped and turned his head and looked peaceably in my direction, his eyes not exactly going to mine as he sniffed. He looked part feline, part canine, his facial features sharp and compact, his body alert.

My heart raced, but I sat perfectly still, fighting the urge to scramble to my feet and leap behind the tree for protection. I didn't know what the fox would do next. I didn't think he would harm me, but I couldn't help but fear that he would. He was barely knee-high, though his strength was irrefutable, his beauty dazzling, his superiority to me apparent down to his every pristine hair. He could be on me in a flash. This was his world. He was as certain as the sky.

"Fox," I whispered in the gentlest possible voice I could, as if by naming him I could both defend myself against him and also draw him nearer. He raised his fine-boned red head, but remained standing as he'd been and studied me for several seconds more before turning away without alarm to continue walking across the clearing and into the trees.

"Come back," I called lightly, and then suddenly shouted, "MOM! MOM! MOM! MOM!" I didn't know the word was going to come out of my mouth until it did.

And then, just as suddenly, I went silent, spent.

The next morning I came to a road. I'd crossed smaller, rougher jeep roads in the previous days that were buried in snow, but none so wide and definitive as this. I almost fell to my knees at the sight of it. The beauty of the snowy mountains was incontestable, but the road was my people. If it was the one I believed it to be, simply arriving there was a victory. It meant I'd followed the path of the PCT. It also meant that there was a town miles away in either direction. I could turn left or right and follow it, and I'd be delivered to a version of early July that made sense to me. I took off my pack and sat down on a grainy mound of snow, pondering what to do. If I was where I thought I was, I'd covered forty-three miles of the PCT in the four days since I'd left Sierra City, though I'd probably hiked more than that, given my shaky abilities with map and compass. Belden Town was another fifty-five mostly snow-covered trail miles away. It was hardly worth thinking about. I had only a few days' worth of food left in my pack. I'd run out if I tried to push on. I began walking down the road in the direction of a town called Quincy.

The road was like the wilderness I'd been hiking through the last several days, silent and snow-covered, only now I didn't have to stop every few minutes to figure out where I was going. I only followed it down, as the snow gave way to mud. My guidebook didn't say how far away Quincy was, only that it was "a long day's walk." I quickened my pace, hoping to reach it by evening, though what I was going to do there with only sixty cents was another question.

By eleven I rounded a bend and saw a green SUV parked on the side of the road.

"Hello," I called, altogether more cautiously than I had in the times I'd bellowed that same word across the white desolation. No one answered. I approached the SUV and looked inside. There was a hooded sweatshirt lying across the front seat and a cardboard coffee cup on the dash, among other thrilling objects reminiscent of my former life. I continued walking down the road for a half hour, until I heard a car approaching behind me and turned.

It was the green SUV. A few moments later, it came to a halt beside me, a man at the wheel and a woman in the passenger seat.

"We're going to Packer Lake Lodge if you want a ride," the woman said after she rolled down the window. My heart sank, though I thanked her and got into the back seat. I'd read about Packer Lake Lodge in my guidebook days before. I could have taken a side trail to it a day out of Sierra City, but I'd decided to pass it by when I opted to stay on the PCT. As we drove, I could feel my northward progress reversing itself—all the miles I'd toiled to gain, lost in less than an hour—and yet to be in that car was a kind of heaven. I cleared a patch in the foggy window and watched the trees blaze past. Our top speed was perhaps twenty miles an hour as we crept around bends in the road, but it still felt to me as if we were moving unaccountably fast, the land made general rather than particular, no longer including me but standing quietly off to the side.

I thought about the fox. I wondered if he'd returned to the fallen tree and wondered about me. I remembered the moment after he'd disappeared into the woods and I'd called out for my mother. It had been so silent in the wake of that commotion, a kind of potent silence that seemed to contain everything. The songs of the birds and the creak of the trees. The dying snow and the unseen gurgling water. The glimmering sun. The certain sky. The gun that didn't have a bullet in its chamber. And the mother. Always the mother. The one who would never come to me.

10

RANGE OF LIGHT

The mere sight of Packer Lake Lodge felt like a blow. It was a restaurant. With food. And I might as well have been a German shepherd. I could smell it as soon as I got out of the car. I thanked the couple who'd given me a ride and walked toward the little building anyway, leaving Monster on the porch before I went inside. The place was crowded with tourists, most of them people who'd rented one of the rustic cabins that surrounded the restaurant. They didn't seem to notice the way I stared at their plates as I made my way to the counter, stacks of pancakes skirted by bacon, eggs in exquisitely scrambled heaps, or—most painful of all—cheeseburgers buried by jagged mounds of French fries. I was devastated by the sight of them.

"What have you heard about the snow levels up north of here?" I asked the woman who worked the cash register. I could tell that she was the boss by the way her eyes followed the waitress as she moved about the room with a coffeepot in hand. I'd never met this woman, but I'd worked for her a thousand times. It occurred to me that I could ask her for a job for the summer and quit the PCT.

"It's socked in pretty much everywhere above here," she replied. "All the thru-hikers have come down off the trail this year. They're all walking along the Gold Lake Highway instead."

"The Gold Lake Highway?" I asked, bewildered. "Was there a man here in the past few days? His name is Greg. He's fortyish? With brown hair and a beard."

She shook her head, but the waitress chimed that she'd talked to a PCT hiker who met that description, though she didn't know his name.

"You can take a seat, if you'd like to eat," the woman said.

A menu sat on the counter and I picked it up just to see. "Do you have anything that costs sixty cents or less?" I asked her in a jesting tone, so quiet my voice barely rose above the din.

"Seventy-five cents will get you a cup of coffee. Free refills," she replied.

"I've got lunch in my pack, actually," I said, and walked toward the door, past pushed-aside plates that were piled with perfectly edible scraps of food that no one but me and the bears and raccoons would have been willing to eat. I continued out to the porch and sat beside Monster. I pulled my sixty cents from my pocket and stared at the silver coins in my palm as if they would multiply if I stared at them hard enough. I thought of the box waiting for me in Belden Town with the twenty-dollar bill inside. I was starving and it was true I had lunch in my pack, but I was too disheartened to eat it. I paged through my guidebook instead, trying yet again to hatch a new plan.

"I overheard you inside talking about the Pacific Crest Trail," a woman said. She was middle-aged and slim, her frosted blonde hair cut in a stylish bob. In each ear she wore a single diamond stud.

"I'm hiking it for a few months," I said.

"I think that's so neat." She smiled. "I always wondered about the people who do that. I know the trail is up there," she said, waving her hand westward, "but I've never been on it." She came closer and for a moment I thought she'd try to give me a hug, but she only patted my arm. "You're not alone, are you?" When I nodded, she laughed and put a hand to her chest. "And what on earth does your mother have to say about that?"

"She's dead," I said, too discouraged and hungry to soften it with a note of apology, the way I usually did.

"My goodness. That's terrible." Her sunglasses sat against her chest, dangling from a string of glittery pastel beads. She reached for them and put them on. Her name was Christine, she told me, and she and her husband and their two teenaged daughters were staying in a cabin nearby. "Would you like to come back there with me and take a shower?" she asked.

Christine's husband, Jeff, made me a sandwich while I showered. When I emerged from the bathroom, it was sitting on a plate, sliced diagonally and rimmed by blue corn tortilla chips and a pickle.

"If you'd like to add more meat to it, feel free," Jeff said, pushing a platter of cold cuts toward me from his seat across the table. He was handsome and chubby, his dark hair wavy and gray at the temples. An attorney, Christine had told me during the short walk from the restaurant to their cabin. They lived in San Francisco, but they spent the first week of July here each year.

"Maybe just a few more slices, thanks," I said, reaching for the turkey with fake nonchalance.

"It's organic, in case that matters to you," said Christine. "And humanely raised. We've gone in that direction as much as we possibly can. You forgot the cheese," she scolded Jeff, and went to the refrigerator to retrieve it. "Would you like some dill Havarti on your sandwich, Cheryl?"

"I'm fine. Thanks," I said to be polite, but she sliced some anyway and brought it to me, and I ate it so fast she went back to the counter and sliced more without saying anything about it. She reached into the chip bag and put another handful on my plate, then cracked open a can of root beer and set it before me. If she'd emptied the contents of the entire refrigerator, I'd have eaten every last thing. "Thank you," I said every time she placed another item on the table.

Beyond the kitchen, I could see Jeff and Christine's two daughters through the sliding-glass door. They were sitting on the deck in twin Adirondack chairs, browsing copies of *Seventeen* and *People* with their headphones in their ears.

"How old are they?" I asked, nodding in their direction.

"Sixteen and almost eighteen," said Christine. "They're going into their sophomore and senior years."

They sensed us looking at them and glanced up. I waved, and they waved shyly back at me before returning to their magazines.

"I'd love it if they did something like you're doing. If they could be as brave and strong as you," said Christine. "But maybe not that brave, actually. I think it would scare me to have one of them out there like you are. Aren't you scared, all by yourself?"

"Sometimes," I said. "But not as much as you'd think." My wet hair dripped onto my dirty shirt at the shoulders. I was conscious that my clothes stank, though beneath them I felt cleaner than I'd ever been. The shower had been an almost holy experience after days of sweating in the cold beneath my clothes, the hot water and soap scorching me clean. I noticed a few books scattered on the far end of the table—Norman Rush's *Mating*, *A Thousand Acres* by Jane Smiley, and *The Shipping News* by E. Annie Proulx. They were books I'd read and loved, their covers like familiar faces to me, the mere sight of them making me feel as if I was somewhere like home. Perhaps Jeff and Christine would let me stay here with them, I thought nonsensically. I could be like one of their daughters, reading magazines while getting a tan on the deck. If they'd offered, I'd have said yes.

"Do you like to read?" Christine asked. "That's what we do when we come up here. That's our idea of relaxation."

"Reading's my reward at the end of the day," I said. "The book I have right now is Flannery O'Connor's *Complete Stories*." I still had the entire book in my pack. I'd not burned it page by page as I went along, mindful that with the snow and the changes in my itinerary I didn't know how long it'd be before I reached my next resupply box. I'd already read the whole thing and started back in on page one the night before.

"Well, you're welcome to one of these," said Jeff, rising to take *Mating* in his hand. "We're done with them. Or if that's not your taste, you could probably take this one," he said, and disappeared into the bedroom off the kitchen. He returned a moment later with a fat paperback by James Michener that he set near my now-empty plate.

I looked at the book. It was called *The Novel*, which I'd never heard of or read, though James Michener had been my mother's favorite author. It wasn't until I'd gone off to college that I learned there was anything wrong with that. *An entertainer for the masses,* one of my professors had scoffed after inquiring what books I'd read. Michener, he advised me, was not the kind of writer I should bother with if I truly wanted to be a writer myself. I felt like a fool. All those years as a teen, I'd thought myself sophisticated when I'd been absorbed in *Poland* and *The Drifters*, *Space* and *Sayonara*. In my first month at college, I quickly learned that I knew nothing about who was important and who was not.

"You know that isn't a *real* book," I'd said disdainfully to my mother when someone had given her Michener's *Texas* as a Christmas gift later that year.

"Real?" My mother looked at me, quizzical and amused.

"I mean serious. Like actual literature worth your time," I replied.

"Well, my time has never been worth all that much, you might like to know, since I've never made more than minimum wage and more often than not, I've slaved away for free." She laughed lightly and swatted my arm with her hand, slipping effortlessly away from my judgment, the way she always did.

When my mother died and the woman Eddie eventually married moved in, I took all the books I wanted from my mother's shelf. I took the ones she'd bought in the early 1980s, when we'd first moved onto our land: *The Encyclopedia of Organic Gardening* and *Double Yoga*. *Northland Wildflowers* and *Quilts to Wear*. *Songs for the Dulcimer* and *Bread Baking Basics*. *Using Plants for Healing* and *I Always Look Up the Word Egregious*. I took the books she'd read to me, chapter by chapter, before I could read to myself: the unabridged *Bambi* and *Black Beauty* and *Little House in the Big Woods*. I took the books that she'd acquired as a college student in the years right before she died: Paula Gunn Allen's *The Sacred Hoop* and Maxine Hong Kingston's *The Woman Warrior* and Cherríe Moraga and Gloria Anzaldúa's *This Bridge Called My Back*. Herman Melville's *Moby-Dick* and Mark Twain's *Huckleberry Finn* and Walt Whitman's *Leaves of Grass*. But I did not take the books by James Michener, the ones my mother loved the most.

"Thank you," I said now to Jeff, holding *The Novel*. "I'll trade this for the Flannery O'Connor if you'd like. It's an incredible book." I stopped short of mentioning that I'd have to burn it that night in the woods if he said no.

"Absolutely," he replied, laughing. "But I think I'm getting the better deal."

After lunch, Christine drove me to the ranger station in Quincy, but when we got there, the ranger I spoke to seemed only dimly aware of the PCT. He hadn't been on it this year, he told me, because it was still covered with snow. He was surprised to learn I had. I returned to Christine's car and studied my guidebook to get my bearings. The only reasonable place to get back on the PCT was where it crossed a road fourteen miles west of where we were.

"Those girls look like they might know something," said Christine. She pointed across the parking lot to a gas station, where two young women stood next to a van with the name of a camp painted on its side.

I introduced myself to them, and a few minutes later I was hugging Christine goodbye and clambering into the back of their van. The women were college students who worked at a summer camp; they were going right past the place where the PCT crossed the road. They said they'd be happy to give me a ride, so long as I was willing to wait while they did their errands. I sat in the shade of their lumbering camp van, reading *The Novel* in the parking lot of a grocery store as they shopped. It was hot and humid—summertime in a way that it hadn't been up in the snow just that morning. As I read, I could feel my mother's presence so acutely, her absence so profoundly, that it was hard to focus on the words. Why had I mocked her for loving Michener? The fact is, I'd loved Michener too—when I was fifteen I'd read *The Drifters* four times. One of the worst things about losing my mother at the age I did was how very much there was to regret. Small things that stung now: all the times I'd scorned her kindness by rolling my eyes or physically recoiled in response to her touch; the time I'd said, "Aren't you amazed to see how much more sophisticated I am at twenty-one than you were?" The thought of my youthful lack of humility made me nauseous now. I had been an arrogant asshole and, in the midst of that, my mother died. Yes, I'd been a loving daughter and yes, I'd been there for her when it mattered, but I could have been better. I could have been what I'd begged her to say I was: the best daughter in the world.

I shut *The Novel* and sat almost paralyzed with regret until the women reappeared, rolling a cart. Together we loaded their bags into the van. The women were four or five years younger than me, their hair and faces shiny and clean. Both wore sporty shorts and tank tops and colorful strands of braided yarn around their ankles and wrists.

"So we were talking. It's pretty intense you're hiking alone," said one of them after we'd finished with the bags.

"What do your parents think of you doing it?" asked the other.

"They don't. I mean—I don't have parents. My mom's dead and I don't have a father—or I do, technically, but he's not in my life." I climbed into the van and tucked *The Novel* into Monster so I wouldn't have to see the discomfort sweep across their sunny faces.

"Wow," said one of them.

"Yeah," said the other.

"The upside is that I'm free. I get to do whatever I want to do."

"Yeah," said the one who'd said wow.

"Wow," said the one who'd said yeah.

They got into the front and we drove. I looked out the window, at the towering trees whipping past, thinking of Eddie. I felt a bit guilty that I hadn't mentioned him when the women asked about my parents. He'd become like someone I used to know. I loved him still and I'd loved him instantly, from the very first night that I met him when I was ten. He wasn't like any of the men my mother dated in the years after she divorced my father. Most of those men had lasted only a few weeks, each scared off, I quickly understood, by the fact that allying himself with my mother meant also allying himself with me, Karen, and Leif. But Eddie loved all four of us from the start. He worked at an auto parts factory at the time, though he was a carpenter by trade. He had soft blue eyes and a sharp German nose and brown hair that he kept in a ponytail that draped halfway down his back.

The first night I met him, he came for dinner at Tree Loft, the apartment complex where we lived. It was the third such apartment complex we'd lived in since my parents' divorce. All of the apartment buildings were located within a half-mile radius of one another in Chaska, a town about an hour outside of Minneapolis. We moved whenever my mom could find a cheaper place. When Eddie arrived, my mother was still making dinner, so he played with Karen, Leif, and me out on the little patch of grass in front of our building. He chased us and caught us and held us upside down and shook us to see if any coins would fall from our pockets; if they did, he would take them from the grass and run, and we would run after him, shrieking with a particular joy that had been denied us all of our lives because we'd never been loved right by a man. He tickled us and watched as we performed dance routines and cartwheels. He taught us whimsical songs and complicated hand jives. He stole our noses and ears and then showed them to us with his thumb tucked between his fingers, eventually giving them back while we laughed. By the time my mother called us in to dinner, I was so besotted with him that I'd lost my appetite.

We didn't have a dining room in our apartment. There were two bedrooms, one bathroom, and a living room with a little alcove in one corner where there was a countertop, a stove, a refrigerator, and some cabinets. In the center of the room was a big round wooden table whose legs had been cut off so it was only knee-high. My mother had purchased it for ten dollars from the people who'd lived in our apartment before us. We sat on the floor around this table to eat. We said we were Chinese, unaware that it was actually the Japanese who ate meals seated on the floor before low tables. We weren't allowed to have pets at Tree Loft, but we did anyway, a dog named Kizzy and a canary named Canary, who flew free throughout the apartment.

He was a mannerly bird. He shat on a square of newspaper in a cat-litter pan in the corner. Whether he'd been trained to do it by my mother or did it of his own volition, I don't know. A few minutes after we all sat down on the floor around the table, Canary landed on Eddie's head. Usually when he landed on us, he'd perch there for only a moment and then fly away, but on top of Eddie's head, Canary stayed. We giggled. He turned to us and asked, with false obliviousness, what we were laughing at.

"There's a canary on your head," we told him.

"What?" he said, looking around the room in pretend surprise.

"There's a canary on your head," we yelled.

"Where?" he asked.

"There's a canary on your head!" we yelled, now in delighted hysterics.

There was a canary on his head and, miraculously, the canary stayed there, all through dinner, all through afterwards, falling asleep, nestling in.

So did Eddie.

At least he did until my mother died. Her illness had initially brought the two of us closer than we'd ever been. We'd become comrades in the weeks that she was sick—playing tag team at the hospital, consulting each other about medical decisions, weeping together when we knew the end was near, meeting with the funeral home director together after she died. But soon after that, Eddie pulled away from my siblings and me. He acted like he was our friend instead of our father. Quickly, he fell in love with another woman and soon she moved into our house with her children. By the time the first anniversary of my mother's death rolled around, Karen, Leif, and I were essentially on our own; most of my mother's things were in boxes I'd packed up and stored. He loved us, Eddie said, but life moved on. He was still our father, he claimed, but he did nothing to demonstrate that. I railed against it, but eventually had no choice but to accept what my family had become: not a family at all.

You can't squeeze blood from a turnip, my mother had often said.

By the time the young women pulled their van over to the side of the narrow highway, the tall trees that lined the road almost entirely blotted out the setting sun. I thanked them for the ride and looked around as they drove away. I was standing next to a forest service sign that said WHITEHORSE CAMPGROUND. The PCT was just beyond it, the women had told me as I'd climbed out of their van. I hadn't bothered to look at my map as we drove. After days of constant vigilance, I was tired of checking the guidebook and checking again. I'd simply enjoyed the ride, lulled by the women's confidence that they knew where they were going. From the campground they said I could hike a short trail that would take me up to the PCT. I read the fresh pages that I'd ripped from my guidebook as I walked the paved loops of the campground, straining to see the words in the dying light. My heart leapt with relief when I came across the words WHITEHORSE CAMPGROUND, then it fell when I read on and realized I was nearly two miles away from the PCT. The words "just beyond it" had meant something different to the women in the van than they did to me.

I looked around at the water spigots, the sets of brown outhouses, and the big sign that explained how one should go about paying for a spot for the night by leaving money in an envelope that should then be deposited through a slot in a wooden box. Aside from a few RVs and a smattering of tents, the campground was eerily empty. I walked another paved loop, wondering what to do. I didn't have money to pay to camp, but it was too dark to walk into the woods. I came to a campsite on the very edge of the campground, the one that was farthest away from the sign detailing how to pay. Who would even see me?

I set up my tent and cooked and ate my dinner in luxury on the picnic table with only my headlamp to light my way and peed in perfect comfort in the pit toilet, and then got into my tent and opened up *The Novel.* I'd read perhaps three pages when my tent was flooded with light. I unzipped my door and stepped out to greet the elderly couple who stood in the blinding headlights of a pickup truck.

"Hi," I said tentatively.

"You need to pay for this spot," the woman barked in response.

"I need to *pay?*" I said, with false innocence and surprise. "I thought only people who had cars had to pay the fee. I'm on foot. I just have my backpack." The couple listened in silence, their wrinkled faces indignant. "I'll be leaving first thing in the morning. By six at the latest."

"If you're going to stay here, you need to pay," the woman repeated.

"It's twelve dollars for the night," the man added in a gasping voice.

"The thing is," I said, "I don't happen to have any cash on me. I'm on this big trip. I'm hiking the Pacific Crest Trail—the PCT?—and there's all this snow up in the mountains—it's a record year—and anyway, I got off the trail and I didn't plan to be here because these women who gave me a ride accidentally dropped me off in the wrong place and it was—"

"None of that changes the fact you have to pay, young lady," the man bellowed with surprising power, his voice silencing me like a great horn from the fog.

"If you can't pay, you've got to pack up and leave," said the woman. She wore a sweatshirt that had a pair of baby raccoons peeping coyly from a burrow in a tree on her chest.

"There's no one even here! It's the middle of the night! What harm would it do if I simply—"

"Them are the rules," heaved the man. He turned away and got back into the truck, done with me.

"We're sorry, miss, but we're the camp hosts and keeping everyone to the rules is what we're here to do," said the woman. Her face softened for a moment in apology before she pursed her lips and added, "We'd hate to have to call the police."

I lowered my eyes and addressed her raccoons. "I just—I can't believe that I'm doing any harm. I mean, no one would even be using this site if I weren't here," I said quietly, trying to make one last appeal, woman to woman.

"We're not saying you have to *leave*," she shouted, as if she were scolding a dog to hush up. "We're saying you've got to *pay*."

"Well, I *can't*."

"There's a trail to the PCT that starts up just past the bathrooms," the woman said, gesturing behind her. "Or you can walk on the side of the road, about a mile or so up. I think the road's more direct than the trail. We'll keep the lights on while you pack," she said, and got back into the truck beside her husband, their faces now invisible to me behind the headlights.

I turned to my tent, stunned. I'd yet to meet a stranger on my trip who'd been anything but kind. I scrambled inside, put on my headlamp with shaking hands, and shoved everything I'd unpacked back into my pack without the usual orderly care for what went where. I didn't know what I should do. It was full dark by now, the half moon in the sky. The only thing scarier than the thought of hiking along an unknown trail in the dark was walking along an unknown road in the dark. I put on Monster and waved to the couple in the truck, unable to see whether they waved back.

I walked with my headlamp in my hand. It barely lit the way for each step; the batteries were dying. I followed the pavement to the bathrooms and saw the trail the woman had mentioned leading off behind it. I took a few tentative steps onto it. I'd become used to feeling safe in the woods, safe even through all the nights, but walking in the woods in the dark felt like a different matter altogether because I couldn't see. I could run into nocturnal animals or trip over a root. I could miss a turn and continue on where I didn't plan to go. I walked slowly, nervously, as I had the very first day of my hike, when I'd been braced for a rattlesnake to lunge at me any second.

After a while, the outlines of the landscape revealed themselves dimly to me. I was in a forest of tall pines and spruces, their limbless straight trunks culminating in clusters of dense branches high above me. I could hear a stream gurgling off to my left and feel the soft blanket of dry pine needles crackling beneath my boots. I walked with a kind of concentration I'd never had before, and because of it I could feel the trail and my body more acutely, as if I were walking barefoot and naked. It reminded me of being a child and learning how to ride a horse. My mother had taught me on her horse, Lady, letting me sit in the saddle while she stood holding a lead rope attached to Lady's bridle. I clutched Lady's mane with my hands at first, scared even when she walked, but eventually I relaxed and my mother implored me to close my eyes so I could feel the way the horse moved beneath me and the way my body moved with the horse. Later, I did the same thing with my arms held out wide on either side, going round and round, my body surrendering to Lady's as we moved.

I made my way along the trail for twenty minutes until I came to a place where the trees opened up. I took off my pack and got down on my hands and knees with my headlamp to explore a spot that seemed like a reasonable place to sleep. I set up my tent, crawled inside, and zipped myself into my sleeping bag, though now I wasn't even remotely tired, energized by the eviction and the late-night hike.

I opened up *The Novel,* but my headlamp was flickering and dying, so I turned it off and lay in the dark. I smoothed my hands over my arms, hugging myself. I could feel my tattoo beneath my right fingers; could still trace the horse's outline. The woman who'd inked it had told me that it would stand up on my flesh for a few weeks, but it had remained that way even after a few months, as if the horse were embossed rather than inked into my skin. It wasn't just a horse, that tattoo. It was Lady—the horse my mother had asked the doctor at the Mayo Clinic if she could ride when he'd told her she was going to die. Lady wasn't her real name—it was only what we called her. She was a registered American Saddlebred, her official name spelled out in grandiose glory on the breeder's association certificate that came with her: Stonewall's Highland Nancy, sired by Stonewall Sensation and foaled by Mack's Golden Queen. My mother had managed, against all reason, to buy Lady in the horrible winter when she and my father were finally and forever breaking up. My mother had met a couple at the restaurant where she worked as a waitress. They wanted to sell their purebred twelve-year-old mare for cheap, and even though my mother couldn't afford even cheap, she went to see the horse and struck a deal with the couple to pay them three hundred dollars over the course of six months, and then she struck another deal with another couple who owned a stable nearby, doing work in exchange for Lady's board.

"She's breathtaking," my mother said each time she described Lady, and she was. Over sixteen hands tall, lean and long-limbed, high-stepping and elegant as a queen. She had a white star on her forehead, but the rest of her coat was the same red chestnut as the fox I'd seen in the snow.

I was six when my mother bought her. We were living on the basement level of an apartment complex called Barbary Knoll. My mother had just left my father for the last time. We barely had enough money to live, but my mother had to have that horse. I knew instinctively, even as a child, that it was Lady who saved my mother's life. Lady who made it possible for her not only to walk away from my father, but also to keep going. Horses were my mother's religion. It was with them she'd wanted to be on all those Sundays as a child, when she'd been made to put on dresses to go to mass. The stories she told me about horses were a counterpoint to the other stories she'd told me about her Catholic upbringing. She did anything she could to ride them. She raked stalls and polished tack, hauled hay and spread straw, any kind of odd job that came her way, so that she would be allowed to hang out at whatever stable happened to be nearest and ride someone's horse.

Images of her past cowgirl life came to me from time to time, captured in freeze-frame moments, as clear and concise to me as if I'd read them in a book. The overnight backcountry rides she'd done in New Mexico with her father. The daredevil rodeo tricks she'd practiced and performed with her girlfriends. At sixteen she got her own horse, a palomino named Pal, whom she rode in horse shows and rodeos in Colorado. She still had the ribbons when she died. I packed them in a box that was now in Lisa's basement in Portland. A yellow third for barrel racing, a pink fifth for walk, trot, canter; green for showmanship and participation; and a single blue ribbon for riding her horse through all of the gaits smoothly over a course lined with mud pits and tight corners, laughing clowns and blaring horns, while she balanced an egg on a silver spoon in her outstretched hand for longer than anyone else could or did.

In the stable where Lady first lived when she became ours, my mother did the same work she'd done as a kid, cleaning stalls and spreading hay, hauling things to and fro in a wheelbarrow. Often, she brought Karen, Leif, and me with her. We played in the barn while she did her chores. Afterwards, we watched her ride Lady around and around the ring, each of us getting a turn when she was done. By the time we moved to our land in northern Minnesota, we had a second horse, a mixed-breed gelding named Roger, whom my mother had bought because I'd fallen in love with him and his owner was willing to let him go for next to nothing. We hauled them both up north in a borrowed trailer. Their pasture was a quarter of our forty acres.

When I went home one day to visit Eddie in early December nearly three years after my mother died, I was shocked by how thin and weak Lady had become. She was nearly thirty-one, old for a horse, and even if nursing her back to health had been possible, no one was around enough to do it. Eddie and his girlfriend had begun splitting their time between the house where I'd grown up and a trailer in a small town outside the Twin Cities. The two dogs, two cats, and four hens we'd had when my mother died had either died themselves or been given away to new homes. Only our two horses, Roger and Lady, remained. Often, they were cared for in the most cursory way by a neighbor whom Eddie had enlisted to feed them.

When I visited that early December, I talked to Eddie about Lady's condition. He was belligerent at first, telling me that he didn't know why the horses were his problem. I didn't have the heart to argue with him about why, as my mother's widower, he was responsible for her horses. I spoke only about Lady, persistent about making a plan, and after a while he softened his tone and we agreed that Lady should be put down. She was old and sickly; she'd lost an alarming amount of weight; the light in her eyes had faded. I'd consulted with the veterinarian already, I told him. The vet could come to our place and euthanize Lady with an injection. That, or we could shoot her ourselves.

Eddie thought we should do the latter. We were both flat broke. It was how horses had been put down for generations. It seemed to both of us a strangely more humane thing to do—that she'd die at the hands of someone she knew and trusted, rather than a stranger. Eddie said he'd do it before Paul and I returned for Christmas in a few weeks. We wouldn't be coming for a family occasion: Paul and I would be in the house alone. Eddie planned to spend Christmas at his girlfriend's place with her and her kids. Karen and Leif had plans of their own too—Leif would be in St. Paul with his girlfriend and her family, and Karen with the husband she'd met and married within the span of a few weeks earlier that year.

I felt ill as Paul and I pulled into the driveway a few weeks later, on the afternoon of Christmas Eve. Over and over again, I'd been imagining how it would feel to look out to the pasture and see only Roger. But when I got out of the car, Lady was still there, shivering in her stall, her flesh hanging from her skeletal frame. It hurt to even look at her. The weather had turned brutally cold, breaking records with lows that hovered around 25 degrees below zero, with the wind chill plunging the temperature colder still.

I didn't call Eddie to ask why he hadn't followed through on what we'd decided. I called my mother's father in Alabama instead. He'd been a horseman all his life. We talked for an hour about Lady. He asked me one question after another, and by the end of our conversation he was adamant that it was time to put her down. I told him I'd sleep on it. The next morning the phone rang shortly after dawn.

It wasn't my grandfather calling to wish me a merry Christmas. It was my grandfather calling to implore me to act now. To let Lady die naturally was cruel and inhumane, he insisted, and I knew he was right. I also knew that it was up to me to make sure it was done. I didn't have money to pay for the veterinarian to come out and give her an injection, and even if I did, it was Christmas and I doubted he would come. My grandfather described to me in specific detail how to shoot a horse. When I expressed trepidation, he assured me this was the way it had been done for years. I also worried about what to do with Lady's corpse. The ground was so deeply frozen that burial was impossible.

"Leave her," he instructed. "The coyotes will drag her away."

"What should I do?" I cried to Paul after I hung up the phone. We didn't know it, but it was our last Christmas together. A couple of months later, I'd tell him about my infidelities and he'd move out. By the time Christmas came again we were discussing divorce.

"Do what you think is right," he said on that Christmas morning. We were sitting at the kitchen table—its every crack and groove familiar to me, and yet it seemed as if I were as far as I could be from home, alone on an ice floe.

"I don't know what's right," I said, though I did. I knew exactly what I had to do. It was what I'd had to do so many times now: choose the best of two horrible things. But I couldn't do it without my brother. Paul and I had shot a gun before—Leif had taught us both the previous winter—but neither of us could do it with any confidence. Leif wasn't an avid hunter, but at least he'd done it often enough that he knew what he was doing. When I called him, he agreed to drive home that evening.

In the morning, we discussed in detail what we'd do. I told him everything our grandfather had told me.

"Okay," he said. "Get her ready."

Outside, the sun was bright, the sky crystal blue. By eleven it had warmed to 17 degrees below zero. We bundled ourselves in layers of clothes. It was so cold the trees were cracking open, freezing and exploding in great bursts that I'd heard from my bed the sleepless night before.

I whispered to Lady as I put her halter on, telling her how much I loved her as I led her out of her stall. Paul shut the gate behind us, trapping Roger inside so he couldn't follow. I led her across the icy snow, turning back to watch her walk one last time. She still moved with an unspeakable grace and power, striding with the long, grand high-stepping gait that always took my mother's breath away. I led her to a birch tree that Paul and I had chosen the previous afternoon and tied her to it by her lead rope. The tree was on the very edge of the pasture, beyond which the woods thickened in earnest, far enough away from the house that I hoped the coyotes would approach and take her body that night. I spoke to her and ran my hands over her chestnut coat, murmuring my love and sorrow, begging her forgiveness and understanding.

When I looked up, my brother was standing there with his rifle.

Paul took my arm and together we stumbled through the snow to stand behind Leif. We were only six feet away from Lady. Her warm breath was like a silk cloud. The frozen crust of the snow held us for a moment, then collapsed so we all sank up to our knees.

"Right between her eyes," I said to Leif, repeating yet again the words our grandfather had said to me. If we did that, he promised, we'd kill her in one clean shot.

Leif crouched, kneeling on one knee. Lady pranced and scraped her front hooves on the ice and then lowered her head and looked at us. I inhaled sharply and Leif fired the gun. The bullet hit Lady right between her eyes, in the middle of her white star, exactly where we hoped it would. She bolted so hard her leather halter snapped into pieces and fell away from her face, and then she stood unmoving, looking at us with a stunned expression.

"Shoot her again," I gasped, and immediately Leif did, firing three more bullets into her head in quick succession. She stumbled and jerked, but she didn't fall and she didn't run, though she was no longer tied to the tree. Her eyes were wild upon us, shocked by what we'd done, her face a constellation of bloodless holes. In an instant I knew we'd done the wrong thing, not in killing her, but in thinking that we should be the ones to do it. I should have insisted Eddie do this one thing, or paid for the veterinarian to come out. I'd had the wrong idea of what it takes to kill an animal. There is no such thing as one clean shot.

"Shoot her! *Shoot her!*" I pleaded in a guttural wail I didn't know was mine.

"I'm out of bullets," Leif yelled.

"Lady!" I shrieked. Paul grabbed my shoulders to pull me toward him and I batted him away, panting and whimpering as if someone were beating me to death.

Lady took one wobbling step and then fell onto her front knees, her body tilting hideously forward as if she were a great ship slowly sinking into the sea. Her head swayed and she let out a deep moan. Blood gushed from her soft nostrils in a sudden, great torrent, hitting the snow so hot it hissed. She coughed and coughed, tremendous buckets of blood coming each time, her back legs buckling in excruciating slow motion beneath her. She hovered there, struggling to stay grotesquely up, before she finally toppled over onto her side, where she kicked her legs and flailed and twisted her neck and fought to rise again.

"Lady!" I howled. "Lady!"

Leif grabbed me. "Look away!" he shouted, and together we turned away.

"LOOK AWAY!" he hollered to Paul, and Paul obeyed.

"Please come take her," Leif chanted, as tears streaked down his face. "Come take her. Come take her. Come take her."

When I turned, Lady had dropped her head to the ground at last, though her sides still heaved and her legs twitched. The three of us staggered closer, breaking through the snow's crust to sink miserably to our knees again. We watched as she breathed enormous slow breaths and then finally she sighed and her body went still.

Our mother's horse. Lady. Stonewall's Highland Nancy was dead.

Whether it had taken five minutes or an hour, I didn't know. My mittens and hat had fallen off, but I could not bring myself to retrieve them. My eyelashes had frozen into clumps. Strands of hair that had blown onto my tear- and snot-drenched face had frozen into icicles that clinked when I moved. I pushed them numbly away, unable even to register the cold. I knelt beside Lady's belly and ran my hands along her blood-speckled body one last time. She was still warm, just as my mother had been when I'd come into the room at the hospital and seen that she'd died without me. I looked at Leif and wondered if he was remembering the same thing. I crawled to her head and touched her cold ears, soft as velvet. I put my hands over the black bullet holes in her white star. The deep tunnels of blood that had burned through the snow around her were already beginning to freeze.

Paul and I watched as Leif took out his knife and cut bundles of reddish-blonde hair from Lady's mane and tail. He handed one to me.

"Mom can go to the other side now," he said, looking into my eyes as if it were only the two of us in the entire world. "That's what the Indians believe—that when a great warrior dies you've got to kill their horse so he can cross over to the other side of the river. It's a way of showing respect. Maybe Mom can ride away now."

I imagined our mother crossing a great river on Lady's strong back, finally leaving us nearly three years after she died. I wanted it to be true. It was the thing I wished for when I had a wish to make. Not that my mother would ride back to me—though, of course, I wanted that—but that she and Lady would ride away together. That the worst thing I'd ever done had been a healing instead of a massacre.

I slept finally that night in the woods somewhere outside the Whitehorse Campground. And when I did, I dreamed of snow. Not the snow in which my brother and I had killed Lady, but the snow I'd just passed through up in the mountains, the memory of it more frightening than the experience of it had been. All night long, I dreamed of the things that could have happened but didn't. Skidding and sliding down a treacherous slope and off the side of a cliff or crashing into rocks below. Walking and never coming to that road, but wandering lost and starving instead.

I studied my guidebook as I ate my breakfast the next morning. If I walked up to the PCT as planned, I'd be walking into more snow. The idea of that spooked me, and as I gazed at my map I saw that I didn't have to do it. I could walk back to the Whitehorse Campground and west farther still to Bucks Lake. From there I could follow a jeep road that wended its way north, ascending to the PCT at a place called Three Lakes. The alternate route was about the same distance as the PCT, approximately fifteen miles, but it was at a low enough elevation that it had a chance of being snow-free. I packed up my camp, walked back down the trail I'd come on the night before, and strode defiantly through the Whitehorse Campground.

All morning, as I walked west to Bucks Lake, then north and west again along its shore before coming to the rugged jeep road that would take me back up to the PCT, I thought of the resupply box that waited for me in Belden Town. Not so much the box, but the twenty-dollar bill that would be inside. And not so much the twenty-dollar bill, but the food and beverages I could buy with it. I spent hours in a half-ecstatic, half-tortured reverie, fantasizing about cake and cheeseburgers, chocolate and bananas, apples and mixed-green salads, and, more than anything, about Snapple lemonade. This did not make sense. I'd had only a few Snapple lemonades in my pre-PCT life and liked them well enough, but they hadn't stood out in any particular way. It had not been *my drink*. But now it haunted me. Pink or yellow, it didn't matter. Not a day passed that I didn't imagine in vivid detail what it would be like to hold one in my hand and bring it to my mouth. Some days I forbade myself to think about it, lest I go entirely insane.

I could see that the road to Three Lakes had only recently become free of snow. Great gashes had split open in places across it and streams of melting snow flowed in wide gaping gullies along its sides. I followed it up beneath a dense canopy of trees without seeing anyone. Midafternoon, I felt a familiar tug inside me. I was getting my period, I realized. My first on the trail. I'd almost forgotten it could come. The new way I'd been aware of my body since beginning my hike had blunted the old ways. No longer was I concerned about the delicate intricacies of whether I felt infinitesimally fatter or thinner than I had the day before. There was no such thing as a bad hair day. The smallest inner reverberations were obliterated by the frank pain I always felt in the form of my aching feet or the muscles of my shoulders and upper back that knotted and burned so hard and hot that I had to pause several times an hour to do a series of moves that would offer a moment of relief. I took off my pack, dug through my first aid kit, and found the jagged hunk of natural sponge I'd put in a small ziplock bag before my trip began. I'd used it only a few times experimentally before I took it on the PCT. Back in Minneapolis, the sponge had seemed like a sensible way to deal with my period given my circumstances on the trail, but now that I held it, I was less than sure. I attempted to wash my hands with water from my bottle, dousing the sponge as I did so, and then squeezed it out, pulled down my shorts, squatted on the road, and pushed the sponge into my vagina as far as I could, wedging it against my cervix.

As I pulled up my shorts, I heard the sound of an engine approaching, and a moment later a red pickup truck with an extended cab and oversized tires rounded a bend. The driver hit the brakes when he saw me, startled at the sight. I was startled too, and deeply grateful that I wasn't still squatting and half naked with my hand jammed into my crotch. I waved nervously as the truck pulled up beside me.

"Howdy," a man said, and reached through his open window. I took his hand and shook it, conscious of where mine had just been. There were two other men in the truck with him—one in the front and another in the back seat with two boys. The men looked to be in their thirties, the boys about eight.

"You headed up to Three Lakes?" the man asked.

"Yeah."

He was handsome and clean-cut and white, like the man beside him and the boys in the back. The other man was Latino and long-haired, a hard round belly rising before him.

"We're headed up there to do some fishing. We'd give you a ride, but we're packed," he said, pointing to the back of the truck, which was covered by a camper.

"That's okay. I like to walk."

"Well, we're having Hawaiian screwdrivers tonight, so stop on by."

"Thanks," I said, and watched them drive off.

I hiked the rest of the afternoon thinking about Hawaiian screwdrivers. I didn't know exactly what they were but they didn't sound all that different from Snapple lemonade to me. When I reached the top of the road, the red pickup and the men's camp came into view, perched above the westernmost of the Three Lakes. The PCT was just beyond it. I followed a scant trail east along the lake's shore, finding a secluded spot among the boulders that were scattered around the lake. I set up my tent and ducked into the woods to squeeze out my sponge and put it in again. I walked down to the lake to filter water and wash my hands and face. I thought about diving in to bathe, but the water was ice-cold and I was already chilled in the mountain air. Before coming on the PCT, I'd imagined countless baths in lakes and rivers and streams, but in reality, only rarely did I plunge in. By the end of the day, I often ached with fatigue and shook with what felt like a fever but was only exhaustion and the chill of my drying sweat. The best I could do most days was splash my face and strip off my sweat-drenched T-shirt and shorts before swaddling myself in my fleece anorak and leggings for the night.

I removed my boots and pulled the duct tape and 2nd Skin off my feet and soaked them in the icy water. When I rubbed them, another blackened toenail came off in my hand, the second I'd lost so far. The lake was calm and clear, rimmed by towering trees and leafy bushes among the boulders. I saw a bright green lizard in the mud; it froze in place for a moment before scampering away at lightning speed. The men's camp was not far beyond me along the lakeshore, but they hadn't yet detected my presence. Before going to see them, I brushed my teeth, put on lip balm, and pulled a comb through my hair.

"There she is," shouted the man who'd been in the passenger seat when I ambled up. "And just in time too."

He handed me a red plastic cup full of a yellow liquid that I could only assume was a Hawaiian screwdriver. It had ice cubes. It had vodka. It had pineapple juice. When I sipped it I thought I would faint. Not from the alcohol hitting me, but from the sheer fabulousness of the combination of liquid sugar and booze.

The two white men were firefighters. The Latino man was a painter by passion but a carpenter by trade. His name was Francisco, though everyone called him Paco. He was the cousin of one of the white guys, visiting from Mexico City, though the three of them had grown up together on the same block in Sacramento, where the firefighters still lived. Paco had gone to visit his great-grandmother in Mexico ten years before, fallen in love with a Mexican woman while there, and stayed. The firefighters' sons flitted past us, playing war while we sat around a fire ring filled with logs the men had yet to light, making intermittent shouts, gasps, and explosive sounds as they shot each other with plastic guns from behind the boulders.

"You've got to be kidding me! *You've got to be kidding me!*" the firefighters took turns exclaiming when I explained to them what I was doing and showed them my battered feet with their eight remaining toenails. They asked me question after question while marveling and shaking their heads and plying me with another Hawaiian screwdriver and tortilla chips.

"Women are the ones with the *cojones*," said Paco as he made a bowl of guacamole. "We guys like to think we're the ones, but we're wrong." His hair was like a snake down his back, a long thick ponytail bound in sections all the way down with plain rubber bands. After the fire was lit and after we had eaten the trout that one of them had caught in the lake and the stew made with venison from a deer one of them had shot last winter, it was only me and Paco sitting by the fire as the other men read to their sons in the tent.

"You want to smoke a joint with me?" he asked as he took one from his shirt pocket. He lit it up, took a hit, and handed it to me. "So this is the Sierras, eh?" he said, looking out over the dark lake. "All that time growing up I never made it up here before."

"It's the Range of Light," I said, passing the joint back to him. "That's what John Muir called it. I can see why. I've never seen light like I have out here. All the sunsets and sunrises against the mountains."

"You're on a spirit walk, aren't you?" Paco said, staring into the fire.

"I don't know," I said. "Maybe you could call it that."

"That's what it is," he said, looking at me intensely. He stood. "I've got something I want to give you." He went to the back of the truck and returned with a T-shirt. He handed it to me and I held it up. On the front was a giant picture of Bob Marley, his dreadlocks surrounded by images of electric guitars and pre-Columbian effigies in profile. On the back was a picture of Haile Selassie, the man Rastafarians thought was God incarnate, rimmed by a red and green and gold swirl. "That is a sacred shirt," Paco said as I studied it by the firelight. "I want you to have it because I can see that you walk with the spirits of the animals, with the spirits of the earth and the sky."

I nodded, silenced by emotion and the half-drunk and entirely stoned certitude that the shirt really was sacred. "Thank you," I said.

When I walked back to my camp, I stood gazing up at the stars with the shirt in my hand before crawling into my tent. Away from Paco, sobered by the cool air, I wondered about walking with the spirits. What did that even mean? Did I walk with the spirits? Did my mom? Where had she gone after she died? Where was Lady? Had they really ridden together across the river to the other side? Reason told me that all they'd done was die, though they'd both come to me repeatedly in my dreams. The Lady dreams were the opposite of those I'd had about my mother—the ones in which she'd ordered me to kill her over and over again. In the dreams of Lady, I didn't have to kill anyone. I had only to accept a giant and fantastically colorful bouquet of flowers that she carried to me clenched in her soft mouth. She would nudge me with her nose until I took it, and in that offering, I knew that I was forgiven. But was I? Was that her spirit or was it only my subconscious working it out?

I wore the shirt from Paco the next morning as I hiked back to the PCT and on to Belden Town, catching glimpses of Lassen Peak as I went. It was about fifty miles to the north, a snowy volcanic mountain rising to 10,457 feet—a landmark to me not only because of its size and majesty, but because it was the first of the peaks I'd pass in the Cascade Range, which I'd enter just north of Belden Town. From Lassen northward, the mountains of the High Cascades lined up in a rough row among hundreds of other, less prominent mountains, each one marking the progress of my journey in the coming weeks. Each of those peaks seemed in my mind's eye to be like a set of monkey bars I'd swung on as a child. Every time I got to one, the next would be just out of reach. From Lassen Peak to Mount Shasta to Mount McLoughlin to Mount Thielsen to the Three Sisters—South, Middle, and North—to Mount Washington to Three Fingered Jack to Mount Jefferson and finally to Mount Hood, which I'd traverse fifty-some miles before I reached the Bridge of the Gods. They were all volcanoes, ranging in elevation from a little under 8,000 to just over 14,000 feet. They were a small portion of the Pacific Ring of Fire, a 25,000-mile-long series of volcanoes and oceanic trenches that rim the Pacific Ocean in a horseshoe shape from Chile, up along the western edge of Central and North America, across to Russia and Japan, and down through Indonesia and New Zealand, before culminating in Antarctica.

Down, down, down the trail went on my last full day of hiking in the Sierra Nevada. It was only seven miles to Belden from Three Lakes, but the trail descended a merciless 4,000 feet in the space of five of them. By the time I reached Belden, my feet were injured in an entirely new way: the tips of my toes were blistered. They'd slid forward with each step, pressed relentlessly against the toe ends of my boots. This was supposed to be my easy day, but I dragged into Belden Town limping in agony, observing that, in fact, it wasn't a town. It was a rambling building near a railroad track. The building contained a bar and a small store, which also served as a post office, a tiny laundromat, and a shower house. I pulled off my boots on the store's porch, put my camp sandals on, and hobbled inside to collect my box. Soon I had my envelope with twenty dollars, the sight of it such a tremendous relief that I forgot about my toes for a minute. I bought two bottles of Snapple lemonade and returned to the porch to drink them, one after the other.

"Cool shirt," a woman said. She had short curly gray hair and a big white dog on a leash. "This is Odin." She bent to scratch his neck, then stood and pushed her little round glasses back into place on her nose and fixed me in her curious gaze. "Are you, by chance, hiking the PCT?"

Her name was Trina. She was a fifty-year-old high school English teacher from Colorado who'd begun her hike only a couple of days before. She'd left Belden Town, hiking north on the PCT, only to be met by enough snow on the trail that she'd returned. Her report filled me with gloom. Would I ever escape the snow? As we talked, another hiker walked up—a woman named Stacy who had also begun her hike the day before, coming up the same road I had to reach Three Lakes.

At last I'd met some women on the trail! I was dumbfounded with relief as we exchanged in a flurry the quick details of our lives. Trina was an avid weekend backpacker, Stacy an experienced trekker who'd hiked the PCT with a friend from Mexico to Belden Town the previous summer. Stacy and I talked about the places on the trail we'd both been, about Ed in Kennedy Meadows, whom she'd met the summer before, and about her life in a desert town in southern California, where she worked as a bookkeeper for her father's company and took her summers off to hike. She was thirty and from a big Irish family, pale, pretty, and black-haired.

"Let's camp together for the night and make a plan," said Trina. "There's a spot over in that meadow." She pointed to a place visible from the store. We walked there and pitched our tents. I unpacked my box while Trina and Stacy talked on the grass. Waves of pleasure came over me as I picked up each item and held it instinctively to my nose. The pristine packets of Lipton noodles or dehydrated beans and rice that I ate for dinner, the still shiny Clif bars and immaculate ziplock bags of dried fruit and nuts. I was sick to death of these things, but seeing them new and unsullied restored something in me. There was the fresh T-shirt I didn't need now that I had my Bob Marley shirt, two brand-new pair of wool socks, and a copy of Margaret Drabble's *A Summer Bird-Cage,* which I wasn't quite ready for yet—I'd burned my way through only about half the pages of *The Novel,* tossing them that morning in Paco's fire. And, most important, a fresh supply of 2nd Skin.

I took off my boots and sat down, doctoring my chawed-up feet. When Trina's dog began to bark, I looked up and saw a young man, blond, blue-eyed, and lanky. I knew in an instant that he was a PCT hiker by the drag of his gait. His name was Brent, and once he introduced himself I greeted him like an old friend, though I'd never met him. I'd heard stories about him back in Kennedy Meadows. He'd grown up in a small town in Montana, Greg, Albert, and Matt had told me. He'd once gone into a deli in a town near the trail in southern California, ordered a sandwich with two pounds of roast beef in it, and eaten it in six bites. He laughed when I reminded him about it, and then he took his pack off and squatted down to get a closer look at my feet.

"Your boots are too small," he said, echoing what Greg had told me back in Sierra City. I stared at him vacantly. My boots *couldn't* be too small. They were the only boots I had.

"I think it was just all that descending from Three Lakes," I said.

"But that's the point," replied Brent. "With the right size boots, you'd be able to descend without hashing up your feet. That's what boots are for, so you *can descend.*"

I thought of the good people of REI. I remembered the man who made me walk up and down a small wooden ramp in the store for just this reason: to make sure my toes didn't bang up against the ends of my boots when I went down and that my heels didn't rub against the backs when I went up. They hadn't seemed to in the store. There was no question now that I'd been wrong or that my feet had grown or that there was any denying that as long as I had these boots on my feet, I was in a living hell.

But there was nothing to be done. I didn't have the money to buy a new pair or any place to do it if I did. I put on my camp sandals and walked back to the store, where I paid a dollar to take a shower and dressed in my rain gear while my clothes washed and dried in the two-machine laundromat. I called Lisa while I waited and was elated when she answered the phone. We talked about her life and I told her what I could convey of mine. Together we went over my new itinerary. After we hung up, I signed the PCT hiker register and scanned it to see when Greg had passed through. His name wasn't there. It seemed impossible that he was behind me.

"Have you heard anything about Greg?" I asked Brent when I returned wearing my clean clothes.

"He dropped out because of the snow."

I looked at him, stunned. "Are you sure?"

"That's what the Australians told me. Did you ever meet them?"

I shook my head.

"They're a married couple on their honeymoon. They decided to ditch the PCT too. They took off to go hike the AT instead."

It was only once I'd decided to hike the PCT that I learned about the AT—the Appalachian Trail, the far more popular and developed cousin of the PCT. Both were designated national scenic trails in 1968. The AT is 2,175 miles long, approximately 500 miles shorter than the PCT, and follows the crest of the Appalachian Mountains from Georgia to Maine.

"Did Greg go to the AT too?" I squeaked.

"Nah. He didn't want to keep missing so much of the trail, doing all these bypasses and taking alternate routes, so he's coming back to hike it next year instead. That's what the Australians told me, anyway."

"Wow," I said, feeling sick at the news. Greg had been a talisman for me since the day I met him in the very hour I'd decided to quit. He'd believed that if he could do this, I could too, and now he was gone. So were the Australians, a pair I'd never met, but a picture of them formed instantly in my mind anyway. I knew without knowing that they were buff and Amazonian, dazzlingly fit for the rugged outdoors by virtue of their Australian blood in ways I would never be. "Why aren't *you* going to hike the AT instead?" I asked, worried he'd reveal that in fact he was.

He thought about it for a while. "Too much traffic," he said. He continued looking at me, at Bob Marley's face so big on my chest, as if he had more to say. "That's a seriously awesome shirt, by the way."

I'd never set foot on the AT, but I'd heard much about it from the guys at Kennedy Meadows. It was the PCT's closest kin and yet also its opposite in many ways. About two thousand people set out to thru-hike the AT each summer, and though only a couple hundred of them made it all the way, that was far more than the hundred or so who set out on the PCT each year. Hikers on the AT spent most nights camping in or near group shelters that existed along the trail. On the AT, resupply stops were closer together, and more of them were in real towns, unlike those along the PCT, which often consisted of nothing but a post office and a bar or tiny store. I imagined the Australian honeymooners on the AT now, eating cheeseburgers and guzzling beer in a pub a couple of miles from the trail, sleeping by night under a wooden roof. They'd probably been given trail names by their fellow hikers, another practice that was far more common on the AT than on the PCT, though we had a way of naming people too. Half the time that Greg, Matt, and Albert had talked about Brent they'd referred to him as the Kid, though he was only a few years younger than me. Greg had been occasionally called the Statistician because he knew so many facts and figures about the trail and he worked as an accountant. Matt and Albert were the Eagle Scouts, and Doug and Tom the Preppies. I didn't think I'd been dubbed anything, but I got the sinking feeling that if I had, I didn't want to know what it was.

Trina, Stacy, Brent, and I ate dinner in the bar that adjoined the Belden store that evening. After paying for a shower, laundry, the Snapple, and a few snacks and incidentals, I had about fourteen bucks left. I ordered a green salad and a plate of fries, the two items on the menu that both were cheap and satisfied my deepest cravings, which veered in opposite directions: fresh and deep-fried. Together they cost me five dollars, so now I had nine left to get me all the way to my next box. It was 134 miles away at McArthur-Burney Falls Memorial State Park, which had a concessionaire's store that allowed PCT hikers to use it as a resupply stop. I drank my ice water miserably while the others sipped their beers. As we ate, we discussed the section ahead. By all reports, long stretches of it were socked in. The handsome bartender overheard our conversation and approached to tell us that rumor had it that Lassen Volcanic National Park was still buried under seventeen feet of snow. They were dynamiting the roads so they could open it for even a short tourist season this year.

"You want a drink?" he said to me, catching my eye. "On the house," he added when he saw my hesitation.

He brought me a glass of cold pinot gris, filled to the rim. When I sipped it I felt instantly dizzy with pleasure, just as I had when I drank the Hawaiian screwdriver the night before. By the time we paid our bill, we'd decided that when we hiked away from Belden in the morning, we'd follow a combination of lower-elevation jeep roads and the PCT for about fifty miles before hitchhiking a bypass of a socked-in section of the trail in Lassen Volcanic National Park, catching the PCT again at a place called Old Station.

After we returned to our camp, I sat in my chair writing a letter to Joe on a piece of paper I'd torn from my journal. His birthday was approaching and the wine had made me nostalgic for him. I remembered walking with him one night a year before with a miniskirt on and nothing underneath and having sex with him against a stone wall in a private cove of a public park. I remembered the giddy surge of emotion I'd felt every time we scored another bit of heroin and how the dye from his hair had stained my pillowcase blue. I didn't let myself write those things in the letter. I sat holding my pen, only thinking of them and also of the things I could tell him about my time on the PCT. It seemed impossible to make him understand all that had happened in the month since I'd seen him in Portland. My memories of last summer felt as foreign to me as my description of this summer would likely seem to him, so instead I mostly asked him a long list of questions, wondering how he was, what he was doing, who he was spending time with, and if he'd yet made the escape he'd alluded to in the postcard he'd sent me at Kennedy Meadows and gotten clean. I hoped he had. Not for me, but for him. I folded the letter and put it into an envelope that Trina had given me. I picked a few wildflowers from the meadow and pressed them inside before sealing the envelope shut.

"I'm going to mail this," I said to the others, and followed the light of my headlamp over the grass and along the dirt path to the mailbox outside the shuttered store.

"Hey, good-looking," a man's voice called to me after I put the letter in the box. I saw only the burning end of a cigarette on the dark porch.

"Hi," I answered uncertainly.

"It's me. The bartender," the man said, stepping forward into the faint light so I could see his face. "How'd you like your wine?" he asked.

"Oh. Hi. Yeah. That was really nice of you. Thanks."

"I'm still working," he said, flicking the ash of his cigarette into a planter. "But I'll be off in a bit. My trailer's just across the way, if you wanna come over and party. I can get a whole bottle of that pinot gris you liked."

"Thanks," I said. "But I've got to get up early and hike in the morning."

He took another drag of his cigarette, the end burning brightly. I'd watched him a bit after he'd brought me the wine. I guessed he was thirty. He looked good in his jeans. Why shouldn't I go with him?

"Well, you've got time to think about it, if you change your mind," he said.

"I've got to hike nineteen miles tomorrow," I replied, as if that meant anything to him.

"You could sleep at my place," he said. "I'd give you my bed. I could sleep on the couch, if you wanted. I bet a bed would feel good after you've been sleeping on the ground."

"I'm all set up over there." I gestured toward the meadow.

I walked back to my camp feeling queasy, equal parts flustered and flattered by his interest, a shot of bald desire quaking through me. The women had zipped themselves into their tents for the night by the time I returned, but Brent was still awake, standing in the dark, gazing up at the stars.

"Beautiful, huh?" I whispered, gazing up with him. As I did so, it occurred to me that I'd not cried once since I'd set foot on the trail. How could that be? After all the crying I'd done, it seemed impossible that it was true, but it was. I almost burst into tears with the realization, but I laughed instead.

"What's so funny?" Brent asked.

"Nothing." I looked at my watch. It was 10:15. "I'm usually sound asleep by now."

"Me too," said Brent.

"But I'm wide awake tonight."

"It's 'cause we're so excited to be in town," he said.

We both laughed. I'd been savoring the company of the women all day, grateful for the kinds of conversation that I'd seldom had since starting the PCT, but it was Brent I felt oddly the closest to, if only because he felt familiar. As I stood next to him, I realized he reminded me of my brother, who, in spite of our distance, I loved more than anyone.

"We should make a wish," I said to Brent.

"Don't you have to wait till you see a shooting star?" he asked.

"Traditionally, yes. But we can make up new rules," I said. "Like, I want boots that don't hurt my feet."

"You're not supposed to say it out loud!" he said, exasperated. "It's like blowing out your birthday candles. You can't tell anyone what your wish is. Now it's not going to come true. Your feet are totally fucked."

"Not necessarily," I said indignantly, though I felt sick with the knowledge that he was right.

"Okay, I made mine. Now it's your turn," he said.

I stared at a star, but my mind only went from one thing to the next. "How early are you taking off tomorrow?" I asked.

"At first light."

"Me too," I said. I didn't want to say goodbye to him the next morning. Trina, Stacy, and I had decided to hike and camp together the next couple of days, but Brent hiked faster than us, which meant he'd go on alone.

"So did you make your wish?" he asked.

"I'm still thinking."

"It's a good time to make one," he said. "It's our last night in the Sierra Nevada."

"Goodbye, Range of Light," I said to the sky.

"You could wish for a horse," Brent said. "Then you wouldn't have to worry about your feet."

I looked at him in the dark. It was true—the PCT was open to both hikers and pack animals, though I hadn't yet encountered any horseback riders on the trail. "I used to have a horse," I said, turning my gaze back to the sky. "I had two, actually."

"Well then, you're lucky," he said. "Not everyone gets a horse."

We were silent together for several moments.

I made my wish.

PART FOUR

WILD

When I had no roof I made
Audacity my roof.

ROBERT PINSKY,
"Samurai Song"

Never never never give up.

WINSTON CHURCHILL

11

THE LOU OUT OF LOU

I was standing by the side of the highway just outside the town of Chester, trying to hitch a ride, when a man driving a silver Chrysler LeBaron pulled over and got out. Over the past fifty-some hours, I'd hiked fifty miles with Stacy and Trina and the dog, from Belden Town to a place called Stover Camp, but we'd split up ten minutes before when a couple in a Honda Civic had stopped, announcing that they only had room for two of us. "You go," we'd each said to the other; "no, *you* go"—until I insisted and Stacy and Trina got in, Odin lumbering behind them to sit wherever he could, while I assured them I'd be fine.

And I *would* be fine, I thought, as the man who drove the Chrysler LeBaron made his way toward me on the gravel shoulder of the road, though I felt a sick flutter in my gut as I attempted to discern, in the flash of a second, what his intentions were. He looked like a nice enough guy, a few years older than me. He *was* a nice guy, I decided, when I glanced at the bumper of his car. On it, there was a green sticker that said IMAGINE WHIRLED PEAS.

Has there ever been a serial killer who imagined whirled peas?

"Hey there," I called amiably. I was holding the world's loudest whistle, my hand having traveled to it unconsciously over the top of Monster and around to the nylon cord that dangled from my backpack's frame. I hadn't used the whistle since I'd seen that first bear on the trail, but ever since then, I had a constant and visceral awareness of where it was in relation to me, as if it weren't only attached to my backpack by a cord, but another, invisible cord attached it to me.

"Good morning," the man said, and held his hand out to shake mine, his brown hair flopping over his eyes. He told me his name was Jimmy Carter, no relation, and that he couldn't give me a ride because there was no room in his car. I looked and saw it was true. Every inch except the driver's seat was crammed with newspapers, books, clothes, soda cans, and a jumble of other things that came up all the way to the windows. He wondered, instead, if he could talk to me. He said he was a reporter for a publication called the *Hobo Times*. He drove around the country interviewing "folks" who lived the hobo life.

"I'm not a hobo," I said, amused. "I'm a long-distance hiker." I let go of the whistle and extended my arm toward the road, jabbing my upright thumb at a passing van. "I'm hiking the Pacific Crest Trail," I explained, glancing at him, wishing he'd get in his car and drive away. I needed to catch two rides on two different highways to get to Old Station and he wasn't helping the cause. I was filthy and my clothes were even filthier, but I was still a woman alone. Jimmy Carter's presence complicated things, altered the picture from the vantage point of the drivers passing by. I remembered how long I'd had to stand by the side of the road when I'd been trying to get to Sierra City with Greg. With Jimmy Carter beside me, no one was going to stop.

"So how long have you been out on the road?" he asked, pulling a pen and a long, narrow reporter's notebook from the back pocket of his thin corduroy pants. His hair was shaggy and unwashed. His bangs concealed then revealed his dark eyes, depending on how the wind blew. He struck me as someone who had a PhD in something airy and indescribable. The history of consciousness, perhaps, or comparative studies in discourse and society.

"I *told* you. I'm not on the road," I said, and laughed. Eager as I was to get a ride, I couldn't help but feel a little delighted by Jimmy Carter's company. "I'm hiking the Pacific Crest Trail," I repeated, gesturing by way of elaboration to the woods that edged up near the road, though in fact the PCT was about nine miles west of where we stood.

He stared at me blankly, uncomprehending. It was midmorning and hot already, the kind of day that would be scorching by noon. I wondered if he could smell me. I was past the point where I could smell myself. I took a step back and dropped my hitchhiking arm in surrender. When it came to getting a ride, until he left I was screwed.

"It's a National Scenic Trail," I offered, but he only continued looking at me with a patient expression on his face, his unmarked notebook in his hand. As I explained to him what the PCT was and what I was doing on it, I saw that Jimmy Carter wasn't bad-looking. I wondered if he had any food in his car.

"So if you're hiking a wilderness trail, what are you doing *here*?" he asked.

I told him about bypassing the deep snow in Lassen Volcanic National Park.

"How long have you been out on the road?"

"I've been on the *trail* about a month," I said, and watched as he wrote this down. It occurred to me that maybe I was perhaps a tiny bit of a hobo, given all the time I'd spent hitchhiking and bypassing, but I didn't think it wise to mention that.

"How many nights have you slept with a roof over your head in that month?" he asked.

"Three times," I answered, after thinking about it—one night at Frank and Annette's and one night each at the motels in Ridgecrest and Sierra City.

"Is this all you have?" he asked, nodding to my backpack and ski pole.

"Yeah. I mean, I have some things in storage too, but for now this is it." I put my hand on Monster. It felt like a friend always, but even more so in the company of Jimmy Carter.

"Well then, I'd say you're a hobo!" he said happily, and asked me to spell my first and last names.

I did and then wished I hadn't.

"No fucking way!" he exclaimed when he had it all down on the page. "Is that really your name?"

"Yeah," I said, and turned away, as if searching for a car, so he wouldn't read the hesitation on my face. It was eerily silent until a logging truck came around the bend and roared by, oblivious to my imploring thumb.

"So," Jimmy Carter said after the truck passed, "we could say you're an *actual* stray."

"I wouldn't say that," I stammered. "Being a hobo and being a hiker are two entirely different things." I looped my wrist into the pink strap of my ski pole and scraped the dirt with the tip, making a line that went nowhere. "I'm not a hiker in the way you might think of a hiker," I explained. "I'm more like an *expert* hiker. I hike fifteen to twenty miles a day, day after day, up and down mountains, far away from roads or people or anything, often going days without seeing another person. Maybe you should do a story on that instead."

He glanced up at me from his notebook, his hair blowing extravagantly across his pale face. He seemed like so many people I knew. I wondered if I seemed that way to him.

"I hardly ever meet hobo women," he half whispered, as if confiding a secret, "so this is fucking cool."

"I'm not a hobo!" I insisted more vehemently this time.

"Hobo women are hard to find," he persisted.

I told him that this was because women were too oppressed to be hobos. That most likely all the women who wanted to be hobos were holed up in some house with a gaggle of children to raise. Children who'd been fathered by hobo men who'd hit the road.

"Oh, I see," he said. "You're a feminist, then."

"Yes," I said. It felt good to agree on something.

"My favorite," he said, and wrote in his notebook without saying his favorite *what.*

"But none of this matters!" I exclaimed. "Because I myself am not a hobo. This is totally legit, you know. What I'm doing. I'm not the only one hiking the PCT. People *do this.* Have you ever heard of the Appalachian Trail? It's like that. Only out west." I stood watching him write what seemed like more words than I'd spoken.

"I'd like to get a picture of you," Jimmy Carter said. He reached into his car and pulled out a camera. "That's a cool shirt, by the way. I love Bob Marley. And I like your bracelet too. A lot of hobos are Nam vets, you know."

I looked down at William J. Crockett's name on my wrist.

"Smile," he said, and snapped a shot. He told me to look for his piece on me in the fall issue of the *Hobo Times,* as if I were a regular reader. "Articles have been excerpted in *Harper's,*" he added.

"*Harper's?*" I asked, dumbfounded.

"Yeah, it's this magazine that—"

"I know what *Harper's* is," I interrupted sharply. "And I don't want to *be* in *Harper's.* Or rather, I really want to be in *Harper's,* but not because I'm a hobo."

"I thought you weren't a hobo," he said, and turned to open the trunk of his car.

"Well, I'm not, so it would be a really bad idea to be in *Harper's,* which means you probably shouldn't even write the article because—"

"Standard-issue hobo care package," he said, turning to give me a can of cold Budweiser beer and a plastic grocery bag weighed down with a handful of items at its bottom.

"But I'm not a hobo," I echoed for the last time, with less fervor than I had before, afraid he'd finally believe me and take the standard-issue hobo care package away.

"Thanks for the interview," he said, and shut the trunk. "Stay safe out here."

"Yeah. You too," I said.

"You have a gun, I assume. At least I *hope* you do."

I shrugged, unwilling to commit either way.

"'Cause, I know you've been south of here, but now you're going north, which means you're soon entering Bigfoot country."

"Bigfoot?"

"Yeah. You know, Sasquatch? No lie. From here all the way up to the border and into Oregon you're in the territory where most of the Bigfoot sightings in the world are reported." He turned to the trees as if one might come barreling out at us. "A lot of folks believe in them. A lot of hobo folks—folks who are *out here*. Folks who *know*. I hear Bigfoot stories all the time."

"Well, I'm okay, I think. At least so far," I said, and laughed, though my stomach did a little somersault. In the weeks preceding my hike on the PCT, when I'd decided not to be afraid of anything, I'd been thinking about bears and snakes and mountain lions and strange people I met along the way. I hadn't pondered hairy humanoid bipedal beasts.

"But you're probably fine. I wouldn't worry. Chances are, they'll leave you alone. Especially if you have a gun."

"Right." I nodded.

"Good luck on your hike," he said, getting into his car.

"Good luck . . . finding hobos," I said, and waved as he drove away.

I stood there for a while, letting cars pass without even trying to get them to give me a ride. I felt more alone than anyone in the whole wide world. The sun beat down on me hot, even through my hat. I wondered where Stacy and Trina were. The man who'd picked them up was only going to take them about twelve miles east, to the junction of the next highway we needed to catch a ride on, which would take us north and then back west to Old Station, where we'd rejoin the PCT. We'd agreed to meet at that junction. I remotely regretted having encouraged them to leave me behind when that ride had come along. I jabbed my thumb at another car and realized only after it passed that it didn't look so good that I was holding a can of beer. I pressed its cool aluminum against my hot forehead and suddenly had the urge to drink it. Why shouldn't I? It would only get warm in my pack.

I hoisted Monster onto my back and ambled through the weeds down into the ditch and then up again, into the woods, which somehow felt like home to me, like the world that was mine in a way that the world of roads and towns and cars was no longer. I walked until I found a good spot in the shade. Then I sat down in the dirt and cracked the beer open. I didn't like beer—in fact, that Budweiser was the first whole beer I'd ever drunk in my life—but it tasted good to me, like beer tastes, I imagine, to those who love it: cold and sharp and crisp and right.

While I drank it I explored the contents of the plastic grocery bag. I took everything out and laid each item before me on the ground: a pack of peppermint gum, three individually wrapped wet wipes, a paper packet containing two aspirin, six butterscotch candies in translucent gold wrappers, a book of matches that said *Thank You Steinbeck Drug,* a Slim Jim sausage sealed in its plastic vacuum world, a single cigarette in a cylindrical faux-glass case, a disposable razor, and a short, fat can of baked beans.

I ate the Slim Jim first, washing it down with the last of my Budweiser, and then the butterscotch candies, all six of them, one after the other, and then—still hungry, always hungry—turned my attention to the can of baked beans. I pried it open in tiny increments with the impossible can-opening device on my Swiss army knife, and then, too lazy to rummage through my pack for my spoon, I scooped them out with the knife itself and ate them—hobo-style—from the blade.

I returned to the road feeling slightly hazy from the beer, chewing two pieces of the peppermint gum to sober up, while cheerfully stabbing my thumb at every vehicle that passed. After a few minutes, an old white Maverick pulled over. A woman sat in the driver's seat with a man beside her and another man and a dog in the back seat.

"Where you headed?" she asked.

"Old Station," I said. "Or at least the junction of 36 and 44."

"That's on our way," she said, and got out of the car, came around the back, and opened the trunk for me. She looked to be about forty. Her hair was frizzy and bleached blonde, her face puffy and pocked with old acne scars. She wore cutoffs and gold earrings in the shape of butterflies and a grayish halter top that seemed to have been made with the strings of a mop. "That's quite a pack you got there, kiddo," she said, and laughed raucously.

"Thanks, thanks," I kept saying, wiping the sweat from my face as we worked together to cram Monster into the trunk. We got it in eventually, and I climbed into the back seat with the dog and the man. The dog was a husky, blue-eyed and gorgeous, standing on the tiny floor in front of the seat. The man was lean and about the same age as the woman, his dark hair woven into a thin braid. He wore a black leather vest without a shirt underneath and a red bandanna tied biker-style over the top of his head.

"Hi," I murmured in his direction as I searched uselessly for the seat belt that was crammed irretrievably into the fold of the seat, my eyes skimming his tattoos: a spiked metal ball on the end of a chain on one arm and the top half of a bare-breasted woman with her head thrown back in either pain or ecstasy on the other; a Latin word I didn't know the meaning of scrawled across his tan chest. When I gave up on finding the seat belt, the husky leaned over and licked my knee avidly with his soft and strangely cool tongue.

"That dog's got some motherfucking good taste in women," said the man. "His name's Stevie Ray," he added. Instantly the dog stopped licking me, closed his mouth up tight, and looked at me with his icy black-rimmed eyes, as if he knew he'd been introduced and wanted to be polite. "I'm Spider. You already met Louise—she goes by Lou."

"Hi!" Lou said, meeting my eyes for a second in the rearview mirror.

"And this here's my brother Dave," he said, gesturing to the man in the passenger seat.

"Hi," I said.

"How about you? You got a name?" Dave turned to ask.

"Oh yeah—sorry. I'm Cheryl." I smiled, though I felt a blurry uncertainty about having accepted this particular ride. There was nothing to do about it now. We were already on our way, the hot wind blowing my hair. I petted Stevie Ray while assessing Spider in my peripheral vision. "Thanks for picking me up," I said to conceal my unease.

"Hey, no problem, sister," Spider said. On his middle finger, he wore a square turquoise ring. "We've all been on the road before. We all know what it's like. I hitched last week and motherfuck if I couldn't get a ride to save my life, so that's why when I saw you I told Lou to stop. Mother-fucking karma, you know?"

"Yeah," I said, reaching up to tuck my hair behind my ears. It felt as coarse and dry as straw.

"What you doing out on the road anyway?" Lou asked from the front.

I went into the whole PCT shebang, explaining about the trail and the record snowpack and the complicated way I had to hitchhike to get to Old Station. They listened with respectful, distant curiosity, all three of them lighting up cigarettes as I spoke.

After I was done talking, Spider said, "I've got a story for you, Cheryl. I think it's along the lines of what you're talking about. I was reading about animals a while back and there was this motherfucking scientist in France back in the thirties or forties or whenever the motherfuck it was and he was trying to get apes to draw these pictures, to make *art* pictures like the kinds of pictures in serious motherfucking paintings that you see in museums and shit. So the scientist keeps showing the apes these paintings and giving them charcoal pencils to draw with and then one day one of the apes finally draws something but it's not the art pictures that it draws. What it draws is the bars of its own motherfucking cage. *Its own motherfucking cage!* Man, that's the truth, ain't it? I can relate to that and I bet you can too, sister."

"I can," I said earnestly.

"We can all relate to that, man," said Dave, and he turned in his seat so he and Spider could do a series of motorcycle blood brother hand jives in the air between them.

"You know something about this dog?" Spider asked me when they were done. "I got him the day Stevie Ray Vaughan died. That's how he got his motherfucking name."

"I love Stevie Ray," I said.

"You like *Texas Flood*?" Dave asked me.

"Yeah," I said, swooning at the thought of it.

"I got it right here," he said, and pulled out a CD and placed it into the boom box that was propped between him and Lou. A moment later, the heaven of Vaughan's electric guitar filled the car. The music felt like sustenance to me, like food, like all the things I'd once taken for granted that had now become sources of ecstasy for me because I'd been denied them. I watched the trees stream past, lost in the song "Love Struck Baby."

When it ended, Lou said, "We're love struck too, me and Dave. We're getting married next week."

"Congrats," I said.

"You wanna marry me, sweetheart?" Spider asked me, momentarily grazing my bare thigh with the back of his hand, his turquoise ring hard against me.

"Just ignore him," said Lou. "He's nothing but a horny old bastard." She laughed and caught my eye in the rearview mirror.

I was a horny old bastard too, I thought, while Stevie Ray the dog licked my knee methodically and the other Stevie Ray launched into a smoking rendition of "Pride and Joy." The place on my leg where Spider had touched me seemed to pulse. I wished he'd do it again, though I knew that was ludicrous. A laminated card with a cross on it dangled from the stem of the rearview mirror, alongside a faded Christmas-tree-shaped air freshener, and when it spun around I saw that on the other side there was a photograph of a little boy.

"Is that your son?" I asked Lou when the song ended, pointing to the mirror.

"That's my little Luke," she said, reaching to tap it.

"Is he going to be in the wedding?" I asked, but she made no reply. She only turned the music down low and I knew instantly that I'd said the wrong thing.

"He died five years ago, when he was eight," said Lou, a few moments later.

"I'm so sorry," I said. I leaned forward and patted her shoulder.

"He was riding his bike and he was hit by a truck," she said plainly. "He wasn't killed right away. He held on for a week in the hospital. None of the doctors could believe it, that he didn't die instantly."

"He was a tough little motherfucker," said Spider.

"He sure was," said Lou.

"Just like his mom," Dave said, grabbing Lou's knee.

"I'm so very sorry," I said again.

"I know you are," said Lou before she turned the music up loud. We drove without talking, listening to Vaughan's electric guitar wail its way through "Texas Flood," my heart clenching at the sound of it.

A few minutes later Lou shouted, "Here's your junction." She pulled over and shut the engine off and looked at Dave. "Why don't you boys take Stevie Ray for a leak?"

They all got out with me and stood around lighting up cigarettes while I pulled my pack out of the trunk. Dave and Spider led Stevie Ray into the trees by the side of the road and Lou and I stood in a patch of shade near the car while I buckled Monster on. She asked me if I had kids, how old I was, if I was married or ever had been.

No, twenty-six, no, yes, I told her.

She said, "You're pretty, so you'll be okay whatever you do. Me, people always just gotta go on the fact that I'm good-hearted. I never did have the looks."

"That's not true," I said. "I think you're pretty."

"You do?" she asked.

"Yeah," I said, though pretty wasn't precisely how I would have described her.

"*You do?* Thanks. That's nice to hear. Usually Dave's the only one who thinks that." She looked down at my legs. "You need a shave, girl!" she bellowed, then laughed in the same raucous way she had when she'd said how big my pack was. "Nah," she said, blowing smoke from her mouth. "I'm just giving you shit. I think it's neat you do what you want. Not enough chicks do that, if you ask me—just tell society and their expectations to go fuck themselves. If more women did that, we'd be better off." She took a drag and blew the smoke out in a hard line. "Anyway, after all that stuff about my son getting killed? After that happened, I died too. Inside." She patted her chest with the hand that held the cigarette. "I look the same, but I'm not the same in here. I mean, life goes on and all that crap, but Luke dying took it out of me. I try not to act like it, but it did. It took the Lou out of Lou, and I ain't getting it back. You know what I mean?"

"I do," I said, looking into her hazel eyes.

"I thought so," she said. "I had that feeling about you."

I said goodbye to them, crossed the intersection, and walked to the road that would take me to Old Station. The heat was so potent it rose in visible waves from the ground. When I got to the road, I saw three figures undulating in the distance.

"Stacy!" I shouted. "Trina!"

They saw me and waved their arms. Odin barked hello.

Together we hitched a ride to Old Station—another tiny village that was more a gathering of buildings than a town. Trina walked to the post office to mail a few things home while Stacy and I waited for her in the air-conditioned café, drinking soda pop and discussing the next section of the trail. It was a slice of the Modoc Plateau called Hat Creek Rim—desolate and famous for its lack of shade and water, a legendary stretch on a trail of legends. Dry and hot, it was scorched clean by a fire in 1987. *The Pacific Crest Trail, Volume 1: California* informed me that although there was no reliable water source from Old Station to Rock Springs Creek thirty miles away, when the book went to print in 1989, the Forest Service was about to install a water tank near the ruins of an old fire lookout tower, fifteen miles in. The book cautioned that this information should be verified and that even if it was installed, such tanks can't always be relied upon because of vandalism in the form of bullet holes.

I sucked on the ice in my tumbler of soda one cube at a time, pondering this information. I'd ditched my dromedary bag back in Kennedy Meadows, since most sections of the trail north of there had adequate water. In anticipation of the dry Hat Creek Rim, I'd planned to buy a large jug of water and strap it to Monster, but for reasons both financial and physical I was hoping that wouldn't be necessary. I hoped to spend my last bits of money on food at that café rather than on a jug of water, not to mention the misery of carrying that jug for thirty miles across the rim. So I almost fell out of my chair in joy and relief when Trina returned from the post office with the news that southbound hikers had written in the trail register that the tank mentioned in the guidebook was there and that it had water in it.

Exuberantly, we walked to a campground a mile away and set up our tents side by side for one last night together. Trina and Stacy were hiking out the next day, but I decided to lay over, wanting to hike alone again and also to rest my feet, which were still recovering from the blistering descent from Three Lakes.

The next morning when I woke, I had the campsite to myself. I sat at the picnic table and drank tea from my cooking pot while burning the last pages of *The Novel*. The professor who'd scoffed about Michener had been right in some regards: he wasn't William Faulkner or Flannery O'Connor, but I'd been utterly absorbed in his book nonetheless and not only for the writing. Its subject hit a chord in me. It was a story about many things, but it centered on the life of one novel, told from the perspectives of its author and editor, its critics and readers. Of all the things I'd done in my life, of all the versions of myself I'd lived out, there was one that had never changed: I was a writer. Someday, I intended to write a novel of my own. I felt ashamed that I hadn't written one already. In the vision I'd had of myself ten years before, I felt sure I'd have published my first book by now. I'd written several short stories and made a serious stab at a novel, but I wasn't anywhere close to having a book done. In the tumult of the past year it seemed as if writing had left me forever, but as I hiked, I could feel that novel coming back to me, inserting its voice among the song fragments and advertising jingles in my mind. That morning in Old Station, as I ripped Michener's book into clumps of five and ten pages so they would burn, crouching next to the fire ring in my campsite to set them aflame, I decided to begin. I had nothing but a long hot day ahead of me anyway, so I sat at my picnic table and wrote until late afternoon.

When I looked up, I saw that a chipmunk was chewing a hole in the mesh door of my tent in an attempt to get to my food bag inside. I chased it away, cursing it while it chattered at me from a tree. By then the campground had filled in around me: most of the picnic tables were now covered with coolers and Coleman stoves; pickup trucks and campers were parked in the little paved pull-ins. I took my food bag out of my tent and carried it the mile back to the café where I'd sat with Trina and Stacy the afternoon before. I ordered a burger, not caring that I'd be spending almost all of my money. My next resupply box was at the state park in Burney Falls, forty-two miles away, but I could get there in two days, now that I was finally able to hike farther and faster—I'd done two nineteen-milers back-to-back out of Belden. It was five on a summer day when the light stretched until nine or ten and I was the only customer, wolfing down my dinner.

I left the restaurant with nothing more than some change in my pocket. I walked past a pay phone and then returned to it, picked up the receiver, and pressed 0, my insides trembling with a mix of fear and excitement. When the operator came on to assist me in placing the call, I gave her Paul's number.

He picked up on the third ring. I was so overcome by the sound of his voice I could barely say hello. "Cheryl!" he exclaimed.

"Paul!" I said finally, and then in a fast jumble I told him where I was and some of what I'd been through since I'd last seen him. We talked for close to an hour, our conversation loving and exuberant, supportive and kind. It didn't seem like he was my ex-husband. It seemed like he was my best friend. When I hung up, I looked down at my food bag on the ground. It was almost empty, robin's-egg blue and tubular, made of a treated material that felt like rubber. I lifted it up, pressed it against my body, and closed my eyes.

I walked back to my camp and sat for a long time on my picnic table with *A Summer Bird-Cage* in my hands, too staggered with emotion to read. I watched the people make their dinners all around me and then I watched the yellow sun melt into pink and orange and the softest lavender in the sky. I missed Paul. I missed my life. But I didn't want to go back to it either. That awful moment when Paul and I fell onto the floor after I told him the truth about my infidelities kept coming to me in waves, and I realized that what I'd started when I'd spoken those words hadn't led only to my divorce but to this: to me sitting alone in Old Station, California, on a picnic table beneath the magnificent sky. I didn't feel sad or happy. I didn't feel proud or ashamed. I only felt that in spite of all the things I'd done wrong, in getting myself here, I'd done right.

I went to Monster and took out the cigarette in the faux-glass case that Jimmy Carter had given me earlier that day. I didn't smoke, but I broke the case open anyway, sat on top of the picnic table, and lit the cigarette. I'd been on the PCT for a little more than a month. It seemed like a long time and also it seemed like my trip had just begun, like I was only now digging into whatever it was I was out here to do. Like I was still the woman with the hole in her heart, but the hole had gotten ever so infinitesimally smaller.

I took a drag and blew the smoke from my mouth, remembering how I'd felt more alone than anyone in the whole wide world that morning after Jimmy Carter drove away. Maybe I *was* more alone than anyone in the whole wide world.

Maybe that was okay.

12

THIS FAR

I woke at first light, moving with precision as I broke camp. I could pack up in five minutes now. Every item that had been in that unfathomable heap on the bed in the motel in Mojave that hadn't already been ditched or burned had its place in or on my pack and I knew exactly where that place was. My hands moved to it on instinct, seeming almost to bypass my brain. Monster was my world, my inanimate extra limb. Though its weight and size still confounded me, I'd come to accept that it was my burden to bear. I didn't feel myself in contradiction to it the way I had a month before. It wasn't me against it. We two were one.

Bearing Monster's weight had changed me on the outside too. My legs had become as hard as boulders, their muscles seemingly capable of anything, rippling beneath my thinning flesh in ways they never had. The patches on my hips and shoulders and tailbone that had repeatedly bled and scabbed over in the places where Monster's straps rubbed my body had finally surrendered, becoming rough and pocked, my flesh morphing into what I can only describe as a cross between tree bark and a dead chicken after it's been dipped in boiling water and plucked.

My feet? Well, they were still entirely, unspeakably fucked.

My two big toes had never recovered from the beating they took on the merciless descent from Three Lakes to Belden Town. Their nails looked near dead. My pinky toes had been rubbed so raw I wondered if they'd eventually just wear clean away from my feet. What seemed like permanent blisters covered the backs of my heels all the way up to my ankles. But I refused to think of my feet that morning in Old Station. So much of being able to hike the PCT depended upon mind control: the stout decision to move forward, regardless. I covered my wounds with duct tape and 2nd Skin, then I put on my socks and boots and hobbled over to the campground's spigot to fill up my two bottles with sixty-four ounces of water, which had to last me for fifteen searing miles across Hat Creek Rim.

It was early but hot already as I walked the road to the place where the PCT crossed it. I felt rested and strong, braced for the day. I spent the morning weaving my way through dry creek beds and bone-hard gullies, pausing to sip water as seldom as I could. By midmorning I was walking across a miles-wide escarpment, a high dry field of weeds and wildflowers that offered barely a scrap of shade. The few trees I passed were dead, killed in the fire years before, their trunks scorched white or charred black, their branches broken and burnt into daggers. Their stark beauty bore down on me with a silent anguished force as I passed them by.

The blue sky was everywhere above me, the sun bright and unrelenting, scorching me even through my hat and the sunscreen I rubbed into my sweaty face and arms. I could see for miles—snowy Lassen Peak nearby to the south and the higher and snowier Mount Shasta rising far to the north. The sight of Mount Shasta filled me with relief. I was going there. I would walk past it and beyond it, all the way to the Columbia River. Now that I'd escaped the snow, it seemed nothing could take me off course. An image of myself hiking with ease and alacrity through the rest of the miles formed in my mind, though the shimmering heat soon eradicated it, reminding me that I knew better. If I made it to the Oregon-Washington border, I knew it would only be with all the hardships that moving at foot speed beneath a monster of a pack entailed.

Foot speed was a profoundly different way of moving through the world than my normal modes of travel. Miles weren't things that blazed dully past. They were long, intimate straggles of weeds and clumps of dirt, blades of grass and flowers that bent in the wind, trees that lumbered and screeched. They were the sound of my breath and my feet hitting the trail one step at a time and the click of my ski pole. The PCT had taught me what a mile was. I was humble before each and every one. And humbler still that day on Hat Creek Rim as the temperature moved from hot to hotter, the wind doing little more than whip the dust into swirls at my feet. It was during one such gust that I heard a sound more insistent than any caused by the wind and realized that it was a rattlesnake shaking its rattle hard and near, warning me off. I scrambled backwards and saw the snake a few steps ahead of me on the trail, its rattle held like a scolding finger slightly above its coiled body, its blunt face darting in my direction. If I'd taken another few steps, I'd have been upon it. It was the third rattlesnake I'd encountered on the trail. I made an almost comically wide arc around it, and continued on.

At midday I found a narrow patch of shade and sat down to eat. I took my socks and boots off and reclined in the dirt to prop up my swollen and battered feet on my pack, as I almost always did on my lunch break. I stared at the sky, watching the hawks and eagles that soared in serene circles above me, but I couldn't quite relax. It wasn't only because of the rattlesnake. The landscape was barren enough that I could see for great distances, though I kept having the vague feeling that something lurked nearby, watching me, waiting to pounce. I sat up and scanned the terrain for mountain lions, then lay back down, telling myself that there was nothing to fear, before I quickly sat up again at what I thought was the snap of a branch.

It was nothing, I told myself. I was not afraid. I reached for my water bottle and took a long drink. I was so thirsty that I chugged it until it was empty, then I opened the other one and drank from that too, unable to stop myself. The thermometer that dangled from the zipper on my pack said it was 100 degrees in my shaded patch.

I sang cool songs as I walked, the sun beating me as if it had an actual physical force that consisted of more than heat. Sweat collected around my sunglasses and streamed into my eyes, stinging them so I had to stop and wipe my face every now and then. It seemed impossible that I'd been up in the snowy mountains wearing all of my clothes only the week before, that I'd awakened to a thick layer of frost on my tent walls each morning. I couldn't rightly remember it. Those white days seemed like a dream, as if all this time I'd been staggering north in the scorching heat into this, my fifth week on the trail, straight through the same heat that had almost driven me off the trail in my second week. I stopped and drank again. The water was so hot it almost hurt my mouth.

Sagebrush and a sprawl of hardy wildflowers blanketed the wide plain. As I walked, scratchy plants I couldn't identify grazed my calves. Others

I knew seemed to speak to me, saying their names to me in my mother's voice. Names I didn't realize I knew until they came so clearly into my mind: Queen Anne's lace, Indian paintbrush, lupine—those same flowers grew in Minnesota, white and orange and purple. When we passed them as we drove, my mother would sometimes stop the car and pick a bouquet from what grew in the ditch.

I stopped walking and looked up at the sky. The birds of prey still circled, hardly seeming to flap their wings. *I will never go home,* I thought with a finality that made me catch my breath, and then I walked on, my mind emptying into nothing but the effort to push my body through the bald monotony of the hike. There wasn't a day on the trail when that monotony didn't ultimately win out, when the only thing to think about was whatever was the physically hardest. It was a sort of scorching cure. I counted my steps, working my way to a hundred and starting over again at one. Each time I completed another set it seemed as if I'd achieved a small thing. Then a hundred became too optimistic and I went to fifty, then twenty-five, then ten.

One two three four five six seven eight nine ten.

I stopped and bent over, pressing my hands to my knees to ease my back for a moment. The sweat dripped from my face onto the pale dirt like tears.

The Modoc Plateau was different from the Mojave Desert, but it didn't feel different. Both teemed with jagged desert plants while being entirely inhospitable to human life. Tiny gray and brown lizards either zipped across the trail as I approached or held their position as I passed. Where did *they* get water? I wondered, trying to stop myself from thinking about how hot and thirsty I was. Where would *I*? I was three miles away from the water tank, I reckoned. I had eight ounces of water left.

Then six.

Then four.

I forced myself not to drink the last two until I had the water tank in sight and by 4:30 there it was: the stilted legs of the burned fire lookout on a rise in the distance. Nearby was a metal tank propped up against a post. As soon as I saw it, I pulled out my bottle and drank the last of my water, thankful that in a matter of minutes I'd be able to drink my fill from the tank. As I approached, I saw that the wooden post near the tank was covered with something that flapped in the wind. It looked like several shredded ribbons at first and then a ripped cloth. It wasn't until I got up close that I saw they were tiny scraps of paper—notes stuck to the post with duct tape and now fluttering in the wind. I lurched forward to read them, knowing what they would say even before my eyes met the paper. They said what they said in various ways, but they all bore the same message: NO WATER.

I stood motionless for a moment, paralyzed with dread. I gazed into the tank to confirm what was true. There was no water. I had no water. Not even a sip.

Nowaternowaternowaternowaternowaternowater.

I kicked the dirt and grabbed fistfuls of sage and threw them, furious with myself for yet again doing the wrong thing, for being the same idiot I'd been the very day I set foot on the trail. The same one who had purchased the wrong size boots and profoundly underestimated the amount of money I'd need for the summer, and even maybe the same idiot who believed I could hike this trail.

I pulled the ripped-out guidebook pages from my shorts pocket and read them again. I wasn't scared in the same way I'd been earlier in the day, when I had the funny feeling that something was lurking nearby. Now I was terrified. This wasn't a feeling. It was a fact: I was miles from water on a hundred-and-something-degree day. I knew that this was the most serious situation I'd been in so far on the trail—more threatening than the marauding bull, more harrowing than the snow. I needed water. I needed it soon. I needed it now. I could feel that need in my every pore. I remembered Albert asking me how many times I urinated each day when I'd first met him. I hadn't peed since I'd left Old Station that morning. I hadn't needed to. Every ounce I'd ingested had been used. I was so thirsty I couldn't even spit.

The authors of *The Pacific Crest Trail, Volume 1: California* said the nearest "reliable" water was fifteen miles away at Rock Spring Creek, but they conceded there was, in fact, water nearer by in a reservoir that they strongly advised against drinking from, calling its quality "questionable at best." That water was nearly five miles farther up the trail.

Unless, of course, the reservoir had also gone dry.

There was a distinct chance that it had, I acknowledged, as I did my version of racing toward it, which, given the condition of my feet and the weight of my pack, was nothing more than a decidedly brisk walk. It felt as if I could see the entire world from the east rim of Hat Creek. A wide valley spread below me into the distance, interrupted by green volcanic mountains to both the north and the south. Even in my anxious state, I couldn't help but feel rapturous at the beauty. I was a big fat idiot, yes, one who might die of dehydration and heat exhaustion, yes, but at least I was in a beautiful place—a place I'd come to love, in spite and because of its hardships—and I'd gotten myself into this place on my own two feet. Consoling myself with this, I walked on, so thirsty that I became nauseated and slightly feverish. *I'll be okay,* I told myself. *It's just another bit farther,* I said around each bend and over every rise as the sun sank toward the horizon until at last I saw the reservoir.

I stopped to gaze at it. It was a miserable-looking mucky pond about the size of a tennis court, but there was water in it. I was laughing with joy as I staggered down the slope toward the little dirt beach that surrounded the reservoir. I'd hiked my first twenty-mile day. I unbuckled Monster and set it onto the ground and went to the muddy shore and squatted to put my hands in the water. It was gray and warm as blood. When I moved my hands, the muck from the bottom rose in weedy tendrils and streaked the water black.

I got my purifier and pumped the questionable liquid into my bottle. My purifier had remained as difficult to use as it had been that first time I used it at Golden Oak Springs, but it was especially difficult in this water, so dense with sludge that it half jammed my filter. By the time I was done filling one bottle, my arms shook with fatigue. I went to my first aid kit and took out my iodine pills and dropped a couple into the water. I'd brought the pills for just this reason, reinforcement should I ever be compelled to drink water that was likely contaminated. Even Albert had thought the iodine pills a good idea back in Kennedy Meadows, when he'd been ruthlessly tossing things into the get-rid-of pile. Albert, who'd been felled by a waterborne illness the very next day.

I had to wait thirty minutes for the iodine to do its work before it was safe to drink. I was desperately thirsty, but I distracted myself by filling my other bottle with water. When I was done, I laid out my tarp on the dirt beach, stood on top of it, and took off my clothes. The wind had mellowed with the fading light. In gentle wafts, it cooled the hot patches on my naked hips. It didn't occur to me that anyone might come along the trail. I hadn't seen a soul all day, and even if someone did come along, I was too catatonic with dehydration and exhaustion to care.

I looked at my watch. Twenty-seven minutes had passed since I'd plopped the iodine pills into my water. Usually I was starving by evening, but the idea of eating was nothing to me now. Water was my only desire.

I sat on my blue tarp and drank one bottle down and then the other. The warm water tasted like iron and mud and yet seldom have I ever consumed anything so amazing. I could feel it moving into me, though even once I'd had two 32-ounce bottles, I wasn't entirely restored. I still wasn't hungry. I felt like I had in those first days on the trail, when I'd been so astoundingly exhausted that all my body wanted was sleep. Now all my body wanted was water. I filled my bottles again, let the iodine purify them, and drank them both.

By the time I was sated, it was dark and the full moon was rising. I couldn't muster the energy to set up my tent—a task that required little more than two minutes' effort, which now seemed Herculean to me. I didn't need a tent. It hadn't rained since my first couple of days on the trail. I put my clothes back on and spread out my sleeping bag on the tarp, but it was too hot still to do anything but lie on top of it. I was too tired to read. Even gazing at the moon felt like a mild effort. I'd consumed 128 ounces of questionable reservoir water since I'd arrived a couple of hours before and I still didn't have to pee. I had done a stupendously dumb thing by setting out across Hat Creek Rim with so little water. *I'll never be so careless again,* I promised the moon before falling asleep.

I woke two hours later with the vaguely pleasant sensation that tiny cool hands were gently patting me. They were on my bare legs and arms and face and in my hair, on my feet and throat and hands. I could feel their cool weight through my T-shirt on my chest and belly. "Hmm," I moaned, turning slightly before I opened my eyes and a series of facts came to me in slow motion.

There was the fact of the moon and the fact that I was sleeping out in the open on my tarp.

There was the fact that I had woken because it seemed like small cool hands were gently patting me and the fact that small cool hands *were* gently patting me.

And then there was the final fact of all, which was a fact more monumental than even the moon: the fact that those small cool hands were not hands, but hundreds of small cool black frogs.

Small cool slimy black frogs jumping all over me.

Each one was the approximate size of a potato chip. They were an amphibious army, a damp smooth-skinned militia, a great web-footed migration, and I was in their path as they hopped, scrambled, leapt, and hurled their tiny, pudgy, bent-legged bodies from the reservoir and onto the scrim of dirt that they no doubt considered their private beach.

Within an instant, I was among them, hopping, scrambling, leaping, and hurling myself, my pack, my tarp, and everything that sat on it into the brush beyond the beach, swatting frogs from my hair and the folds of my T-shirt as I went. I couldn't help but squash a few beneath my bare feet. Finally safe, I stood watching them from the frog-free perimeter, the frantic motion of their little dark bodies apparent in the blazing moonlight. I checked my shorts pockets for errant frogs. I gathered my things into a little clear patch that seemed flat enough for my tent and pulled it from my pack. I didn't need to see what I was doing. My tent was up with the flick of my wrist.

I crawled out of it at 8:30 the next morning. Eight thirty was late for me, like noon in my former life. And this 8:30 felt like noon in my former life too. Like I'd been out drinking into the wee hours. I half stood, looking around groggily. I still didn't have to pee. I packed up and pumped more filthy water and walked north beneath the scorching sun. It was even hotter than it had been the day before. Within an hour, I almost stepped on another rattlesnake, though it too warned me off politely with its rattle.

By late afternoon any thought of making it all the way to McArthur-Burney Falls Memorial State Park by day's end had been shot down entirely by my late start, my throbbing and blistered feet, and the staggering heat. Instead, I took a short detour off the trail to Cassel, where my guidebook promised there would be a general store. It was nearly three by the time I reached it. I took off my pack and sat on a wooden chair on the store's old-fashioned porch, nearly catatonic from the heat. The big thermometer in the shade read 102 degrees. I counted my money, feeling on the verge of tears, knowing that no matter how much I had, it wouldn't be enough for a Snapple lemonade. My desire for one had grown so large that it wasn't even a longing anymore. It was more like a limb growing from my gut. It would cost 99 cents or $1.05 or $1.15— I didn't know how much exactly. I knew I had only 76 cents and that wouldn't be enough. I went into the store anyway, just to look.

"You a PCT hiker?" the woman behind the counter asked.

"Yeah," I said, smiling at her.

"Where you from?"

"Minnesota," I called as I made my way along a bank of glass-fronted doors with cold drinks lined up in neat rows inside. I passed cans of icy beer and soda pop, bottles of mineral water and juice. I stopped at the door where the racks of Snapples were kept. I put my hand to the glass near the bottles of lemonade—there was both yellow and pink. They were like diamonds or pornography. I could look, but I couldn't touch.

"If you're done hiking for the day, you're welcome to camp out in the field behind the store," the woman said to me. "We let all the PCT hikers stay there."

"Thanks, I think I'll do that," I said, still staring at the drinks. Perhaps I could just hold one, I thought. Just press it against my forehead for a moment. I opened the door and pulled out a bottle of pink lemonade. It was so cold it felt like it was burning my hand. "How much is this?" I couldn't keep myself from asking.

"I saw you counting your pennies outside," the woman laughed. "How much you got?"

I gave her everything I had while thanking her profusely and took the Snapple out onto the porch. Each sip sent a stab of heady pleasure through me. I held the bottle with both hands, wanting to absorb every bit of cool I could. Cars pulled up and people got out and went into the store, then came out and drove away. I watched them for an hour in a post-Snapple bliss that felt more like a drugged-up haze. After a while, a pickup slowed in front of the store just long enough for a man to climb out of the back and pull out his backpack behind him before waving the driver away. He turned to me and spotted my pack.

"Hey!" he said, a giant smile spreading across his pink beefy face. "It's one hell of a hot day to hike on the PCT, don't you think?"

His name was Rex. He was a big red-haired guy, gregarious and gay and thirty-eight years old. He struck me as the kind of person who gave a lot of bear hugs. He went into the store and bought three cans of beer and drank them as he sat beside me on the porch, where together we talked into the evening. He lived in Phoenix and held a corporate job he couldn't properly make me understand, but he'd grown up in a little town in southern Oregon. He'd hiked from the Mexican border to Mojave in the spring—getting off the trail at the very place where I'd gotten on and at about the same time as well—to return to Phoenix for six weeks to tend to some business matters before starting back on the trail at Old Station, having elegantly bypassed all the snow.

"I think you need new boots," he said when I showed him my feet, echoing Greg's and Brent's sentiments.

"But I *can't* get new boots. I don't have the money," I told him, no longer too ashamed to admit it.

"Where'd you buy them?" asked Rex.

"REI."

"Call them. They've got a satisfaction guarantee. They'll replace them for free."

"They will?"

"Call the 1-800 number," he said.

I thought about it all through the evening as Rex and I camped together in the field behind the store, and all the next day as I raced faster than ever through twelve mercifully unchallenging miles to McArthur-Burney Falls Memorial State Park. When I arrived, I immediately collected my resupply box from the concessionaire's store and went to the pay phone nearby to call the operator and then REI. Within five minutes, the woman I spoke to had agreed to mail me a new pair of boots, one size larger, via overnight mail, no charge.

"Are you *sure*?" I kept asking her, yammering on about the trouble my too-small boots had caused me.

"Yes," she said placidly, and now it was official: I loved REI more than I loved the people behind Snapple lemonade. I gave her the address of the park store, reading it from my as-yet-unopened box. I'd have jumped with joy after I hung up the phone if my feet had been well enough to do it. I ripped open my box and found my twenty dollars and joined the crowd of tourists in the line, hoping none of them would notice that I reeked. I bought an ice-cream cone and sat at a picnic table eating it with barely restrained glee. Rex walked up as I sat there, and a few minutes after that Trina appeared with her big white dog. We embraced and I introduced her to Rex. She and Stacy had arrived the day before. She'd decided to get off the trail here and return to Colorado to do several day hikes near her home for the rest of the summer instead of hiking the PCT. Stacy would be continuing on as planned.

"I'm sure she'd be happy if you joined her," Trina added. "She'll be hiking out in the morning."

"I can't," I said, and giddily explained that I needed to wait for my new boots.

"We worried about you on Hat Creek Rim," she said. "No water at—"

"I know," I said, and we ruefully shook our heads.

"Come," she said to Rex and me. "I'll show you where we're camped. It's a twenty-minute walk, but it's away from all this," she gestured with an air of disdain toward the tourists, the snack bar, and the store. "Plus, it's free."

My feet had gotten to the point that each time I rested it hurt more the next time I got up to walk, their various sores reopening with every new effort. I limped behind Trina and Rex down a path through the woods that took us back to the PCT, where there was a small clearing among the trees.

"Cheryl!" Stacy called, coming to hug me.

We talked about Hat Creek Rim and the heat, the trail and the lack of water, and what the snack bar had to offer for dinner. I took off my boots and socks and put on my camp sandals and set up my tent and went through the pleasant ritual of unpacking my box while we chatted. Stacy and Rex made fast friends and decided to hike the next section of the trail together. By the time I was ready to walk back up to the snack bar for dinner, my big toes had swollen and reddened so much that they looked like two beets. I couldn't even bear to wear socks anymore, so I hobbled up to the snack bar in my sandals instead, where we sat around a picnic table with paper boats of hot dogs and jalapeño poppers and nachos with fluorescent orange cheese dripping off the sides. It felt like a feast and a celebration. We held up our wax cups of soda pop and made a toast.

"To Trina and Odin's trip home!" we said, and clinked our cups.

"To Stacy and Rex hitting the trail!" we cheered.

"To Cheryl's new boots!" we yelled.

And I drank with solemnity to that.

When I woke the next morning, my tent was the only one in the clearing among the trees. I walked up to the bathhouse meant for the campers in the official park campground, took a shower, and returned to my campsite, where I sat in my camp chair for hours. I ate breakfast and read half of *A Summer Bird-Cage* in one sitting. In the afternoon, I walked to the store near the snack bar to see if my boots were there, but the woman who worked at the counter told me the mail hadn't arrived yet.

I left forlornly, strolling in my sandals down a short paved path to an overlook to see the grand falls that the park is named for. Burney Falls is the most voluminous waterfall in the state of California for most of the year, a sign explained. As I gazed at the thundering water, I felt almost invisible among the people with their cameras, fanny packs, and Bermuda shorts. I sat on a bench and watched a couple feed an entire pack of Breathsavers to a gaggle of overly familiar squirrels who darted around a sign that said DO NOT FEED THE WILDLIFE. It enraged me to see them do that, but my fury was not only about how they were perpetuating the habituation of the squirrels, I realized. It was also that they were a couple. To witness the way they leaned into each other and laced their fingers together and tugged each other tenderly down the paved path was almost unbearable. I was simultaneously sickened by it and envious of what they had. Their existence seemed proof that I would never succeed at romantic love. I'd felt so strong and content while talking on the phone with Paul in Old Station only a few days before, but I didn't feel anything like that anymore. Everything that had rested then was roiling now.

I limped back to my camp and examined my tortured big toes. To so much as graze against them had become excruciating. I could literally see them throbbing—the blood beneath my flesh pulsating in a regular rhythm that flushed my nails white then pink, white then pink. They were so swollen that it looked as if my nails were simply going to pop off. It occurred to me that popping them off might actually be a good idea. I pinched one of the nails, and with a solid tug, followed by a second of searing pain, the nail gave way and I felt instant, almost total, relief. A moment later, I did the same with the other toe.

It was me against the PCT when it came to my toenails, I realized.

The score was 6–4, and I was just barely hanging on to my lead.

By nightfall four other PCT hikers joined my encampment. They arrived as I was burning the last pages of *A Summer Bird-Cage* in my little aluminum pie pan, two couples about my age who'd hiked all the way from Mexico, minus the same section of the socked-in Sierra Nevada I'd skipped. Each couple had set out separately, but they'd met and joined forces in southern California, hiking and bypassing the snow together in a weeks-long wilderness double date. John and Sarah were from Alberta, Canada, and hadn't even been dating a year when they'd started to hike the PCT. Sam and Helen were a married couple from Maine. They were laying over the next day, but I was heading on, I told them, as soon as my new boots arrived.

The next morning I packed up Monster and walked to the store wearing my sandals, my boots tied to the frame of my pack. I sat at one of the nearby picnic tables waiting for the mail to arrive. I was eager to hike away not so much because I felt like hiking, but because I had to. In order to reach each resupply point on roughly the day I'd anticipated, I had a schedule to keep. In spite of all the changes and bypasses, for reasons related to both money and weather, I needed to stick to my plan to finish my trip by mid-September. I sat for hours reading the book that had come in my box—Vladimir Nabokov's *Lolita*—while waiting for my boots to arrive. People came and went in waves, sometimes gathering in little circles around me to ask questions about the PCT when they noticed my pack. As I spoke, the doubts I had about myself on the trail fell away for whole minutes at a time and I forgot all about being a big fat idiot. Basking in the attention of the people who gathered around me, I didn't just feel like a backpacking expert. I felt like a hard-ass motherfucking Amazonian queen.

"I advise you to put this on your résumé," said an old woman from Florida adorned in a bright pink visor and a fistful of gold necklaces. "I used to work in HR. Employers look for things like this. It tells them that you've got character. It sets you apart from the rest."

The mailman pulled up around three. The UPS guy came an hour later. Neither one of them had my boots. My stomach sinking, I went to the pay phone and called REI.

They hadn't yet mailed my boots, the man I spoke to politely informed me. The problem was, they'd learned they could not get them to the state park overnight, so they wanted to send them by regular mail instead, but because they hadn't known how to contact me to tell me this, they'd done nothing at all. "I don't think you understand," I said. "I'm hiking the PCT. I'm sleeping in the woods. *Of course* you couldn't have gotten in touch with me. And I can't wait here for—how long will it take for my boots to come in the regular mail?"

"Approximately five days," he replied, unperturbed.

"Five days?" I asked. I couldn't exactly be upset. They were mailing me a new pair of boots for free, after all, but still I was frustrated and panicked. In addition to maintaining my schedule, I needed the food I had in my bag for the next section of the trail—the eighty-three-mile stretch that took me to Castle Crags. If I stayed in Burney Falls to wait for my boots, I'd have to eat that food because—with little more than five dollars left—I didn't have enough money to spend the next five days eating from the park's snack bar. I reached for my pack, got my guide-book, and found the address for Castle Crags. I couldn't imagine hiking another blistering eighty-three miles in my too-small boots, but I had no choice but to ask REI to send them there.

When I hung up the phone, I didn't feel like a hard-ass motherfucking Amazonian queen anymore.

I stared at my boots with a pleading expression, as if we could possibly work out a deal. They were dangling from my pack by their dusty red laces, evil in their indifference. I'd planned to leave them in the PCT hiker free box as soon as my new boots arrived. I reached for them, but I couldn't bring myself to put them on. Perhaps I could wear my flimsy camp sandals for short stretches on the trail. I'd met a few people who switched off between boots and sandals while they hiked, but their sandals were far sturdier than mine. I'd never intended to wear my sandals to hike. I'd brought them only to give my feet a break from my boots at the end of the day, cheap knockoffs I'd purchased at a discount store for something like $19.99. I took them off and cradled them in my hands, as if by examining them up close I could bestow on them a durability they did not possess. The Velcro was matted with detritus and peeling away from the black straps at the frayed ends. Their blue soles were malleable as dough and so thin that when I walked I could feel the contours of pebbles and sticks beneath my feet. Wearing them was just barely more than having no shoes on at all. And I was going to walk to Castle Crags in these?

Maybe I shouldn't, I thought. Maybe I *wouldn't*. This far was far enough. I could put it on my résumé.

"Fuck," I said. I picked up a rock and whipped it hard as I could at a nearby tree, and then another and another.

I thought of the woman I always thought of in such moments: an astrologer who'd read my natal chart when I was twenty-three. A friend had arranged for the reading as a going-away gift just before I left Min-nesota for New York City. The astrologer was a no-nonsense middle-aged woman named Pat who sat me down at her kitchen table with a piece of paper covered in mysterious markings and a quietly whirring tape recorder between us. I didn't put much faith in it. I thought it would be a bit of fun, an ego-boosting session during which she'd say generic things like *You have a kind heart.*

But she didn't. Or rather, she said those things, but she also said bizarrely specific things that were so accurate and particular, so simultaneously consoling and upsetting, that it was all I could do not to bawl in recognition and grief. "How can you know this?" I kept demanding. And then I would listen as she explained about the planets, the sun and the moon, the "aspects" and the moment I was born; about what it meant to be a Virgo, with a moon in Leo and Gemini rising. I'd nod while thinking, *This is a bunch of crazy New Age anti-intellectual bullshit,* and then she'd say another thing that would blow my brain into about seven thousand pieces because it was so true.

Until she began to speak of my father. "Was he a Vietnam vet?" she asked. No, I told her, he wasn't. He was in the military briefly in the mid-1960s—in fact, he was stationed at the base in Colorado Springs where my mother's father was stationed, which is how my parents met—but he never went to Vietnam.

"It seems he was like a Vietnam vet," she persisted. "Perhaps not literally. But he has something in common with some of those men. He was deeply wounded. He was damaged. His damage has infected his life and it infected you."

I was not going to nod. Everything that had ever happened to me in my whole life was mixed into the cement that kept my head perfectly still at the moment an astrologer told me that my father had infected me.

"Wounded?" was all I could manage.

"Yes," said Pat. "And you're wounded in the same place. That's what fathers do if they don't heal their wounds. They wound their children in the same place."

"Hmm," I said, my face blank.

"I could be wrong." She gazed down at the paper between us. "This isn't necessarily literal."

"Actually, I only saw my father three times after I was six," I said.

"The father's job is to teach his children how to be warriors, to give them the confidence to get on the horse and ride into battle when it's necessary to do so. If you don't get that from your father, you have to teach yourself."

"But—I think I have already," I sputtered. "I'm strong—I face things. I—"

"This isn't about strength," said Pat. "And you may not be able to see this yet, but perhaps there will come a time—it could be years from now—when you'll need to get on your horse and ride into battle and you're going to hesitate. You're going to falter. To heal the wound your father made, you're going to have to get on that horse and ride into battle like a warrior."

I laughed a bit then, a self-conscious puff-croak of a chuckle that sounded more sad than happy. I know because I took the cassette tape home and listened to it over and over again. *To heal the wound your father made, you're going to have to get on that horse and ride into battle like a warrior.* Puff-croak.

Rewind. Repeat.

"Would you like a knuckle sandwich?" my father used to ask me when he was angry, holding his man-fist an inch from my three- and four- and five- and six-year-old face. "Would you? Huh? Huh? HUH?

"ANSWER ME!"

I put on my stupid sandals and began the long walk to Castle Crags.

13

THE ACCUMULATION OF TREES

It was a woman who first thought of the PCT. She was a retired teacher from Bellingham, Washington, named Catherine Montgomery. In a conversation with mountaineer and writer Joseph T. Hazard, she suggested that there should be a border-to-border "high trail winding down the heights of our western mountains." It was 1926. Though a small group of hikers immediately embraced Montgomery's idea, it wasn't until Clinton Churchill Clarke took up the cause six years later that a clear vision of the PCT began to coalesce. Clarke was an oilman who lived in leisure in Pasadena, but he was also an avid outdoorsman. Appalled by a culture that spent "too much time sitting on soft seats in motors, too much sitting in soft seats in movies," Clarke lobbied the federal government to set aside a wilderness corridor for the trail. His vision went far beyond the PCT, which he hoped would be a mere segment of a much longer "Trail of the Americas" that would run from Alaska to Chile. He believed that time in the wilderness provided "a lasting curative and civilizing value," and he spent twenty-five years advocating for the PCT, though when he died in 1957 the trail was still only a dream.

Perhaps Clarke's most important contribution to the trail was making the acquaintance of Warren Rogers, who was twenty-four when the two met in 1932. Rogers was working for the YMCA in Alhambra, California, when Clarke convinced him to help map the route by assigning teams of YMCA volunteers to chart and in some cases construct what would become the PCT. Though initially reluctant, Rogers soon became passionate about the trail's creation, and he spent the rest of his life championing the PCT and working to overcome all the legal, financial, and logistical obstacles that stood in its way. Rogers lived to see Congress designate the Pacific Crest National Scenic Trail in 1968, but he died in 1992, a year before the trail was finished.

I'd read the section in my guidebook about the trail's history the winter before, but it wasn't until now—a couple of miles out of Burney Falls, as I walked in my flimsy sandals in the early evening heat—that the realization of what that story meant picked up force and hit me squarely in the chest: preposterous as it was, when Catherine Montgomery and Clinton Clarke and Warren Rogers and the hundreds of others who'd created the PCT had imagined the people who would walk that high trail that wound down the heights of our western mountains, they'd been imagining me. It didn't matter that everything from my cheap knockoff sandals to my high-tech-by-1995-standards boots and backpack would have been foreign to them, because what mattered was utterly timeless. It was the thing that had compelled them to fight for the trail against all the odds, and it was the thing that drove me and every other long-distance hiker onward on the most miserable days. It had nothing to do with gear or footwear or the backpacking fads or philosophies of any particular era or even with getting from point A to point B.

It had only to do with how it felt to be in the wild. With what it was like to walk for miles for no reason other than to witness the accumulation of trees and meadows, mountains and deserts, streams and rocks, rivers and grasses, sunrises and sunsets. The experience was powerful and fundamental. It seemed to me that it had always felt like this to be a human in the wild, and as long as the wild existed it would always feel this way. That's what Montgomery knew, I supposed. And what Clarke knew and Rogers and what thousands of people who preceded and followed them knew. It was what *I* knew before I even really did, before I could have known how truly hard and glorious the PCT would be, how profoundly the trail would both shatter and shelter me.

I thought about this as I walked into my sixth week on the trail beneath the humid shade of ponderosa pines and Douglas firs. The trail's gravelly surface was palpable to the soles of my feet through the bottoms of my thin sandals. The muscles of my ankles felt strained without my boots to support them, but at least my sore toes weren't bumping up against my boots with each step. I hiked until I came to a wooden bridge that spanned a creek. Unable to find a flat spot nearby, I pitched my tent right on the bridge, which was the trail itself, and slept hearing the delicate thunder of the small waterfall beneath me all night long.

I woke at first light and hiked in my sandals for a few hours, climbing nearly 1,700 feet while catching an occasional view of Burney Mountain to the south when I emerged from the shade of the fir and pine forests I was passing through. When I stopped to eat lunch, I reluctantly untied my boots from my pack, feeling I had no choice but to put them on. I'd begun to see evidence of what the authors of *The Pacific Crest Trail, Volume 1: California* had noted in their introduction to the section describing the miles between Burney Falls and Castle Crags. They'd written that the trail in this section was so ill-maintained that it was "little better than cross-country hiking" in places, and though I hadn't yet seen that, such a warning didn't bode well for my sandals. Already, they'd begun to give out, their bottoms splitting apart and flapping beneath me with each step, catching small twigs and pebbles as I went.

I forced my feet back into my boots and continued on, ignoring the pain as I ascended past an eerie pair of electrical towers that made otherworldly crackling sounds. A few times throughout the day, I saw Bald Mountain and Grizzly Peak to the northwest—dark green and brown mountains covered with smatterings of scraggly windblown trees and bushes—but mostly I walked in a bushy forest, crossing an increasing number of primitive roads cut with the deep treads of tractors. I passed old clear-cuts that were slowly coming back to life, great fields of stumps and roots and small green trees that stood no higher than me, where the trail became untenable in places, difficult to track among the litter of blown-down trees and branches. The trees were the same species as those I'd hiked past often on the trail, but the forest felt different, desultory and somehow darker, in spite of the intermittent expansive views.

Late in the afternoon, I stopped for a break in a spot on the trail with a view over the rolling green land. I was on a slope, the mountain rising above me and descending steeply below. With no other place to sit, I sat on the trail itself, as I often did. I pulled off my boots and socks and massaged my feet as I stared out across the tops of the trees, my perch on the trail essentially a ledge over the forest. I loved the sensation of feeling taller than the trees, of seeing their canopy from above, as a bird would.

The sight of it eased my sense of worry over the state of my feet and the rough trail ahead.

It was in this reverie that I reached for the side pocket of my pack. When I pulled on the pocket's zipper, Monster toppled over onto my boots, clipping the left one in such a way that it leapt into the air as if I'd thrown it. I watched it bounce—it was lightning fast and in slow motion all at once—and then I watched it tumble over the edge of the mountain and down into the trees without a sound. I gasped in surprise and lurched for my other boot, clutching it to my chest, waiting for the moment to reverse itself, for someone to come laughing from the woods, shaking his head and saying it had all been a joke.

But no one laughed. No one would. The universe, I'd learned, was never, ever kidding. It would take whatever it wanted and it would never give it back. I really did have only one boot.

So I stood up and tossed the other one over the edge too. I looked down at my bare feet, staring at them for a long moment, then began repairing my sandals with duct tape as best I could, sealing the bottoms back together and reinforcing the straps where they threatened to detach. I wore my socks inside the sandals to protect my feet from the lines of tape and hiked away feeling sick about the new state of affairs, but reassuring myself that at least I had a new pair of boots waiting for me in Castle Crags.

By evening the forest opened into a wide swath of what can only be called wilderness rubble, a landscape ripped up by its seams and logged clear, the PCT picking its way faintly along its edges. Several times I had to stop walking to search for the trail, obstructed as it was by fallen branches and clumps of turned-up soil. The trees that remained standing on the edge of the clear-cut seemed to mourn, their rough hides newly exposed, their jagged limbs reaching out at absurd angles. I'd never seen anything like it in the woods. It was as if someone had come along with a giant wrecking ball and let it swing. Was this the wilderness corridor Congress had in mind when they'd set it aside? It didn't seem so, but I was hiking through national forest land, which, in spite of its promising name, meant that I was on land that the powers that be could use as they saw fit for the public good. Sometimes that meant that the land would remain untouched, as it had been on most of the PCT. Other times it meant that ancient trees were chopped down to make things like chairs and toilet paper.

The sight of the churned, barren earth unsettled me. I felt sad and angry about it, but in a way that included the complicated truth of my own complicity. I used tables and chairs and toilet paper too, after all. As I picked my way through the rubble, I knew I was done for the day. I mounted a steep berm to reach the flattened clear-cut above and pitched my tent among the stumps and upturned mounds of soil, feeling lonely the way I seldom did on the trail. I wanted to talk to someone, and it wasn't just anyone I wanted to talk to.

I wanted to talk to Karen or Leif or Eddie. I wanted to have a family again, to be folded into something I believed was safe from destruction. Right alongside my longing for them, I felt something as hot as hate for each of them now. I imagined a big machine like the one that had mawed up this forest mawing up our forty acres in the Minnesota woods. I wished with all my heart that it really would. I would be free then, it seemed. Because we had not been safe from destruction after my mom died, total destruction would come now as a relief. The loss of my family and home were my own private clear-cut. What remained was only ugly evidence of a thing that was no more.

I'd last been home the week before I left to hike the PCT. I'd driven up north to say goodbye to Eddie and to visit my mother's grave, knowing I wouldn't return to Minnesota after I finished my hike. I worked my last shift at the restaurant where I waited tables in Minneapolis and drove three hours north, arriving at one in the morning. I'd planned to park in the driveway and sleep in the back of my truck so as not to disturb anyone in the house, but when I arrived, there was a party in progress. The house was lit up, and in the yard there was a bonfire; tents were scattered all around, and loud music blared from speakers propped in the grass. It was the Saturday of Memorial Day weekend. I got out of my truck and walked through throngs of people, most of them unknown to me. I was taken aback, but not surprised—by either the raucous nature of the party or the fact that I hadn't been invited. It was only further evidence of how profoundly things had changed.

"Cheryl!" Leif bellowed when I entered the garage packed with people. I pushed my way toward him through the crowd and we embraced. "I'm tripping on 'shrooms," he told me cheerfully, clutching too hard on my arm.

"Where's Eddie?" I asked.

"I don't know, but I got something to show you," he said, tugging on me. "It's guaranteed to piss you off."

I followed him into the yard and up the front stairs of our house and through the door until we were standing before our kitchen table. It was the same one we'd had in the Tree Loft apartments when we were kids, the one our mother had bought for ten bucks, the one we'd eaten on that first night we met Eddie, when we thought we were Chinese because we sat on the floor. It was the height of a normal table now. After we'd moved out of Tree Loft and into a regular house with Eddie, he'd cut off the short legs and bolted a barrel to the bottom and we'd eaten off of it all these years sitting in chairs. The table had never been fancy, and it had become less so over the years, cracking in places that Eddie repaired with wood putty, but it had been ours.

Or at least it had been until that night the week before I left to go hike the PCT.

Now the surface of the table was smattered with freshly carved words and phrases, and names and initials of people linked by plus signs or rimmed with hearts, obviously made by those at the party. As we looked on, a teenaged boy I didn't know carved into the table's surface with a Swiss army knife.

"Stop it," I commanded, and he looked at me with alarm. "That table is . . ." I couldn't finish what I wanted to say. I only turned and bolted out the door. Leif trailed behind me as we walked past the tents and the bonfire, past the chicken coop that was now devoid of chickens and away from the horse pasture where no horses lived anymore and down a trail into the woods to the gazebo that was back there, where I sat and cried while my brother stayed quietly by my side. I was disgusted with Eddie, but more, I was sick with myself. I'd burned candles and made proclamations in my journal. I'd come to healthy conclusions about acceptance and gratitude, about fate and forgiveness and fortune. In a small, fierce place inside me, I'd let my mother go and my father go and I'd finally let Eddie go as well. But the table was another thing. It hadn't occurred to me that I'd have to let that go too.

"I'm so glad I'm leaving Minnesota," I said, the words bitter in my mouth. "So glad."

"I'm not," said Leif. He put his hand on my hair at the back of my head and then took it away.

"I don't mean I'm glad to be leaving *you*," I said, wiping my face and nose with my hands. "But I hardly ever see you anyway." It was true, much as he claimed that I was the most important person in his life—his "second mother," he sometimes called me—I saw him only intermittently. He was elusive and vague, irresponsible and nearly impossible to track down. His phone was constantly being disconnected. His living situations were always temporary. "You can visit me," I said.

"Visit you where?" he asked.

"Wherever I decide to live in the fall. After I'm done with the PCT."

I thought about where I'd live. I couldn't imagine where it would be. It could be anywhere. The only thing I knew was that it wouldn't be here. *Not in this state! Not in this state!* my mother had disconcertedly insisted in the days before she died, when I'd pressed her to tell me where she'd like us to spread her ashes. I couldn't ever get from her what she meant by that, if she was referring to the state of Minnesota or the state she was in—her weakened and confused condition.

"Maybe Oregon," I said to Leif, and we were quiet for a while.

"The gazebo is cool in the dark," he whispered a few minutes later, and we both looked around, seeing it in the shadowy night light. Paul and I had gotten married in it. We'd built it together for the occasion of our wedding nearly seven years before, along with help from Eddie and my mom. It was the humble castle of our naïve, ill-fated love. The roof was corrugated tin; the sides, unsanded wood that would give you splinters if you touched it. The floor was packed dirt and flat stones we'd hauled through the woods in a blue wheelbarrow my family had owned for ages. After I married Paul in the gazebo, it had become the place in our woods where people would walk to when they walked, congregate when they congregated. Eddie had hung a wide rope hammock across its length, a gift to my mother years before.

"Let's get in this thing," Leif said, gesturing to the hammock. We climbed in and I rocked us gently, pushing off with one foot from the very stone upon which I'd stood when I'd married Paul.

"I'm divorced now," I said without emotion.

"I thought you were divorced before."

"Well, now it's official. We had to send our paperwork to the state so they could process it. I just got the final papers last week with a stamp from the judge."

He nodded and said nothing. It seemed he had little pity for me and the divorce I'd brought on myself. He, Eddie, and Karen liked Paul. I couldn't make them understand why I'd had to smash things up. *But you seemed so happy* was all they could say. And it was true: we had seemed that way. Just as I'd seemed to be doing okay after my mom died. Grief doesn't have a face.

As Leif and I swung in the hammock, we caught glimpses of the house lights and the bonfire through the trees. We could hear the dim voices of the partiers as the party died down and disappeared. Our mother's grave was close behind us, maybe only another thirty steps farther on the trail that continued past the gazebo and out into a small clearing, where we'd made a flowerbed, buried her ashes, and laid a tombstone. I felt her with us and I felt Leif feeling her with us too, though I didn't say a word about it, for fear my words would make the feeling go away. I dozed off without knowing it and roused as the sun began to seep into the sky, turning to Leif with a start, having forgotten for an instant where I was.

"I fell asleep." I said.

"I know," he replied. "I've been awake the whole time. The 'shrooms."

I sat up in the hammock and turned back to look at him. "I worry about you," I said. "With drugs, you know."

"You're the one to talk."

"That was different. It was just a phase and you know it," I said, trying to keep my voice from sounding defensive. There were a lot of reasons I regretted having gotten involved with heroin, but losing credibility with my brother was the thing I regretted the most.

"Let's take a walk," he said.

"What time is it?" I asked.

"Who cares?"

I followed him back along the trail, past the silent tents and cars and down our driveway to the gravel road that passed our house. The light was soft and tinged with the slightest shade of pink, so beautiful that my exhaustion didn't matter. Without discussing it, we walked to the abandoned house a short way down the road beyond our driveway, where we used to go as kids, bored on the long hot summer days before we were old enough to drive. The house had been empty and falling to the ground then. Now it was falling more.

"I think her name was Violet, the woman who lived here," I said to my brother when we mounted the porch, remembering the lore about the house I'd heard from the Finnish old-timers years before. The front door had never been locked and it still wasn't. We pushed it open and went inside, stepping over places where boards were missing from the floor. The same items that had been scattered around the house a dozen years ago were still there, amazingly, only now they were even more decrepit. I picked up a yellowed magazine and saw that it was published by the Communist Party of Minnesota and dated October 1920. A chipped teacup with pink roses on it sat on its side and I bent to right it. The house was so tiny it took only a few steps to have it all in view. I walked to the back and approached a wooden door that hung diagonally from one hinge, a pane of pristine glass in its top half.

"Don't touch it," whispered Leif. "Bad karma if it breaks."

We walked carefully past it and into the kitchen. There were gouges and holes and a giant black stain where the stove used to be. In the corner stood a small wooden table that was missing a leg. "Would you carve your name into that?" I asked, gesturing to the table, my voice suddenly flashing with emotion.

"Don't," said Leif, grabbing my shoulders to give me a firm shake. "Just forget it, Cheryl. It's reality. And reality is what we have to accept, like it or not."

I nodded and he let go of me. We stood side by side, gazing out the windows to the yard. There was a dilapidated shed that used to be the sauna and a trough that was overrun by weeds and moss now. Beyond it, a wide swampy field gave way to a stand of birch trees in the distance, and beyond that a bog we knew was there but couldn't see.

"Of course I wouldn't carve into that table and neither would you," Leif said after a while, turning to me. "You know why?" he asked.

I shook my head, though I knew the answer.

"Because we were raised by Mom."

I hiked away from my camp in the clear-cut at first light and saw no one all morning. By noon I didn't even see the PCT. I'd lost it amid the blow-downs and temporary roads that crisscrossed and eventually obliterated the trail. I wasn't terribly alarmed at first, believing that the road I was following would snake its way back to another place where it intersected the trail, but it didn't. I pulled out my map and compass and got my bearings. Or what I believed were my bearings—my orienteering skills were still rather unreliable. I followed another road, but it only led to another and another until I couldn't clearly recall which one I'd been on before.

I stopped to eat lunch in the midafternoon heat, my monumental hunger slightly deadened by the queasy realization that I didn't know where I was. I silently lambasted myself for having been so careless, for pushing on in my annoyance rather than pausing to consider a course, but there was nothing I could do now. I took off my Bob Marley T-shirt and draped it over a branch to dry, pulled another T-shirt from my pack and put it on. Ever since Paco had given me the Bob Marley shirt, I'd carried two, switching them out during the day the same way I did my socks, though I knew such a practice was a luxury that only added more weight to my pack.

I studied my map and walked on, down one rough logging road and then another, feeling a flutter of hope each time that I'd found my way back on track. But by early evening the road I was on ended in a bull-dozed heap of dirt, roots, and branches as high as a house. I scaled it for a better view and spotted another road across an old clear-cut swath. I made my way across it until one of my sandals fell off, both the duct tape and the strap that held it across the top of my foot having detached from the rest of the shoe.

"AHHHH!" I yelled, and looked around, feeling the strange hush of the trees in the distance. They were like a presence, like a people, protectors who would get me out of this mess, though they did nothing other than silently look on.

I sat in the dirt among the weeds and knee-high saplings and did more than extensive repair on my shoes. I constructed a pair of metal-gray booties by winding the duct tape around and around my socks and the skeletal remains of my sandals, as if I were making a cast for my broken feet. I was careful to wind them tight enough that the booties would stay on while I hiked, but loose enough that I could pry them off at the end of the day without ruining them. They had to last me all the way to Castle Crags.

And now I had no idea how far away that might be or how I would get there.

In my duct tape booties, I continued across the clear-cut to the road and looked around. I wasn't sure anymore in which direction I should go. The only views I had were those afforded me by the clear-cuts and roads. The woods were a dense thicket of fir trees and fallen branches, and the day had taught me that the logging roads were only lines in an inexplicable maze. They'd go west and then northeast and later veer south for a stretch. To make matters more complicated, the section of the PCT between Burney Falls and Castle Crags didn't go north so much as in a wide westerly hook. It seemed unlikely that I could even pretend to be following the trail's course anymore. My only goal now was to find my way out of wherever I was. I knew if I went north I'd eventually run into Highway 89. I walked the road until it was nearly dark, and found a reasonably flat stretch beside it in the woods to pitch my tent.

I was lost but I was not afraid, I told myself as I made my dinner. I had plenty of food and water. Everything I needed to survive for a week or more was in my backpack. If I kept walking I'd find civilization eventually. And yet, when I crawled into my tent, I shivered with palpable gratitude for the familiar shelter of the green nylon and mesh walls that had become my home. I squiggled my feet carefully out of my duct tape booties and set them in the corner. I scanned the maps in my guidebook for the hundredth time that day, feeling frustrated and uncertain. At last I simply gave up and devoured a hundred pages of *Lolita,* sinking into its awful and hilarious reality so thoroughly that I forgot my own.

In the morning, I realized I didn't have my Bob Marley T-shirt. I'd left it on that branch to dry the day before. Losing my boots was bad. But losing my Bob Marley T-shirt was worse. That shirt wasn't just any old shirt. It was, at least according to Paco, a sacred shirt that meant I walked with the spirits of the animals, earth, and sky. I didn't know if I believed that, but the shirt had become an emblem of something I couldn't quite name.

I reinforced my duct tape booties with another layer of tape and walked all through the humid day. The night before, I'd made a plan: I would follow this road wherever it led me. I'd ignore all the others that crossed its path, no matter how intriguing or promising they looked. I'd finally become convinced that if I didn't, I'd only walk an endless maze. By late afternoon I sensed that the road was leading me somewhere. It got wider and less rutted and the forest opened up ahead. Finally, I rounded a bend and saw an unmanned tractor. Beyond the tractor, there was a paved two-lane road. I crossed it, turned left, and walked along its shoulder. I was on Highway 89, I could only assume. I pulled out my maps and traced a route I could hitchhike back to the PCT and then set to work trying to get a ride, feeling self-conscious in my metal-gray boots made of tape. Cars passed in clumps of two and three with long breaks in between. I stood on the highway for half an hour holding out my thumb, feeling a mounting anxiety. At last, a man driving a pickup truck pulled to the side. I went to the passenger door and opened it up.

"You can throw your pack in the back," he said. He was a large bull of a man, in his late forties, I guessed.

"Is this Highway 89?" I asked.

He looked at me, befuddled. "You don't even know what road you're on?"

I shook my head.

"What in the Lord's name have you got on your feet?" he asked.

Nearly an hour later, he dropped me off at a place where the PCT crossed a gravel road in the forest, not unlike those I'd followed when lost the day before. The next day I hiked at what for me was record speed, spurred on by my desire to reach Castle Crags by day's end. My guidebook explained that, as usual, I wouldn't exactly be arriving at a town. The trail emerged at a state park that bordered a convenience store and post office, but that was enough for me. The post office would have my boots and my resupply box. The convenience store had a small restaurant where I could fulfill at least some of my food and beverage fantasies once I retrieved the twenty-dollar bill from my box. And the state park offered a free campsite to PCT hikers, where I could also get a hot shower.

By the time I dragged into Castle Crags at three, I was almost barefoot, my booties disintegrating. I hobbled into the post office with strips of dirt-caked tape flapping along beside me and inquired about my mail.

"There should be two boxes for me," I added, feeling desperate about the package from REI. As I waited for the clerk to return from the back room, it occurred to me that I might have something else besides the boots and my resupply box: letters. I'd sent notifications to all the stops I'd missed when I'd bypassed, instructing that my mail be forwarded here.

"Here you go," said the clerk, setting my resupply box heavily on the counter.

"But, there should be . . . Is there something from REI? It would be—"

"One thing at a time," she called as she returned to the back room.

By the time I walked out of the post office, I was almost whooping out loud with joy and relief. Along with the pristine cardboard box that contained my boots—*my boots!*—I held nine letters, addressed to me at stops along the way I hadn't gone, written in hands I recognized. I sat on the concrete near the little building, shuffling quickly through the envelopes, too overwhelmed to open any yet. One was from Paul. One was from Joe. Another was from Karen. The rest were from friends scattered around the country. I set them aside and ripped the box from REI open with my knife. Inside, carefully wrapped in paper, were my brown leather boots.

The same boots that had gone over the side of the mountain, only new and one size bigger.

"Cheryl!" a woman called, and I looked up. It was Sarah, one of the women from the two couples I'd met in Burney Falls, standing there without her pack. "What are you doing here?" she asked.

"What are *you* doing here?" I replied. I expected her to still be behind me on the trail.

"We got lost. We ended up coming out on the highway and hitching a ride."

"I got lost too!" I said in delighted surprise, grateful that I wasn't the only one who'd managed to lose the trail.

"Everyone got lost," she said. "Come on," she gestured to the entrance of the restaurant at the end of the building. "We're all inside."

"I'll be right in," I said. After she left, I took my new boots out of their box, peeled off my booties for the last time, and tossed them into a nearby garbage can. I opened my resupply box and found a fresh pair of clean, never-worn socks, put them on my filthy feet, and then laced my boots on. They were impeccably clean. They seemed almost a work of art in their perfection as I paced the parking lot. The wonder of their virgin tread; the glory of their unmarked toes. They felt stiff, but roomy; like they would work, though I worried about the fact that I'd be breaking them in on the trail. There was nothing I could do but hope for the best.

"Cheryl!" Rex boomed when I walked into the restaurant. Stacy was sitting beside him, and beside her were Sam and Helen and John and Sarah, the six of them practically filling the small restaurant.

"Welcome to paradise," said John with a bottle of beer in hand.

We ate cheeseburgers and fries, then afterwards walked through the convenience store in postprandial ecstasy, loading our arms full of chips and cookies and beer and double-sized bottles of cheap red wine, pooling our money to pay for it all. The seven of us trooped giddily up a hill to the state park campground, where we crammed our tents close together in a circle in the designated free campsite and spent the evening around the picnic table, laughing and telling story after story as the light faded from the sky. While we talked, two black bears—who actually looked black—emerged from the trees that ringed our campsite, only mildly afraid of us when we shouted at them to go away.

Throughout the evening I repeatedly filled the little paper cup I'd taken from the convenience store, gulping smooth sips of wine as if it were water until it tasted like nothing but water to me. It didn't feel like I'd hiked seventeen miles in midnineties heat that day with a pack on my back and duct tape wound around my feet. It seemed as if I'd floated there instead. Like the picnic table was the best place I'd ever been or would ever be. I didn't realize that I was drunk until we all decided to turn in and I stood up and it struck me that the art of standing had changed. In an instant I was down on my hands and knees, retching miserably onto the dirt in the middle of our camp. In spite of all the ridiculousness of my life in the preceding years, I'd never been sick from alcohol before. When I was done, Stacy placed my water bottle beside me, murmuring that I needed to drink. The real me inside the blur I'd become realized she was right, that I wasn't only drunk but also profoundly dehydrated. I hadn't had a sip of water since I was on the hot trail that afternoon. I forced myself to sit up and drink.

When I took a sip, I instantly retched again.

In the morning, I rose before the others and did what I could to sweep the vomit away with the branch of a fir tree. I went to the shower room, took off my dirty clothes, and stood under the hot spray of water in the concrete stall feeling like someone had beaten me the night before. I didn't have time to be hungover. I planned to be back on the trail by midday. I dressed and returned to camp and sat at the table drinking as much water as I could tolerate, reading all nine of my letters one by one while the others slept. Paul was philosophical and loving about our divorce. Joe was romantic and rash, saying nothing about whether he was in rehab. Karen was brief and workaday, providing me with an update about her life. The letters from friends were a rush of love and gossip, news and funny tales. By the time I finished reading them, the others were emerging from their tents, limping into the day the way I did each morning until my joints warmed up. I was grateful that every last one of them looked at least half as hungover as me. We all smiled at one another, miserable and amused. Helen, Sam, and Sarah left to take showers, Rex and Stacy to pay one more visit to the store.

"They have cinnamon rolls," said Rex, trying to tempt me to join them as they walked away, but I waved him off, and not only because the idea of eating made my stomach roil. Between the burger and the wine and the snacks I'd purchased the afternoon before, I was already, and yet again, down to a little less than five bucks.

When they left, I culled my resupply box, organizing my food into a pile to pack into Monster. I'd be carrying a heavy load of food on this next stretch—one of the longest sections on the PCT: it was 156 miles to Seiad Valley.

"You and Sarah need any dinners?" I asked John, who was sitting at the table, the two of us briefly alone in camp. "I've got extras of these." I held up a packet of something called Fiesta Noodles, a dish I'd tolerated well enough in the early days but now loathed.

"Nah. Thanks," he said.

I pulled out James Joyce's *Dubliners* and put it to my nose, the cover green and tattered. It smelled musty and nice, exactly like the used bookstore in Minneapolis where I'd purchased it months earlier. I opened it and saw my copy had been printed decades before I was born.

"What's this?" John asked, reaching for a postcard I'd bought in the convenience store the afternoon before. It was a photograph of a chainsaw carving of a Sasquatch, the words *Bigfoot Country* emblazoned across the top of the card. "Do you believe they exist?" he asked, putting the card back.

"No. But the people who do claim that this is the Bigfoot capital of the world."

"People say a lot of things," he replied.

"Well, if they're anywhere, I suppose it would be here," I said, and we looked around. Beyond the trees that surrounded us stood the ancient gray rocks called Castle Crags, their crenellated summits rising cathedral-like above us. We'd pass them soon on the trail, as we hiked through a miles-long band of granite and ultramafic rocks that my guidebook described as "igneous in origin and intrusive by nature," whatever that meant. I'd never been much interested in geology, but I didn't need to know the meaning of *ultramafic* to see that I was moving into different country. My transition into the Cascade Range had been like the one I'd experienced crossing into the Sierra Nevada: I'd been hiking for days in each before I felt I was actually entering my idea of them.

"Only one more stop," said John, as if he could read my thoughts. "We've just got Seiad Valley and then it's on to Oregon. We're only about two hundred miles from the border."

I nodded and smiled. I didn't think the words *only* and *two hundred miles* belonged in the same sentence. I hadn't let myself think much beyond the next stop.

"Oregon!" he exclaimed, and the joy in his voice almost lured me in, almost made it seem like those two hundred miles would be a snap, but I knew better. There hadn't been a week on the trail that hadn't been a crucible for me.

"Oregon," I conceded, my face going serious. "But California first."

14

WILD

Sometimes it seemed that the Pacific Crest Trail was one long mountain I was ascending. That at my journey's end at the Columbia River, I'd reach the trail's summit, rather than its lowest point. This feeling of ascension wasn't only metaphorical. It literally felt as if I were almost always, impossibly, going up. At times I almost wept with the relentlessness of it, my muscles and lungs searing with the effort. It was only when I thought I couldn't go up any longer that the trail would level off and descend.

How fabulous down was for those first minutes! Down, down, down I'd go until down too became impossible and punishing and so relentless that I'd pray for the trail to go back up. Going down, I realized, was like taking hold of the loose strand of yarn on a sweater you'd just spent hours knitting and pulling it until the entire sweater unraveled into a pile of string. Hiking the PCT was the maddening effort of knitting that sweater and unraveling it over and over again. As if everything gained was inevitably lost.

When I left Castle Crags at two—an hour behind Stacy and Rex and a few hours ahead of the couples—I was wearing boots that were a whole blissful size bigger than the last pair had been. "*I'm* the Bigfoot!" I'd joked as I said goodbye to the couples. I walked up and up into the searing hot day, feeling exuberant to be on the trail, the last dregs of my hangover soon sweated out of me. Up and up I went, all through that afternoon and the following day, though it wasn't long before my enthusiasm over my new boots faded, replaced by the bleak understanding that, footwise, things weren't going to be any different for me. My new boots had only chawed my feet afresh. I was passing through the beautiful territory I'd come to take for granted, my body finally up to the task of hiking the big miles, but because of my foot troubles, I sank into the grimmest despair. I remembered making that wish upon the star when I was with Brent in Belden Town. It appeared that I really had jinxed myself by saying it aloud. Perhaps my feet would never be okay.

Lost in a spiral of bitter thoughts on my second day out of Castle Crags, I nearly stepped on two rattlesnakes that sat coiled up on the trail within a few miles of each other. Each snake had literally rattled me back from where I was, warning me off at the last minute. Chastened, I tried to rattle myself back too. I marched on, imagining unimaginable things—that my feet were not actually attached to me, say, or that the sensation I was having wasn't really pain but simply a *sensation*.

Hot, angry, sick of myself, I stopped for lunch beneath the shade of a tree, laid out my tarp and reclined on it. I'd camped with Rex and Stacy the night before and planned to meet up with them again that night—the couples were still somewhere behind us—but I'd spent the day hiking alone without seeing a soul. I watched birds of prey soaring far over the rocky peaks, the occasional white wispy cloud traveling slowly across the sky, until I fell asleep without meaning to. I woke up a half hour later with a startled gasp, creeped out by a dream—the same dream I'd had the night before. In it, Bigfoot had kidnapped me. He'd done it in a fairly mannerly fashion, approaching to pull me by the hand deep into the woods, where an entire village of other Bigfoots lived. In the dream I was both astonished and frightened at the sight of them. "How have you hid from humans so long?" I'd asked my Bigfoot captor, but he only grunted. As I looked at him, I realized that he was not a Bigfoot at all but a man wearing a mask and a hairy suit. I could see his pale human flesh beneath the edge of his mask, which terrified me.

I brushed the dream aside when I'd awakened that morning, blaming it on the postcard I'd bought in Castle Crags, but now that I'd had the dream twice, it seemed to carry more weight, as if the dream weren't really a dream but a foreboding sign—of what, I didn't know. I stood up, hoisted Monster back on, and scanned the lined crags, the rocky peaks and high gray and rust-colored cliffs that surrounded me near and far among the patches of green trees, feeling a cool unease. When I met up with Stacy and Rex that evening, I was more than a little relieved to see them. I'd felt jumpy for hours, tentative about the small noises that came from the bushes and unnerved by the long silences.

"How are your feet?" asked Stacy as I pitched my tent near hers. In reply, I only sat in the dirt and pulled my boots and socks off and showed them to her.

"Damn," she whispered. "That looks painful."

"So guess what I heard yesterday morning at the store?" asked Rex. He was stirring a pot of something over the flame of his stove, his face still pink from the day's exertions. "Apparently there's this thing called the Rainbow Gathering up ahead at Toad Lake."

"Toad Lake?" I asked, suddenly remembering the woman I'd met in the restroom at the Reno bus station. She'd been going there.

"Yeah," said Rex. "It's only half a mile off the trail, about nine miles up ahead. I think we should go."

I clapped my hands in glee.

"What's the Rainbow Gathering?" asked Stacy.

I explained it to them while we ate dinner—I'd gone a couple of summers before. The Rainbow Gathering is organized by the Rainbow Family of Living Light, a loose tribe of so-called freethinkers, who share a common goal of peace and love on earth. Every summer they set up an encampment on national forest land that attracts thousands in a celebration that culminates during the Fourth of July week, but simmers all summer long.

"There are drum jams and bonfires and parties," I explained to Rex and Stacy. "But best of all there are these amazing outdoor kitchens where people go and make all these breads and cook vegetables and stews and rice. All sorts of things that anyone can just go and eat."

"Anyone?" asked Rex in a pained voice.

"Yep," I said. "You just bring your own cup and spoon."

While we talked, I decided that I'd stay at the Rainbow Gathering for a few days, my hiking schedule be damned. I needed to let my feet heal and to get my head back in the game, to shake this spooky feeling that had blossomed inside me that I might be abducted by a mythical bipedal humanoid beast.

And possibly, just perhaps, I might get myself laid by a hot hippy.

Later, in my tent, I rummaged through my pack and found the

condom I'd carried all this way—the one I'd rescued back in Kennedy Meadows, when Albert had purged the rest from my pack. It was still unspoiled in its little white packet. It seemed it was high time to put it to use. In the six weeks I'd been on the trail, I hadn't even masturbated, too wrecked by the end of each day to do anything but read and too repulsed by my own sweaty stench for my mind to move in any direction but sleep.

The next day I walked faster than ever, wincing with each step, the trail undulating between 6,500 and 7,300 feet as it offered up views of high pristine lakes below the trail and endless mountains in the near and far distance. It was noon when we started down the little trail that descended from the PCT to Toad Lake.

"It doesn't look like much so far," said Rex as we gazed at the lake 350 feet below.

"It doesn't look like anything," I said. There was only the lake surrounded by a gathering of scraggly pines with Mount Shasta to the east—after having it in sight north of me since Hat Creek Rim, I was now finally moving past the showy 14,000-foot peak.

"Maybe the Gathering is back a ways from the water," said Stacy, though once we reached the lake's shore it was clear that there was no happy encampment, no writhing mass of people jamming and tripping and making hearty stew. There were no dark breads or sexy hippies.

The Rainbow Gathering was a bust.

The three of us lunched dejectedly near the lake, eating the miserable things we always ate. Afterwards, Rex went for a swim and Stacy and I walked without our packs down the steep trail toward a jeep road our guidebook said was there. In spite of the evidence, we hadn't entirely given up hope that we'd find the Rainbow Gathering, but when we came to the rough dirt road after ten minutes, there was nothing. No one. It was all trees, dirt, rocks, and weeds, just like it had always been.

"I guess we got the wrong information," said Stacy, scanning the landscape, her voice high with the same rage and regret that welled in me. My disappointment felt tremendous and infantile, like I might have the sort of tantrum I hadn't had since I was three. I went to a large flat boulder next to the road, lay down on it, and closed my eyes to blot the stupid world out so this wouldn't be the thing that finally brought me to tears on the trail. The rock was warm and smooth, wide as a table. It felt incredibly good against my back.

"Wait," said Stacy after a while. "I thought I heard something."

I opened my eyes and listened. "Probably just the wind," I said, hearing nothing.

"Probably." She looked at me and we smiled wanly at each other. She wore a sun hat that tied under her chin and short shorts with gaiters that went up to her knees, a getup that always made her look like a Girl Scout to me. When I'd first met her, I'd been slightly disappointed that she wasn't more like my friends and me. She was quieter, emotionally cooler, less feminist and artsy and political, more mainstream. If we'd met off the trail I didn't know if we'd have become friends, but by now she'd become dear to me.

"I hear it again," she said suddenly, looking down the road.

I stood up when a small beat-up pickup truck packed full of people rounded the bend. It had Oregon plates. It drove straight up to us and screeched to a sudden stop a few feet away. Before the driver had even turned the engine off, the seven people and two dogs in the truck started leaping out. Ragtag and grubby, dressed in high hippy regalia, these people were unquestionably members of the Rainbow Tribe. Even the dogs were discreetly funked out in bandannas and beads. I reached to touch their furry backs as they darted past me and into the weeds.

"Hi," Stacy and I said in unison to the four men and three women who stood before us, though in return they only gazed at us, squinty-eyed and aggrieved, as if they'd emerged from a cave rather than the bed or the cab of a truck. It seemed as if they'd been up all night or were coming down from hallucinogenics or both.

"Is this the Rainbow Gathering?" the man who'd been behind the wheel demanded. He was tan and small-boned. A strange grungy white headband that covered most of his head held his long wavy hair back from his face.

"That's what we were looking for too, but we're the only ones here," I replied.

"Oh my fucking GOD!" moaned a pale waif of a woman with a bare, skeletal midriff and a collage of Celtic tattoos. "We drove all the way from fucking Ashland for *nothing*?" She went to lie across the boulder I'd recently vacated. "I'm so hungry I'm seriously going to die."

"I'm hungry too," whined another of the women—a black-haired dwarf who wore a string belt with little silver bells attached to it. She went and stood by the waif and petted her head.

"Fucking *folkalizers*!" bellowed the headband man.

"Fucking right," mumbled a man with a green Mohawk and a big silver nose ring like the kind you see every now and then on a bull.

"You know what I'm gonna do?" asked the headband man. "I'm gonna make my own fucking Gathering up at Crater Lake. I don't need those fucking folkalizers to tell me where to go. I got major *influence* around here."

"How far is Crater Lake?" asked the last of the women in an Australian accent. She was tall, beautiful, and blonde, everything about her a spectacle—her hair in a heap of dreadlocks bundled on top of her head, her ears pierced with what looked like actual bird bones, her every last finger clad in extravagant rings.

"Not too far, toots," said the headband man.

"Don't call me 'toots,'" she replied.

"Is 'toots' offensive in Australia?" he asked.

She sighed, then made a growling sound.

"All right, baby, I won't call you 'toots,' then." He cackled to the sky. "But I *will* call you 'baby' if I damn well please. Like Jimi Hendrix said: 'I call *everybody* baby.'"

My eyes met Stacy's.

"We were trying to find the Gathering too," I said. "We heard it was here."

"We're hiking the Pacific Crest Trail," added Stacy.

"I. Need. *Food!*" wailed the waif on the rock.

"I've got some you're welcome to," I said to her. "But it's up at the lake."

She only looked at me, her face expressionless, her eyes glazed. I wondered how old she was. She seemed to be my age, and yet she could've passed for twelve.

"Do you have room in your car?" asked the Australian confidentially. "If you two are headed back to Ashland, I'd catch a ride with you."

"We're on foot," I said to her blank stare. "We have backpacks. We left them up at the lake."

"Actually, we *are* going to Ashland," said Stacy. "But it'll take us about twelve days to get there." The two of us laughed, though no one else did.

They all piled back into the truck and drove away a few minutes later, and Stacy and I walked the trail back to Toad Lake. The two couples were sitting with Rex when we returned and we all hiked back up to the PCT together, though it wasn't long before I was bringing up the rear, the last to limp into camp that night near dark, hindered by the catastrophe of my feet.

"We didn't think you were going to make it," said Sarah. "We thought you'd already stopped to camp."

"Well, I'm here," I replied, feeling stung, though I knew she meant only to console me about my foot troubles. In the midst of our drinking and storytelling back in Castle Crags, Sam had joked that my trail name should be the Hapless Hiker after I'd told them about my various misadventures. I'd laughed at the time—the Hapless Hiker seemed a fairly apt name—but I didn't want to be that hiker. I wanted to be the hard-ass motherfucking Amazonian queen.

In the morning, I rose before the others, quietly mixing my Better Than Milk into my pot with cold water and mildly stale granola and raisins. I'd woken from another Bigfoot dream, almost exactly the same as the two previous ones. As I ate my breakfast, I found myself listening carefully for sounds in the still-dark trees. I hiked away before the others even emerged from their tents, happy to get a head start. Exhausted, slow, and footsore as I was, hapless as I might be, I was keeping up with the others—the people I thought of as real hikers. Seventeen and nineteen miles a day, day after day, had become de rigueur.

An hour out, I heard an enormous crashing in the bushes and trees beside me. I froze, unsure of whether to yell or remain perfectly quiet. I couldn't help it: silly as it was, that man with the Bigfoot mask in my dreams flashed through my mind.

"Ah!" I yelled when a hairy beast materialized in front of me on the trail, so close I could smell him. A bear, I realized a moment later. His eyes passed blandly over me before he snorted and reeled and ran northward up the trail.

Why did they always have to run in the direction I was going?

I waited a few minutes and then hiked on, picking my way trepidatiously along, belting out lines from songs. "Oh I could drink a case of *youuuuu*, darling, and I would still be on my feet," I crooned loudly.

"She was a fast machine, she kept her motor clean . . . !" I growled.

"Time out for tiny little tea leaves in Tetley Tea!" I chirped.

It worked. I didn't run into the bear again. Or Bigfoot.

Instead, I came upon something I actually had to fear: a wide sheaf of icy snow covering the trail at a 40-degree angle. Hot as it was, not all the snow had melted off the north-facing slopes. I could see to the other side of the snow. I could practically throw a stone across it. But I couldn't do the same with myself. I had to walk it. I looked down the mountain, my eyes following the course of the snow, should I slip and slide. It ended far below at a gathering of jagged boulders. Beyond them there was only air.

I began to chip my way across, kicking each step with my boots, bracing myself with my ski pole. Instead of feeling more confident on the snow, given the experience I'd had with it in the Sierra, I felt more shaken, more aware of what could go wrong. One foot slipped out from beneath me and I fell onto my hands; slowly I stood again with my knees bent. *I'm going to fall* was the thought that came into my head, and with it I froze and looked down at the boulders below me, imagining myself careening into them. I looked at the place I'd come from and the place I was going, the two equidistant from me. I was too far from either, so I forced my way forward. I went down on my hands and crawled the rest of the way across, my legs shaking uncontrollably, my ski pole clanging along beside me, dangling from my wrist by its pink nylon strap.

When I reached the trail on the other side, I felt stupid and weak and sorry for myself, vulnerable in a way I hadn't felt on the trail before, envious of the couples who had each other, and of Rex and Stacy who had so easily become a hiking pair—when Rex left the trail in Seiad Valley, Stacy would be meeting her friend Dee so they could hike through Oregon together, but I'd forever be alone. And why? What did being alone do? *I'm not afraid,* I said, calling up my old mantra to calm my mind. But it didn't feel the same as it usually did to say it. Perhaps because that wasn't entirely true anymore.

Perhaps by now I'd come far enough that I had the guts to be afraid.

When I stopped for lunch, I lingered until the others caught up to me. They told me they'd met a backcountry ranger who warned them of a forest fire to the west and north, near Happy Valley. It hadn't affected the PCT so far, but he'd told them to be on alert. I let them all hike ahead, saying I'd catch up to them by nightfall, and walked alone into the heat of the afternoon. A couple of hours later, I came to a spring in an idyllic meadow and stopped to get water. It was too beautiful a spot to leave, so afterwards I lingered, soaking my feet in the spring until I heard an ever-loudening jangle of bells. I had only just scrambled to my feet when a white llama rounded the bend and came bounding straight up to me with a toothy grin on his face.

"Ah!" I yelled, the same as I had when I saw the bear, but I reached for the lead rope that dangled from his halter anyway, an old habit from my childhood with horses. The llama wore a pack that was strung with silver bells, not so unlike the belt on the woman I'd met at Toad Lake. "Easy," I said to him as I stood, barefoot and stunned, wondering what to do next.

He looked stunned too, his expression both comical and stern. It occurred to me that he might bite me, but I had no way to know. I'd never been so close to a llama. I'd never even been far from a llama. I'd had so little experience with llamas that I wasn't even 100 percent sure that a llama was what he was. He smelled like burlap and morning breath. I pulled him discreetly in the direction of my boots and stuffed my feet into them and then petted his long bristly neck in a vigorous manner that I hoped struck him as commanding. After a few minutes, an old woman with two gray braids down the sides of her head came along.

"You got him! Thank you," she called, smiling broadly, her eyes twinkling. With the exception of the small pack on her back, she looked like a woman out of a fairy tale, elfin, plump, and rosy-cheeked. A small boy walked behind her and a big brown dog followed him. "I let go for a moment and off he went," the woman said, laughing and taking the llama's rope from me. "I figured you'd catch him—we met your friends up the way and they said you'd be coming along. I'm Vera and this is my friend Kyle," she said, pointing to the boy. "He's five."

"Hello," I said, gazing down at him. "I'm Cheryl." He had an empty glass maple syrup bottle full of water slung over his shoulder on a thick string, which was odd to see—glass on the trail—and it was also odd to see him. It had been ages since I'd been in the company of a child.

"Hello," he replied, his seawater-gray eyes darting up to meet mine.

"And you've already met Shooting Star," said Vera, patting the llama's neck.

"You forgot Miriam," Kyle said to Vera. He placed his small hand on the dog's head. "This is Miriam."

"Hello, Miriam," I said. "Are you having a good time hiking?" I asked Kyle.

"We're having a wonderful time," he answered in a strangely formal tone, then went to splash his hands in the spring.

I chatted with Vera while Kyle tossed blades of grass into the water and watched them float away. She told me she lived in a little town in central Oregon and backpacked as often as she could. Kyle and his mother had been in a horrible situation, she said in a low voice, living on the streets of Portland. Vera had met them only a few months before, through something they were all involved in called Basic Life Principles. Kyle's mother had asked Vera to take Kyle on this hike while she got her life straightened out.

"You promised not to tell people about my problems!" Kyle yelled vehemently, charging over to us.

"I'm not telling about your problems," Vera said amiably, though it wasn't true.

"Because I've got big problems and I don't want to tell people I don't know about them," Kyle said, his eyes going to mine again.

"A lot of people have big problems," I said. "*I've* had big problems."

"What kinds of problems?" he asked.

"Like problems with my dad," I said uncertainly, wishing I hadn't said it. I hadn't spent enough time with children to be exactly sure how honest one should be with a five-year-old. "I didn't really have a dad," I explained in a mildly cheerful tone.

"I don't have a dad either," Kyle said. "Well, everybody has a dad, but I don't know mine anymore. I used to know him when I was a baby, but I don't remember it." He opened his palms and looked down at them. They were full of tiny blades of grass. We watched as they fluttered away in the wind. "What about your mommy?" he asked.

"She's dead."

His face shot up to mine, his expression moving from startled to serene. "My mommy likes to sing," he said. "You wanna hear a song she taught me?"

"Yes," I said, and without a moment's hesitation he sang every last lyric and verse of "Red River Valley" in a voice so pure that I felt gutted. "Thank you," I said, half demolished by the time he finished. "That might be the best thing I've ever heard in my whole life."

"My mother has taught me many songs," he said solemnly. "She's a singer."

Vera snapped a photograph of me and I cinched Monster back on. "Goodbye, Kyle. Goodbye, Vera. Goodbye, Shooting Star," I called as I walked up the trail.

"Cheryl!" Kyle hollered when I was nearly out of sight.

I stopped and turned.

"The dog's name is Miriam."

"Adios, Miriam," I said.

Late in the afternoon, I came to a shady spot where there was a picnic table—a rare luxury on the trail. As I approached, I saw that there was a peach on top of the table and beneath it a note.

Cheryl!
We yogied this from day hikers for you. Enjoy!
Sam and Helen

I was thrilled about the peach, of course—fresh fruit and vegetables competed with Snapple lemonade in my food fantasy mind—but more so, I was touched that Sam and Helen had left it for me. They no doubt had food fantasies every bit as all-consuming as my own. I sat on top of the picnic table and bit blissfully into the peach, its exquisite juice seeming to reach my every cell. The peach made it not so bad that my feet were a throbbing mass of pulp. The kindness with which it was given blunted the heat and tedium of the day. As I sat eating it, I realized I wasn't going to be able to thank Sam and Helen for leaving it for me. I was ready to be alone again; I was going to camp by myself that night.

When I tossed the peach pit, I saw that I was surrounded by hundreds of azaleas in a dozen shades of pink and pale orange, a few of their petals blowing off in the breeze. They seemed to be a gift to me, like the peach, and Kyle singing "Red River Valley." As difficult and maddening as the trail could be, there was hardly a day that passed that didn't offer up some form of what was called trail magic in the PCT vernacular— the unexpected and sweet happenings that stand out in stark relief to the challenges of the trail. Before I stood to put Monster on, I heard footsteps and turned. There was a deer walking toward me on the trail, seemingly unaware of my presence. I made a small sound, so as not to startle her, but instead of bolting away she only stopped and looked at me, sniffing in my direction before slowly continuing toward me. With each step, she paused to assess whether she should continue forward, and each time she did, coming closer and closer until she was only ten feet away. Her face was calm and curious, her nose extending as far as it dared in my direction. I sat still, watching her, not feeling even a little bit afraid, as I'd been weeks before when the fox had stood to study me in the snow.

"It's okay," I whispered to the deer, not knowing what I was going to say until I said it: "You're safe in this world."

When I spoke, it was as if a spell had been broken. The deer lost all interest in me, though she still didn't run. She only lifted her head and stepped away, picking through the azaleas with her delicate hooves, nibbling on plants as she went.

I hiked alone the next few days, up and down and up again, over Etna Summit and into the Marble Mountains on the long hot slog to Seiad Valley, past lakes where I was compelled by mosquitoes to slather myself in DEET for the first time on my trip and into the paths of day hikers who gave me reports about the wildfires that were raging to the west, though still not encroaching on the PCT.

One night I made camp in a grassy spot from which I could see the evidence of those fires: a hazy scrim of smoke blanketing the westward view. I sat in my chair for an hour, looking out across the land as the sun faded into the smoke. I'd seen a lot of breathtaking sunsets in my evenings on the PCT, but this one was more spectacular than any in a while, the light made indistinct, melting into a thousand shades of yellow, pink, orange, and purple over the waves of green land. I could've been reading *Dubliners* or falling off to sleep in the cocoon of my sleeping bag, but on this night the sky was too mesmerizing to leave. As I watched it, I realized I'd passed the midpoint of my hike. I'd been out on the trail for fifty-some days. If all went as planned, in another fifty days I'd be done with the PCT. Whatever was going to happen to me out here would have happened.

"Oh remember the Red River Valley and the cowboy who loved you so true . . . ,'" I sang, my voice trailing off, not knowing the rest of the words. Images of Kyle's little face and hands came to me, reverberations of his flawless voice. I wondered if I would ever be a mother and what kind of "horrible situation" Kyle's mother was in, where his father might be and where mine was. *What is he doing right this minute?* I'd thought occasionally throughout my life, but I was never able to imagine it. I didn't know my own father's life. He was there, but invisible, a shadow beast in the woods; a fire so far away it's nothing but smoke.

That was my father: the man who hadn't fathered me. It amazed me every time. Again and again and again. Of all the wild things, his failure to love me the way he should have had always been the wildest thing of all. But on that night as I gazed out over the darkening land fifty-some nights out on the PCT, it occurred to me that I didn't have to be amazed by him anymore.

There were so many other amazing things in this world.

They opened up inside of me like a river. Like I didn't know I could take a breath and then I breathed. I laughed with the joy of it, and the next moment I was crying my first tears on the PCT. I cried and I cried and I cried. I wasn't crying because I was happy. I wasn't crying because I was sad. I wasn't crying because of my mother or my father or Paul. I was crying because I was full. Of those fifty-some hard days on the trail and of the 9,760 days that had come before them too.

I was entering. I was leaving. California streamed behind me like a long silk veil. I didn't feel like a big fat idiot anymore. And I didn't feel like a hard-ass motherfucking Amazonian queen. I felt fierce and humble and gathered up inside, like I was safe in this world too.

PART FIVE

BOX OF RAIN

I'm a slow walker, but I never walk back.

ABRAHAM LINCOLN

Tell me, what is it you plan to do
With your one wild and precious life?

MARY OLIVER,
"The Summer Day"

15

BOX OF RAIN

I woke in the darkness on my second-to-last night in California to the sound of wind whipping the branches of the trees and the tap-tapping of rain against my tent. It had been so dry all summer long that I'd stopped putting the rain cover on, sleeping with only a wide pane of mesh between the sky and me. I scrambled barefoot into the dark to pull my rain cover over my tent, shivering, though it was early August. It had been in the nineties for weeks, sometimes even reaching a hundred, but with the wind and the rain, the weather had suddenly shifted. Back in my tent, I put on my fleece leggings and anorak, crawled into my sleeping bag, and zipped it all the way up to my chin, cinching its hood tight around my head. When I woke at six, the little thermometer on my backpack said that it was 37 degrees.

I hiked along a high ridgeline in the rain, dressed in most of what I had. Each time I stopped for more than a few minutes, I grew so chilled that my teeth chattered comically until I walked on and began to sweat again. On clear days, my guidebook claimed, Oregon was in view to the north, but I couldn't see anything for the thick fog that obscured anything beyond ten feet. I didn't need to see Oregon. I could feel it, huge before me. I would walk its entire length if I made it all the way to the Bridge of the Gods. Who would I be if I did? Who would I be if I didn't?

Midmorning, Stacy appeared out of the mist, walking southbound on the trail. We'd hiked away from Seiad Valley together the day before, after spending a night with Rex and the couples. In the morning, Rex had caught a bus back to his real life, while the rest of us walked on, splitting up a few hours out. I was fairly certain I wouldn't see the couples on the trail again, but Stacy and I had made plans to meet up in Ashland, where she was going to lay over for a few days waiting for her friend Dee to arrive before they began their hike through Oregon. Seeing her now startled me, as if she were part woman, part ghost.

"I'm heading back to Seiad Valley," she said, and explained that she was cold, her feet were blistered, and her down sleeping bag had gotten drenched the night before and she had no hope of drying it out before nightfall. "I'm taking a bus to Ashland," she said. "Come find me at the hostel when you get there."

I hugged her before she walked away, the fog enveloping her again in seconds.

The next morning I woke earlier than normal, the sky the palest gray. It had stopped raining and the air had warmed up. I felt excited as I strapped on Monster and walked away from my camp: these were my last miles in California.

I was less than a mile away from the border when a branch that hung along the edge of the trail caught on my William J. Crockett bracelet and sent it flying off into the dense brush. I scanned the rocks and bushes and trees, panicky, knowing as I pushed into the weeds that it was a lost cause. I wouldn't find the bracelet. I hadn't seen where it had gone. It had only made the faintest *ping* as it flew away from me. It seemed absurd that I'd lose the bracelet at this very moment, a clear omen of trouble ahead. I tried to twist it around in my mind and make the loss represent something good—a symbol of things I didn't need anymore, perhaps, of lightening the figurative load—but then that idea flattened out and I thought only of William J. Crockett himself, the man from Minnesota who'd been about my age when he died in Vietnam, whose remains had never been found, whose family no doubt still grieved him. My bracelet wasn't anything but a symbol of the life he lost too young. The universe had simply taken it into its hungry, ruthless maw.

There was nothing to do but go on.

I reached the border only minutes later, stopping to take it in: California and Oregon, an end and a beginning pressed up against each other. For such a momentous spot, it didn't look all that momentous. There was only a brown metal box that held a trail register and a sign that said WASHINGTON: 498 MILES—no mention of Oregon itself.

But I knew what those 498 miles were. I'd been in California two months, but it seemed like I'd aged years since I'd stood on Tehachapi Pass alone with my pack and imagined reaching this spot. I went to the metal box, pulled out the trail register, and paged through it, reading the entries from the previous weeks. There were notes from a few people whose names I'd never seen and others from people I hadn't met, but whom I felt I knew because I'd been trailing them all summer. The most recent entries were from the couples—John and Sarah, Helen and Sam. Beneath their jubilant entries, I wrote my own, so overwhelmed with emotion that I opted to be concise: "I made it!"

Oregon. Oregon. *Oregon.*

I was here. I walked into it, catching views of the peaks of majestic Mount Shasta to the south and the lower but sterner Mount McLoughlin to the north. I hiked high on a ridgeline, coming to short icy patches of snow that I crossed with the help of my ski pole. I could see cows grazing in the high green meadows not far below me, their big square bells clanking as they moved. "Hello, Oregon cows," I called to them.

That night I camped under a nearly full moon, the sky bright and cool. I opened J. M. Coetzee's *Waiting for the Barbarians,* but read only a few pages because I couldn't concentrate; my mind wandered to thoughts of Ashland instead. It was finally so close that I could bear to let myself think about it. In Ashland there would be food, music, and wine, and people who knew nothing of the PCT. And most important, there'd be money, and not just my usual twenty bucks. I'd put $250 in traveler's checks into my Ashland box, originally believing that it would be the box that greeted me at the very end of my trip. It didn't contain food or resupplies. It had only traveler's checks and a "real world" outfit to wear—my favorite faded blue Levi's and a slim-fitting black T-shirt; a brand-new black lace bra and matching underwear. It was in these things that months before I thought I'd celebrate the end of my trip and catch a ride back to Portland. When I'd changed my itinerary, I'd asked Lisa to put that small box into another of the boxes I'd loaded down with food and supplies and readdress it to Ashland, instead of one of the stops I wasn't going to make in the Sierra Nevada. I couldn't wait to get my hands on it—that box within the box—and spend the weekend wearing nontrail clothes.

I arrived in Ashland the next day around lunchtime, after hitching a ride from the trail with a group of AmeriCorps volunteers.

"Did you hear the big news?" one of them had asked after I'd climbed into their van.

I shook my head without explaining that I'd heard little news, big or small, for two months.

"You know the Grateful Dead?" he asked, and I nodded. "Jerry Garcia is dead."

I stood on a sidewalk in the center of town and bent to see an image of Garcia's face in psychedelic colors on the front page of the local paper, reading what I could through the newspaper box's clear plastic window, too broke to spring for a copy. I'd liked several of the Grateful Dead's songs, but I'd never collected tapes of their live shows or followed them around the country like some of my Deadhead friends had. Kurt Cobain's death the year before had felt closer to me—his sad and violent end a cautionary tale not only of my generation's excesses, but of my own as well. And yet Garcia's death felt bigger, as if it was the end of not just a moment, but an era that had lasted all of my life.

I walked with Monster on my back a few blocks to the post office, passing homemade signs propped in store windows that said: WE LOVE YOU, JERRY, RIP. The streets were alive with a mix of well-dressed tourists pouring in for the weekend and the radical youth of the lower Pacific Northwest, who congregated in clumps along the sidewalks emitting a more intense vibe than usual because of the news. "Hey," several of them said to me as I passed, some adding "sister" to the end. They ranged in age from teenager to senior citizen, clad in clothing that placed them somewhere along the hippy/anarchist/punk rock/funked-out artist continuum. I looked just like one of them—hairy, tan, and tattooed; weighed down by all of my possessions—and I smelled like one of them too, only worse, no doubt, since I hadn't had a proper bath since I'd showered at that campground in Castle Crags when I'd been hungover a couple of weeks before. And yet I felt so outside of them, of everyone, as if I'd landed here from another place and time.

"Hey!" I exclaimed with surprise when I passed one of the quiet men who'd been in the truck that had pulled up at Toad Lake, where Stacy and I had been searching for the Rainbow Gathering, but he replied with a stony nod, not seeming to remember me.

I reached the post office and pushed its doors open, grinning with anticipation, but when I gave the woman behind the counter my name, she returned with only a small padded envelope addressed to me. No box. No box within the box. No Levi's or black lace bra or $250 in traveler's checks or the food I needed to hike to my next stop at Crater Lake National Park.

"There should be a box for me," I said, holding the little padded envelope.

"You'll have to check back tomorrow," the woman said without concern.

"Are you sure?" I stammered. "I mean . . . It should definitely be there."

The woman only shook her head unsympathetically. She cared nothing for me. I was a dirty, smelly radical youth of the lower Pacific Northwest. "Next," she said, signaling to the man standing at the head of the line.

I staggered outside, half blind with panic and rage. I was in Ashland, Oregon, and I had only $2.29. I needed to pay for a room at the hostel that night. I needed my food before I hiked on. But more than anything—after sixty days of walking beneath my pack, eating dehydrated foods that tasted like warmed-up cardboard, and being utterly without human contact for sometimes weeklong stretches while hiking up and down mountains in an astonishing range of temperatures and terrains—I needed things to be easy. Just for a few days. *Please.*

I went to a pay phone nearby, took Monster off and set it down, and shut myself into the phone booth. It felt incredibly good to be inside, like I didn't ever want to leave this tiny transparent room. I looked at the padded envelope. It was from my friend Laura in Minneapolis. I opened the envelope and pulled its contents out: a letter folded around a necklace she'd made for me in honor of my new name. STRAYED it said in blocky silver letters on a ball-link chain. At first glance it looked like it said STARVED because the Y was slightly different from all the other letters— fatter and squatter and cast from a different mold, and my mind scrambled the letters into a familiar word. I put the necklace on and looked at the distorted reflection of my chest in the telephone's glossy metal face. It hung beneath the one I'd been wearing since Kennedy Meadows—the turquoise-and-silver earring that used to belong to my mother.

I picked up the phone and attempted to make a collect call to Lisa to inquire about my box, but there was no answer.

I strolled the streets miserably, trying not to want anything. Not lunch, not the muffins and cookies that sat on display in the windows, not the lattes in the paper cups that the tourists held in their spotless hands. I walked to the hostel to see if I could find Stacy. She wasn't there, the man who worked the desk told me, but she'd be back later—she'd already checked in for that night. "Would you like to check in too?" he asked me, but I only shook my head.

I walked to the natural food cooperative, the front of which the radical youth of the lower Pacific Northwest had made into something of a daytime encampment, gathering on the grass and sidewalks in front of the store. Almost immediately, I spotted another of the men I'd seen up at Toad Lake—the headband man, the leader of the pack who, like Jimi Hendrix, called everybody *baby*. He sat on the sidewalk near the entrance to the store holding a little cardboard sign that had a request for money scrawled in marker across it. In front of him there was an empty coffee can with a smattering of coins.

"Hi," I said, pausing before him, feeling buoyed to see a familiar face, even if it was his. He still wore his strange grubby headband.

"Howdy," he replied, obviously not remembering me. He didn't ask me for money. Apparently, I exuded the fact that I had none. "You traveling around?" he asked.

"I'm hiking the Pacific Crest Trail," I said to jog his memory.

He nodded without recognition. "A lot of people from out of town are showing up for the Dead festivities."

"Are there festivities?" I asked.

"Tonight there's something."

I wondered if he'd convened a mini–Rainbow Gathering at Crater Lake, like he'd said he'd do, but not enough to ask him. "Take it easy," I said, walking away.

I went into the co-op, the air-conditioned air so strange on my bare limbs. I'd been in convenience stores and small tourist-oriented general stores in a few of my resupply stops along the PCT, but I hadn't been in a store like this since I'd begun my trip. I walked up and down the aisles looking at things I couldn't have, stupefied by their offhand plenitude. How was it that I had ever taken these things for granted? Jars of pickles and baguettes so fresh they were packed in paper bags, bottles of orange juice and cartons of sorbet, and, most of all, the produce, which sat so brightly in bins I felt almost blinded by it. I lingered, smelling things—

tomatoes and heads of butter lettuce, nectarines and limes. It was all I could do not to slip something into my pocket.

I went to the health and beauty section and pumped free samples of lotion into my palms, rubbing several kinds all over my body, their discrete fragrances making me swoon—peach and coconut, lavender and tangerine. I pondered the sample tubes of lipstick and applied one called Plum Haze with one of the natural, organic, made-from-recycled-material Q-tip knockoffs that sat nearby in a medicinal-looking glass jar with a silver lid. I blotted with a natural, organic, made-from-recycled-material tissue and gazed at myself in a round mirror that stood on a pedestal near the lipstick display. I'd chosen Plum Haze because its shade was similar to the lipstick I wore in my regular, pre-PCT life, but now, with it on, I seemed to look like a clown, my mouth showy and manic against my weathered face.

"Can I help you?" a woman with granny glasses and a nametag that said JEN G. asked me.

"No, thanks," I said. "I'm just looking."

"That shade is nice on you. It totally brings out the blue of your eyes."

"Do you think so?" I asked, feeling suddenly shy. I looked at myself in the little round mirror, as if I were genuinely contemplating whether to purchase Plum Haze.

"I like your necklace too," Jen G. said. "Starved. That's funny."

I put my hand to it. "It says *Strayed*, actually. That's my last name."

"Oh, yeah," Jen G. said, stepping closer to see it. "I just looked at it wrong. It's funny both ways."

"It's an optical illusion," I said.

I walked down the aisles to the deli, where I pulled a coarse napkin from a dispenser and wiped the Plum Haze off my lips, and then perused the lemonade selection. They didn't carry Snapple, much to my chagrin. I bought a natural, organic, fresh-squeezed, no-preservatives lemonade with the last money I had and returned with it to sit in front of the store. In my excitement to reach town, I hadn't eaten lunch, so I got a protein bar and some stale nuts from my pack and ate them while forbidding myself to think about the meal I'd planned to have instead: a Caesar salad with a grilled chicken breast and a basket of crusty French bread that I'd dunk into olive oil and a Diet Coke to drink, with a banana split for dessert. I drank my lemonade and chatted with whoever approached: I spoke to a man from Michigan who'd moved to Ashland to attend the local college, and another who played the drums in a band; one woman who was a potter who specialized in goddess figures, and another who asked me in a European accent if I was going to the Jerry Garcia memorial celebration that night.

She handed me a flyer that said *Remembering Jerry* across the top.

"It's at a club near the hostel, if that's where you're staying," she told me. She was plump and pretty, her flaxen hair tied into a loose bun at the back of her head. "We're traveling around too," she added, gesturing to my pack. I didn't understand who the "we" referred to until a man appeared by her side. He was her physical opposite—tall and almost painfully thin, dressed in a maroon wrap skirt that hung barely past his bony knees, his shortish hair bound into four or five pigtails scattered around his head.

"Did you hitchhike here?" asked the man. He was American.

I explained to them about hiking the PCT, about how I planned to lay over in Ashland for the weekend. The man was indifferent, but the woman was astounded.

"My name is Susanna and I am from Switzerland," she said, taking my hand in hers. "We call what you're doing *the pilgrim way.* If you'd like, I would rub your feet."

"Oh, that's sweet, but you don't have to do that," I said.

"I *want* to. It would be my honor. It is the Swiss way. I will return." She turned and walked into the co-op, as I called after her telling her she was too kind. When she was gone, I looked at her boyfriend. He reminded me of a Kewpie doll, with his hair like that.

"She really likes to do this, so no worries," he said, sitting down beside me.

When Susanna emerged a minute later, she held her hands cupped before her, a puddle of fragrant oil in her palms. "It's peppermint," she said, smiling at me. "Take off your boots and socks!"

"But my feet," I hesitated. "They're in pretty rough shape and dirty—"

"This is my calling!" she yelled, so I obeyed; soon she was slathering me with peppermint oil. "Your feet, they are very strong," said Susanna. "Like those of an animal. I can feel their strength in my palms. And also how they are battered. I see you miss the toenails."

"Yes," I murmured, reclining on my elbows in the grass, my eyes fluttering shut.

"The spirits told me to do this," she said as she pressed her thumbs into the soles of my feet.

"The spirits told you?"

"Yes. When I saw you, the spirits whispered that I had something to give you, so that is why I approached with the flyer, but then I understood there was something else. In Switzerland, we have great respect for people who travel the pilgrim way." Rolling my toes one by one between her fingers, she looked up at me and asked, "What does this mean on your necklace—that you are starved?"

And so it went, for the next couple of hours, as I hung out in front of the co-op. I *was* starved. I didn't feel like myself anymore. I felt only like a bucket of desire, a hungry, wilted thing. One person gave me a vegan muffin, another a quinoa salad that had grapes in it. Several approached to admire my horse tattoo or inquire about my backpack. Around four, Stacy came along and I told her my predicament; she offered to loan me money until my box arrived.

"Let me try at the post office again," I said, loath to take her up on her offer, grateful as I was for it. I returned to the post office and stood in line, disappointed to see that the same woman who'd told me my box wasn't there was still working the counter. When I approached her, I asked for my box as if I hadn't been there only a few hours before. She went into a back room and returned holding it, pushing it across the counter to me without apology.

"So it was here all along," I said, but she didn't care, replying that she simply must not have seen it before.

I was too ecstatic to be angry as I walked with Stacy to the hostel, holding my box. I checked in and followed Stacy up the stairs and through the main women's dorm room to a small, private alcove that sat under the eaves of the building. Inside, there were three single beds. Stacy had one, her friend Dee had another, and they'd saved the third for me. Stacy introduced me to Dee and we talked while I opened my box. There were my clean old jeans, my new bra and underwear, and more money than I'd had since I started my trip.

I went to the shower room and stood under the hot water scrubbing myself. I hadn't showered for two weeks, during which the temperatures had ranged from the thirties to the low hundreds. I could feel the water washing the layers of sweat away, as if they were an actual layer of skin. When I was done, I gazed at myself naked in the mirror, my body leaner than the last time I'd looked, my hair lighter than it had been since I was a little girl. I put on the new black bra, underwear, and T-shirt and my faded Levi's, which were loose on me now, though I hadn't quite been able to fit into them three months before, and returned to the alcove and put on my boots. They were no longer new—dirty and hot, heavy and painful—but they were the only shoes I had.

At dinner with Stacy and Dee, I ordered everything I desired. Afterwards, I went to a shoe store and bought a black and blue pair of Merrell sports sandals, the kind I should've sprung for before my trip. We returned to the hostel, but within minutes Stacy and I were out again, headed for the Jerry Garcia memorial celebration at a nearby club, leaving Dee behind to sleep. We sat at a table in a little roped-off area that bordered the dance floor, drinking white wine and watching women of all ages, shapes, and sizes and an occasional man spinning to the Grateful Dead songs that played one after another. Behind the dancers, there was a screen upon which a series of images were projected, some abstract, psychedelic swirls, others literal, drawn renditions of Jerry and his band.

"We love you, Jerry!" a woman at the next table belted out when an image of him appeared.

"Are you going to dance?" I asked Stacy.

She shook her head. "I've got to get back to the hostel. We're heading out early in the morning."

"I think I'm going to stay for a bit," I said. "Wake me up to say goodbye if I'm still sleeping tomorrow." After she left, I ordered another glass of wine and sat listening to the music, watching people, feeling a profound happiness to simply be in a room among others on a summer evening with music playing. When I rose to leave half an hour later, the song "Box of Rain" came on. It was one of my favorite Dead songs and I was a bit buzzed, so I impulsively shot out to the dance floor and began to dance, and then regretted it almost as quickly. My knees felt stiff and creaky from all the hiking, my hips strangely inflexible, but just as I was about to leave, the man from Michigan, whom I'd met earlier in the day, was suddenly upon me, seemingly dancing with me, spinning in and out of my orbit like a hippy gyroscope, drawing an imaginary box in the air with his fingers while nodding at me, as if I knew what the hell that meant, and so it seemed rude to leave.

"I always think of Oregon when I hear this song," he shouted over the music as I moved my body in a faux boogie. "Get it?" he asked. "Box of rain? Like Oregon is a box of rain too?"

I nodded and laughed, attempting to seem as if I were having a fun time, but the moment the song ended, I bolted away to stand near a low wall that ran alongside the bar.

"Hey," a man said to me after a while, and I turned. He stood on the other side of the waist-high wall holding a marker and a flashlight—an employee of the club, apparently manning the territory in which you could drink—though I hadn't noticed him there before.

"Hey," I said back. He was handsome and looked a bit older than me, his dark curls skimming the tops of his shoulders. WILCO it said across the front of his T-shirt. "I love that band," I said, gesturing to his shirt.

"You *know* them?" he asked.

"Of course I know them," I said.

His brown eyes crinkled into a smile. "Rad," he said, "I'm Jonathan," and he shook my hand. The music started up before I could tell him my name, but he leaned into my ear to ask in a delicate shout where I was from. He seemed to know I wasn't from Ashland. I shouted back at him, explaining as concisely as I could about the PCT, and then he leaned toward my ear again and yelled a long sentence that I couldn't make out over the music, but I didn't mind because of the wonderful way his lips brushed against my hair and his breath tickled my neck so I could feel it all the way down my body.

"What?" I yelled back at him when he was done, and so he did it again, talking slower and louder this time, and I understood that he was telling me that he worked late tonight, but that tomorrow night he'd be off at eleven and would I like to come see the band that was performing and then go out with him afterwards?

"Sure!" I shouted, though I half wanted to make him repeat what he'd said so his mouth would do that thing to my hair and my neck again. He handed the marker to me and mimed that I should write my name on his palm so he'd be able to put me on the guest list. *Cheryl Strayed,* I wrote as neatly as I could, my hands shaking. When I was done, he looked at it and gave me a thumbs-up, and I waved and walked out the door feeling ecstatic.

I had a date.

Did I have a date? I walked the warm streets second-guessing myself. Maybe my name wouldn't be on the list, after all. Maybe I'd misheard him. Maybe it was ridiculous to go on a date with someone I'd barely spoken to and whose main appeal was that he was good-looking and he liked Wilco. I'd certainly done such things with men based on far less, but this was different. *I* was different. Wasn't I?

I went back to the hostel and walked quietly past the beds where women unknown to me lay sleeping and into the little alcove under the eaves, where Dee and Stacy slept too, and I took off my clothes and got into the real actual bed that was astoundingly mine for the night. I lay awake for an hour, running my hands over my body, imagining what it would feel like to Jonathan if he touched it the next night: the mounds of my breasts and the plain of my abdomen, the muscles of my legs and the coarse hair on my pudenda—all of that seemed passably okay—but when I got to the palm-sized patches on my hips that felt like a cross between tree bark and a plucked dead chicken, I realized that under no circumstances while on my date tomorrow could I take off my pants. It was probably just as well. God knows I'd taken off my pants too many times to count, certainly more than was good for me.

I spent the next day talking myself out of seeing Jonathan that night. All the time that I was doing my laundry, feasting at restaurants, and wandering the streets watching people, I asked myself, *Who is this good-looking Wilco fan to me anyway?* And yet all the while, my mind kept imagining the things we might do.

With my pants still on.

That evening I showered, dressed, and walked to the co-op to put on some Plum Haze lipstick and ylang-ylang oil from the free samples before strolling up to the woman who staffed the door at the club where Jonathan worked. "I might be on the list," I said casually, and gave her my name, ready to be rebuffed.

Without a word, she stamped my hand with red ink.

Jonathan and I spotted each other the moment I entered; he waved at me from his unreachable place on a raised platform, working the lights. I got a glass of wine and stood sipping it in what I hoped was an elegant way, listening to the band near the low wall where I'd met Jonathan the night before. They were a fairly famous bluegrass band from the Bay Area. They dedicated a song to Jerry Garcia. The music was good, but I couldn't focus on it because I was trying so hard to seem content and perfectly at ease, as if I would be at this very club listening to this very band whether Jonathan had invited me to or not, and, most of all, to be neither looking nor not looking at Jonathan, who was looking at me every time I looked at him, which then made me worry that he thought I was always looking at him because what if it was only a coincidence that every time I looked at him he was looking at me and he wasn't actually looking at me always, but only in the moments that I looked at him, which would compel him to wonder, *Why is this woman always looking at me?* So then I didn't look at him for three whole long bluegrass songs, one of which featured an improvisational, seemingly endless fiddle solo until the audience clapped in appreciation and I couldn't take it anymore and I looked and not only was he looking at me, but he also waved again.

I waved back.

I turned away and stood extra still and upright, acutely aware of myself as an object of hot and exquisite beauty, feeling Jonathan's eyes on my 100-percent-muscle ass and thighs, my breasts held high by the sweet bra beneath my slim-fitting shirt, my extra-light hair and bronze skin, my blue eyes made even bluer by the Plum Haze lipstick—a feeling which lasted for about the length of one song, at which point it reversed itself and I realized that I was a hideous beast with tree-bark-plucked-dead-chicken flesh on my hips and a too-tan, chawed-up face and weather-beaten hair and a lower abdomen that—in spite of all the exercise and deprivation and the backpack strap that for two months had squeezed it into what you'd guess would be oblivion—still had an indisputably rounded shape unless I was lying down or holding it in. In profile, my nose was so prominent a friend had once observed that I was reminiscent of a shark. And my lips—my ludicrous and ostentatious lips! Discreetly, I pressed them to the back of my hand to obliterate the Plum Haze while the music bleated on.

There was, thank God, an intermission. Jonathan materialized by my side, squeezing my hand solicitously, saying he was glad I'd come, asking if I wanted another glass of wine.

I did not. I only wanted it to be eleven o'clock so he'd leave with me and I could stop wondering whether I was a babe or a gargoyle and whether he was looking at me or he thought I was looking at him.

We still had an hour and a half to go.

"So what should we do, afterwards?" he asked. "Have you had dinner?"

I told him I had, but that I was up for anything. I didn't mention I was currently capable of eating approximately four dinners in a row.

"I live on an organic farm about fifteen miles from here. It's pretty cool at night, to walk around. We could go out there and I'll drive you back when you're ready."

"Okay," I said, running my little turquoise-and-silver earring neck-lace along its delicate chain. I'd opted not to wear my Strayed/Starved necklace, in case Jonathan thought it was the latter. "Actually, I think I'm going to step out for some air," I said. "But I'll be back at eleven."

"Rad," he said, reaching over to give my hand another squeeze before he returned to his station and the band started up.

I walked giddily out into the night, the tiny red nylon bag that nor-mally held my stove swinging on its cord from my wrist. I'd ditched most such bags and containers back in Kennedy Meadows, unwilling to carry the extra weight, but this bag I'd held on to, believing the stove needed its protection. I'd changed it into a purse for my days in Ashland, though it smelled faintly of gasoline. The things inside it were all secured in a ziplock bag that served as a very unfancy inner purse—my money, my driver's license, lip balm and a comb, and the card that the workers at the hostel had given me so I could get Monster and my ski pole and my box of food out of their storage area.

"Howdy," said a man who stood on the sidewalk outside the bar. "You like the band?" he asked in a quiet voice.

"Yeah." I smiled at him politely. He looked to be in his late forties, dressed in jeans and suspenders and a frayed T-shirt. He had a long frizzy beard that went to his chest and a straight rim of graying hair that reached his shoulders from beneath the bald dome on top of his head.

"I came down here from the mountains. I like to come and hear music sometimes," the man said.

"I did too. Came down from the mountains, I mean."

"Where do you live?"

"I'm hiking the Pacific Crest Trail."

"Oh, sure." He nodded. "The PCT. I've been up on it before. My place is in the other direction. I've got a tepee up there that I live in about four or five months out of the year."

"You live in a tepee?" I asked.

He nodded. "Yep. Just me. I like it, but it gets lonely sometimes. My name's Clyde, by the way." He held out his hand.

"I'm Cheryl," I said, shaking it.

"You want to come and have a cup of tea with me?"

"Actually, thanks, but I'm waiting for a friend to get off work." I glanced at the club's door, as if Jonathan would emerge from it any moment.

"Well, my truck's right here, so we wouldn't be going anywhere," he said, gesturing to an old milk truck in the parking lot. "That's where I live when I'm not in my tepee. I've been experimenting with being a hermit for years, but sometimes it's nice to come to town and hear a band."

"I know what you mean," I said. I liked him and his gentle way. He reminded me of a few of the men I knew in northern Minnesota. Guys who'd been friends with my mom and Eddie, searching and open-hearted, solidly outside the mainstream. I'd rarely seen any of them since my mom died. It felt now as if I'd never known them and I couldn't know them again. It seemed to me that whatever had existed back in the place where I'd grown up was so far away now, impossible to retrieve.

"Well, nice to meet you, Cheryl," Clyde said. "I'm going to go put my kettle on for tea. You're welcome to join me, like I say."

"Sure," I said immediately. "I'll take a cup of tea."

I've never seen a house inside a truck that failed to strike me as the coolest thing in the world and Clyde's was no different. Orderly and efficient, elegant and artful, funky and utilitarian. There was a woodstove and a tiny kitchen, a row of candles and a string of Christmas lights that cast enchanting shadows around the room. A shelf lined with books wound around three sides of the truck, with a wide bed tucked against it. I kicked off my new sandals and lay across the bed, pulling books off the shelf as Clyde put the kettle on. There were books about being a monk and others about people who lived in caves; about people who lived in the Arctic and the Amazon forest and on an island off the coast of Washington State.

"It's chamomile that I grew myself," Clyde said, pouring the hot water into a pot once it boiled. While it steeped, he lit a few of the candles and came over and sat next to me on the bed, where I lay belly-down and propped up on my elbows, paging through an illustrated book about Hindu gods and goddesses.

"Do you believe in reincarnation?" I asked as we looked together at the intricate drawings, reading bits about them in the paragraph of text on each page.

"I don't," he said. "I believe we're here once and what we do matters. What do you believe?"

"I'm still trying to figure out what I believe," I answered, taking the hot mug he held out to me.

"I have something else for us, if you'd like, a little something I harvested up in the woods." He pulled a gnarly root that looked like ginger from his pocket and showed it to me in his palm. "It's chewable opium."

"Opium?" I asked.

"Except it's way more mellow. It just gives you a relaxed high. You want some?"

"Sure," I said reflexively, and watched as he sliced off a piece and handed it to me, sliced another piece off for himself and put it in his mouth.

"You chew it?" I asked, and he nodded. I put it into my mouth and chewed. It was like eating wood. It took a moment for me to realize that maybe it would be best to steer entirely clear of opium, or any root that a strange man gave me, for that matter, regardless of how nice and non-threatening he seemed. I spit it into my hand.

"You don't like it?" he said, laughing and lifting a small trash can so I could toss it in.

I sat talking to Clyde in his truck until eleven, when he walked me to the front door of the club. "Good luck up there in the woods," he said, and we embraced.

A moment later, Jonathan appeared and led me to his car, an old Buick Skylark he called Beatrice.

"So how was work?" I asked. Sitting beside him at last, I didn't feel nervous the way I had when I'd been in the bar and he'd been watching me.

"Good," he said. As we drove into the darkness beyond Ashland, he told me about living on the organic farm, which was owned by friends of his. He lived there free in exchange for some work, he explained, glancing over at me, his face softly lit by the glow of the dash. He turned down one road and another until I had absolutely no sense of where I was in relation to Ashland, which for me really meant where I was in relation to Monster. I regretted not having brought it. I hadn't been so far from my pack since I began the PCT, and it felt strange. Jonathan turned in to a driveway, drove past an unlit house where a dog barked, and followed a rutted dirt road that took us back among rows of corn and flowers until finally the headlights swooped across a large boxy tent that was erected on a wooden platform and he parked.

"That's my place," he said, and we got out. The air was cooler than it had been in Ashland. I shivered and Jonathan put his arm around me so casually it felt like he'd done it a hundred times before. We walked among the corn and the flowers under the full moon, discussing the various bands and musicians one or the other or both of us loved, recounting stories from shows we'd seen.

"I've seen Michelle Shocked live three times," Jonathan said.

"Three times?"

"One time I drove through a snowstorm for the show. There were only like ten people in the audience."

"Wow," I said, realizing there was no way I was going to keep my pants on with a man who'd seen Michelle Shocked three times, no matter how repulsive the flesh on my hips was.

"Wow," he said back to me, his brown eyes finding mine in the dark.

"Wow," I said.

"Wow," he repeated.

We'd said only one word, but I felt suddenly confused. We didn't seem to be talking about Michelle Shocked anymore.

"What kind of flowers are these?" I asked, pointing to the stalks that blossomed all around us, suddenly terrified that he was going to kiss me. It wasn't that I didn't want to kiss him. It was that I hadn't kissed anyone since I'd kissed Joe more than two months before, and every time I'd gone that long without kissing, I'd become sure that I'd forgotten how to do it. To delay the kiss, I asked him about his job at the farm and his job at the club, and about where he was from and who his family was, and who his last girlfriend was and how long they'd been together and why they'd broken up, and all the while he barely answered me and asked me nothing in return.

It didn't matter much to me. His hand around my shoulder felt good, and then it felt even better when he moved it to my waist and by the time we'd circled back to his tent on the platform and he turned to kiss me and I realized I still did, indeed, know how to kiss, all the things he hadn't exactly answered or asked me fell away.

"This has been really cool," he said, and we smiled at each other in that daffy way two people who just kissed each other for the first time do. "I'm glad you came out here."

"Me too," I said. I was intensely aware of his hands on my waist, so warm through the thin fabric of my T-shirt, skimming the top edge of my jeans. We were standing in the space between Jonathan's car and his tent. They were the two directions I could go: either back to my bed under the eaves in the hostel in Ashland alone, or into his bed with him.

"Look at the sky," he said. "All the stars."

"It's beautiful," I said, though I didn't look at the sky. Instead, I scanned the dark land, punctuated by tiny dots of light, houses and farms spread out over the valley. I thought of Clyde, all alone under this same sky, reading good books in his truck. I wondered where the PCT was. It seemed far away. I realized that I hadn't said anything to Jonathan about it other than the bit I'd shouted into his ear over the music the night before. He hadn't asked.

"I don't know what it was," Jonathan said. "The minute I saw you, I knew I had to come over and talk to you. I knew you'd be totally rad."

"You're rad too," I said, though I never used the word *rad*.

He leaned forward and kissed me again and I kissed him back with more fervor than I had before, and we stood there kissing and kissing between his tent and his car with the corn and the flowers and the stars and the moon all around us, and it felt like the nicest thing in the world, my hands running slowly up into his curly hair and down over his thick shoulders and along his strong arms and around to his brawny back, holding his gorgeous male body against mine. There hasn't ever been a time that I've done that that I haven't remembered all over again how much I love men.

"Do you want to go inside?" Jonathan asked.

I nodded and he told me to wait so he could go in and turn on the lights and the heat, then he returned a moment later, holding the door flaps of the tent open for me, and I stepped inside.

It wasn't a tent like the sort of tent I'd spent any time in. It was a luxury suite. Warmed by a tiny heater and tall enough to stand up in, with room to walk around in the area that wasn't consumed by the double bed that sat in the center. On either side of the bed there were little cardboard dressers on top of which sat two battery-operated lights that looked like candles.

"Sweet," I said, standing next to him in the small space between the door and the end of his bed, then he pulled me toward him and we kissed again.

"I feel funny asking this," he said after a while. "I don't want to presume, because it's fine with me if we just, you know, hang out—which would be totally rad—or if you want me to take you back to the hostel—right now, even, if that's what you want to do, though I hope it isn't what you want to do. But . . . before—I mean, not that we're necessarily going to do this—but in case we . . . I mean, I don't have anything, any diseases or anything, but if we . . . Do you happen to have a condom?"

"You don't have a condom?" I asked.

He shook his head.

"*I* don't have a condom," I said, which seemed the most ridiculous thing ever, since in fact I had carried a condom over scorching deserts and icy slopes and across forests, mountains, and rivers, and through the most agonizing, tedious, and exhilarating days only to arrive here, in a heated luxury tent with a double bed and battery-operated candle lights, staring into the eyes of a hot, sweet, self-absorbed, brown-eyed, Michelle Shocked–loving man without that condom just because I had two palm-sized patches of mortifyingly rough skin on my hips and I'd vowed so fiercely not to take my pants off that I'd purposely left it behind in my first aid kit in my backpack in the town that was located in God-knows-what direction instead of doing the reasonable, rational, realistic thing and putting it in my little faux purse that smelled like white gasoline.

"It's okay," he whispered, taking both of my hands into his. "We can just hang out. There are a lot of things we can do, actually."

And so we recommenced kissing. And kissing and kissing and kissing, his hands running everywhere over my clothes, my hands running everywhere over his.

"Do you want to take your shirt off?" he whispered after a while, pulling away from me, and I laughed because I did want to take my shirt off, so then I took it off and he stood there looking at me in the black lace bra I'd packed months before because I thought when I got to Ashland I might want to wear it and I laughed again, remembering that.

"What's so funny?" he asked.

"Just . . . do you like my bra?" I waved my hands in a flourish, as if to model it. "It traveled a long way."

"I'm glad it found its way here," he said, and reached over and touched his finger very delicately to the edge of one of its straps, near my collarbone, but instead of pushing it down and off my shoulder as I thought he would, he ran his finger slowly along the upper edge of my bra in front and then traced it all the way down around the bottom. I watched his face while he did this. It seemed more intimate than kissing him had.

By the time he'd finished outlining the whole thing, he'd barely touched me and yet I was so wet I could hardly stand up.

"Come here," I said, pulling him to me and then down onto his bed, kicking off my sandals as we went. We were still in our jeans, but he whipped his shirt off and I undid my bra and tossed it into the corner of the tent and we kissed and rolled on top of each other at a feverish pitch until we grew languid and lay side by side kissing some more. His hands traveled all this while from my hair to my breasts to my waist and finally to unbutton the top button of my jeans, which is when I remembered about my hideous patches on my hips and rolled away from him.

"I'm sorry," he said. "I thought you—"

"It isn't that. It's . . . There's something I should tell you first."

"You're married?"

"No," I said, though it took me a moment to realize I was telling the truth. Paul flashed into my mind. Paul. And suddenly, I sat up. "Are *you* married?" I asked, turning back to Jonathan, lying on the bed behind me.

"Not married. No kids," he replied.

"How old are you?" I asked.

"Thirty-four."

"I'm twenty-six."

We sat contemplating this. It seemed exotic and perfect to me that he was thirty-four. Like in spite of the fact that he'd failed to ask me anything about myself, at least I was in bed with a man who wasn't a boy anymore.

"What do you want to tell me?" he asked, and placed his hand on my naked back. When he did, I became aware that I was trembling. I wondered if he could feel that too.

"It's something I feel self-conscious about. The skin on my hips . . . it's kind of . . . Well, you know how last night I told you that I'm in the middle of hiking this trail called the PCT? So I have to wear my back-pack all the time and where the hip belt of my pack rubs against my skin, it's become"—I searched for a way to explain it that avoided the phrases *tree bark* and *plucked dead chicken flesh*—"roughened up. Sort of cal-loused from so much hiking. I just don't want you to be shocked if . . ."

I trailed off, out of breath, my words absorbed entirely in the immac-ulate pleasure of his lips on the small of my back while his hands reached around the front to finish the task of unbuttoning my jeans. He sat up, his naked chest against me, pushing my hair aside to kiss my neck and shoulders until I turned and pulled him down onto me as I wriggled out of my pants while he kissed his way down my body from my ear to my throat to my collarbone to my breasts to my navel to the lace of my underwear, which he nudged down as he worked his way to the patches over my hip bones that I hoped he would never touch.

"Oh, baby," he whispered, his mouth so soft against the roughest part of me. "You don't have to worry about a thing."

It was fun. It was more than fun. It was like a festival in that tent. We fell asleep at six and woke two hours later, exhausted, but awake, our bodies too out of whack to sleep any more.

"It's my day off," said Jonathan, sitting up. "You wanna go to the beach?"

I consented without knowing where exactly the beach might be. It was my day off too, my last one. Tomorrow I'd be back on the trail, headed for Crater Lake. We dressed and drove on a long arcing road that took us a couple of hours through the forest and up over the coastal mountains. We drank coffee and ate scones and listened to music as we drove, sticking to the same narrow conversation we'd had the night before: music, it seemed, was the one thing we had to discuss. By the time we pulled into the coastal town of Brookings, I half regretted agreeing to come and not only because my interest in Jonathan was waning, but because we'd been driving three hours. It seemed odd to be so far from the PCT, as if I were betraying it in a way.

The magnificence of the beach muted that feeling. As I walked along the ocean beside Jonathan, I realized that I'd been at this very beach before, with Paul. We'd camped in the nearby state park campground when we'd been on our long post-NYC road trip—the one on which we'd gone to the Grand Canyon and Vegas, Big Sur and San Francisco, and that had ultimately taken us to Portland. We'd stopped to camp at this beach along the way. We'd made a fire, cooked dinner, and played cards at a picnic table, then crawled into the back of my truck to make love on the futon that was there. I could feel the memory of it like a cloak on my skin. Who I'd been when I'd been here with Paul and what I'd thought would happen and what did and who I was now and how everything had changed.

Jonathan didn't ask what I was thinking about, though I'd gone quiet. We only walked silently together, passing few people, though it was a Sunday afternoon, walking and walking until there was no one but us.

"How about here?" Jonathan asked when we came to a spot that was backed by a cove of dark boulders. I watched as he laid out a blanket, set the bag of lunch things he'd bought at Safeway on top of it, and sat down.

"I want to walk a bit farther, if you don't mind," I said, leaving my sandals near the blanket. It felt good to be alone, the wind in my hair, the sand soothing my feet. As I walked, I collected pretty rocks that I wouldn't be able to take with me. When I'd gone so far that I couldn't make out Jonathan in the distance, I bent and wrote Paul's name in the sand.

I'd done that so many times before. I'd done it for years—every time I visited a beach after I fell in love with Paul when I was nineteen, whether we were together or not. But as I wrote his name now, I knew I was doing it for the last time. I didn't want to hurt for him anymore, to wonder whether in leaving him I'd made a mistake, to torment myself with all the ways I'd wronged him. What if I forgave myself? I thought. What if I forgave myself even though I'd done something I shouldn't have? What if I was a liar and a cheat and there was no excuse for what I'd done other than because it was what I wanted and needed to do? What if I was sorry, but if I could go back in time I wouldn't do anything differently than I had done? What if I'd actually wanted to fuck every one of those men? What if heroin taught me something? What if *yes* was the right answer instead of *no*? What if what made me do all those things everyone thought I shouldn't have done was what also had got me here? What if I was never redeemed? What if I already was?

"Do you want these?" I asked Jonathan when I returned to him, holding out the rocks I'd collected.

He smiled, shook his head, and watched as I let them fall back onto the sand.

I sat down beside him on the blanket, and he pulled things from the Safeway bag—bagels and cheese, a little plastic bear of honey, bananas and oranges, which he peeled for us. I ate them until he reached over with his finger full of honey, spread it on my lips, and kissed it off, biting me ever so gently at the end.

And so began a seaside honey fantasia. Him, me, the honey with some inevitable sand mixed in. My mouth, his mouth, and all the way up the tender side of my arm to my breasts. Across the broad plain of his bare shoulders and down to his nipples and navel and along the top edge of his shorts, until finally I couldn't take it anymore.

"Wow," I gasped because it seemed to be our word. It stood in for what I didn't say, which was that for a guy who wasn't much of a conversationalist, he was ass-kickingly good in bed. And I hadn't even fucked him yet.

Without a word, he took a box of condoms from the Safeway bag and ripped it open. When he stood, he reached for my hand and pulled me up too. I let him lead me across the sand to the gathering of boulders that formed a cove and we circled back into it, to what passed for private on a public beach—a cranny among the dark rocks in the broad light of day. It wasn't the kind of thing I was into, having sex outside. I'm sure there's a woman on the planet who'd choose the outdoors over even the most slipshod and temporary quarters, but I haven't met her, though I decided for this day that the protection of the rocks would suffice. After all, over the course of the past couple of months, I'd done everything else outside. We took each other's clothes off and I reclined with my bare rump against a sloped boulder, wrapping my legs around Jonathan until he turned me over and I gripped the rock. Alongside the remnants of honey, there was the mineral scent of salt and sand and the reedy scent of moss and plankton. It wasn't long before I forgot about being outside, before I couldn't even remember the honey, or whether he'd asked me a single question or not.

There wasn't much to say as we made the long drive back to Ashland. I was so tired from sex and lack of sleep, from sand and sun and honey, that I could hardly speak anyway. We were quiet and peaceful together, blasting Neil Young all the way to the hostel, where, without ceremony, we ended our twenty-two-hour date.

"Thanks for everything," I said, kissing him. It was past dark already, nine o'clock on a Sunday night, the town quieter than it had been the night before, hunkered down and settled in, half the tourists gone home.

"Your address," he said, handing me a scrap of paper and a pen. I wrote down Lisa's, feeling a mounting sense of something that wasn't quite sorrow, wasn't quite regret, and wasn't quite longing, but was a mix of them all. It had been an indisputably good time, but now I felt empty. Like there was something I didn't even know I wanted until I didn't get it.

I handed him the scrap of paper.

"Don't forget your purse," he said, picking up my little red stove bag.

"Bye," I said, taking it from him and reaching for the door.

"Not so fast," he said, pulling me toward him. He kissed me hard and I kissed him back harder, like it was the end of an era that had lasted all of my life.

The next morning I dressed in my hiking clothes—the same old stained sports bra and threadbare navy blue hiking shorts I'd been wearing since day 1, along with a new pair of wool socks and the last fresh T-shirt I'd have all the way to the end, a heather gray shirt that said UNIVERSITY OF CALIFORNIA BERKELEY in yellow letters across the chest. I walked to the co-op with Monster on my back, my ski pole dangling from my wrist, and a box in my arms, taking over a table in the deli section of the store to organize my pack.

When I was done, Monster sat tidily loaded down next to the small box that held my jeans, bra, and underwear, which I was mailing back to Lisa, and a plastic grocery bag of meals I couldn't bear to eat any longer, which I planned to leave in the PCT hiker free box at the post office on my way out of town. Crater Lake National Park was my next stop, about 110 trail miles away. I needed to get back on the PCT and yet I was reluctant to leave Ashland. I dug through my pack, found my Strayed necklace, and put it on. I reached over and touched the raven feather Doug had given me. It was still wedged into my pack in the place I'd first put it, though it was worn and straggly now. I unzipped the side pocket where I kept my first aid kit, pulled it out, and opened it up. The condom I'd carried all the way from Mojave was still there, still like new. I took it out and put it in the plastic grocery bag with the food I didn't want, and then I hoisted Monster onto my back and left the co-op carrying the box and the plastic grocery bag.

I hadn't gone far when I saw the headband man I'd met up at Toad Lake, sitting on the sidewalk where I'd seen him before, his coffee can and little cardboard sign in front of him. "I'm heading out," I said, stopping before him.

He looked up at me and nodded. He still didn't seem to remember me—either from our encounter at Toad Lake or from a couple of days before.

"I met you when you were looking for the Rainbow Gathering," I said. "I was there with another woman named Stacy. We talked to you."

He nodded again, shaking the change in his can.

"I've got some food here that I don't need, if you want it," I said, setting the plastic grocery bag down beside him.

"Thanks, baby," he said as I began to walk away.

I stopped and turned.

"Hey," I called. "Hey!" I shouted until he looked at me.

"Don't call me baby," I said.

He pressed his hands together, as if in prayer, and bowed his head.

16

MAZAMA

Crater Lake used to be a mountain. Mount Mazama, it was called. It was not so unlike the chain of dormant volcanoes I'd be traversing on the PCT in Oregon—Mount McLoughlin, the Three Sisters peaks, Mount Washington, Three Fingered Jack, Mount Jefferson, and Mount Hood—except that it was bigger than them all, having reached an elevation that's estimated at a little under 12,000 feet. Mount Mazama blew up about 7,700 years ago in a cataclysmic eruption that was forty-two times more voluminous than the eruption that decapitated Mount St. Helens in 1980. It was the largest explosive eruption in the Cascade Range going back a million years. In the wake of Mazama's destruction, ash and pumice blanketed the landscape for 500,000 square miles—covering nearly all of Oregon and reaching as far as Alberta, Canada. The Klamath tribe of Native Americans who witnessed the eruption believed it was a fierce battle between Llao, the spirit of the underworld, and Skell, the spirit of the sky. When the battle was over, Llao was driven back into the underworld and Mount Mazama had become an empty bowl. A caldera, it's called—a sort of mountain in reverse. A mountain that's had its very heart removed. Slowly, over hundreds of years, the caldera filled with water, collecting the Oregon rain and snowmelt, until it became the lake that it is now. Reaching a maximum depth of more than 1,900 feet, Crater Lake is the deepest lake in the United States and among the deepest in the world.

I knew a little something about lakes, having come from Minnesota, but as I walked away from Ashland, I couldn't quite imagine what I would see at Crater Lake. It would be like Lake Superior, I supposed, the lake near which my mother had died, going off blue forever into the horizon. My guidebook said only that my first view of it from the rim, which rose 900 feet above the lake's surface, would be "one of disbelief."

I had a new guidebook now. A new bible. *The Pacific Crest Trail, Volume 2: Oregon and Washington,* though back at the co-op in Ashland, I'd ripped off the last 130 of the book's pages because I didn't need the Washington part. My first night out of Ashland, I paged through the book before falling asleep, reading bits here and there, the same as I had with the California guidebook in the desert on my first night on the PCT.

As I walked during those first days out of Ashland, I caught a couple of glimpses of Mount Shasta to the south, but mostly I walked in forests that obscured views. Among backpackers, the Oregon PCT was often referred to as the "green tunnel" because it opened up to far fewer panoramas than the California trail did. I no longer had the feeling that I was perched above looking down on everything, and it felt odd not to be able to see out across the terrain. California had altered my vision, but Oregon shifted it again, drew it closer in. I hiked through forests of noble, grand, and Douglas fir, pushing past bushy lakes through grasses and weedy thistles that sometimes obscured the trail. I crossed into the Rogue River National Forest and walked beneath tremendous ancient trees before emerging into clear-cuts like those I'd seen a few weeks before, vast open spaces of stumps and tree roots that had been exposed by the logging of the dense forest. I spent an afternoon lost amid the debris, walking for hours before I emerged onto a paved road and found the PCT again.

It was sunny and clear but the air was cool, and it grew progressively cooler with each day as I passed into the Sky Lakes Wilderness, where the trail stayed above 6,000 feet. The views opened up again as I walked along a ridgeline of volcanic rocks and boulders, glimpsing lakes occasionally below the trail and the land that spread beyond. In spite of the sun, it felt like an early October morning instead of a mid-August afternoon. I had to keep moving to stay warm. If I stopped for more than five minutes the sweat that drenched the back of my T-shirt turned icy cold. I'd seen no one since I left Ashland, but now I encountered a few day hikers and overnight backpackers who'd climbed up to the PCT on one of the many trails that intersected it, which led to peaks above or lakes below. Mostly I was alone, which wasn't unusual, but the cold made the trail seem even more vacant, the wind clattering the branches of the persevering trees. It felt colder too, even colder than it had been up in the snow above Sierra City, though I saw only small patches of snow here and there. I realized it was because back then the mountains had been moving toward summer, and now, only six weeks later, they were already moving away from it, reaching toward autumn, in a direction that pushed me out.

One night I stopped to camp, stripped off my sweaty clothes, dressed in every other piece of clothing I had, and quickly made dinner, zipping myself into my sleeping bag as soon as I finished eating, chilled to the bone, too cold even to read. I lay curled into myself in a fetal position with my hat and gloves on all night long, barely able to sleep. When the sun rose at last, it was 26 degrees and my tent was covered in a thin layer of snow; the water in my bottles was frozen, though they'd been beside me inside the tent. As I broke camp without a sip of water, eating a protein bar instead of my regular granola mixed with Better Than Milk, I thought again of my mother. She'd been looming for days, riding low and heavy in my mind since Ashland, and now finally, on the day of the snow, she was undeniably here.

It was August 18. Her birthday. She'd have been fifty that day, if she'd lived.

She didn't live. She didn't get to be fifty. She would never be fifty, I told myself as I walked under the cold and bright August sun. *Be fifty, Mom. Be fucking fifty,* I thought with increasing rage as I forged on. I couldn't believe how furious I was at my mother for not being alive on her fiftieth birthday. I had the palpable urge to punch her in the mouth.

Her previous birthdays hadn't brought up the same rage. In past years, I'd been nothing but sad. On the first birthday without her—on the day that she'd have been forty-six—I'd spread her ashes with Eddie, Karen, Leif, and Paul in the little rock-lined flowerbed we'd made for her in a clearing on our land. On her three subsequent birthdays, I'd done nothing but cry as I sat very still listening with great attention to the entire Judy Collins album *Colors of the Day,* its every note seeming to be one of my cells. I could bear to listen to it only once each year, for all the memories of my mother playing it when I was a child. The music made it feel like my mother was right there with me, standing in the room—only she wasn't and would never be again.

I couldn't allow even a line of it now on the PCT. I deleted each and every song from the mix-tape radio station in my head, pressing an imaginary rewind in a desperate scramble, forcing my mind to go static instead. It was my mother's not-fiftieth birthday and there would be no song. Instead, I passed by high lakes and crossed over blocky volcanic rocks as the night's snow melted on the hardy wildflowers that grew among them, hiking faster than ever while thinking uncharitable thoughts about my mother. Dying at forty-five had only been the worst thing she'd done wrong. As I hiked, I made a catalogue of the rest, listing them painstakingly in my head:

1. She'd gone through a phase during which she'd smoked pot on an occasional but regular basis and had no qualms about doing it in front of my siblings and me. Once, stoned, she'd said, "It's only an herb. Like tea."

2. It hadn't been uncommon for my brother, sister, and me to be left alone when we lived in the apartment buildings full of single moms. She told us we were old enough to look after ourselves for a few hours because she couldn't afford a baby-sitter. Plus, there were all those other moms we could go to if something went wrong, she said. But we needed *our* mom.

3. During this same period, when she became really mad, she often threatened to spank us with a wooden spoon, and a few times, she'd followed through.

4. Once she said it was perfectly okay with her if we wanted to call her by her first name instead of calling her Mom.

5. She could be cool and often distant with her friends. She loved them, but she kept them at arm's length. I don't think she truly let any one of them all the way in. She held to her belief that "blood was thicker than water," in spite of the fact that my family was rather short of blood relations who didn't live hundreds of miles away. She maintained an air of insularity and privacy, participating in the community of friends, but also sealing off our family from it. This was why no one had swooped in when she died, I supposed, why her friends had left me in peace in my inevitable exile. Because she had

not held any of them very close, none of them held me. They wished me well, but they didn't invite me to Thanksgiving dinner or call me up on my mom's birthday to say hello after she died.

6. She was optimistic to an annoying degree, given to saying those stupid things: *We're not poor because we're rich in love!* or *When one door closes, another one opens up!* Which always, for a reason I couldn't quite pin down, made me want to throttle her, even when she was dying and her optimism briefly and desolately expressed itself in the belief that in fact she wouldn't die, so long as she drank a tremendous amount of wheatgrass juice.

7. When I was a senior in high school, she didn't ask where I would like to go to college. She didn't take me on a tour. I didn't even know people went on tours until I went to college and others told me they'd gone on them. I was left to figure it out on my own, applying to a single college in St. Paul for no reason whatsoever other than it looked nice on the brochure and it was only a three-hour drive away from home. Yes, I had slacked a bit in high school, playing the dumb blonde so I wouldn't be socially ostracized because my family lived in a house with a honey bucket for a toilet and a woodstove for heat; and my stepfather had long hair and a big bushy beard and drove around in a demolished car that he'd made into a pickup truck by himself with a blowtorch, a chain saw, and a few two-by-fours; and my mother opted not to shave under her arms and to say things to the red-blooded gun-loving locals like *Actually, I think hunting is murder.* But she knew I was secretly smart. She knew I was intellectually avid, devouring books by the day. I'd scored in the upper percentiles on every standardized test I ever took, to everyone's surprise but hers and mine. Why hadn't she said, *Hey, maybe you should apply to Harvard? Maybe you should apply to Yale?* The thought of Harvard and Yale hadn't even crossed my mind back then. They seemed to be utterly fictitious schools. It was only later that I realized that Harvard and Yale were real. And even though the reality is they wouldn't have let me in—

I honestly wasn't up to their standards—something inside me was smashed by the fact that there'd never even been the question that I could give them a shot.

But it was too late now, I knew, and there was only my dead, insular, overly optimistic, non-college-preparing, occasionally-child-abandoning, pot-smoking, wooden-spoon-wielding, feel-free-to-call-me-by-my-name mom to blame. She had failed. She had failed. She had so profoundly failed me.

Fuck her, I thought, so mad that I stopped walking.

And then I wailed. No tears came, just a series of loud brays that coursed through my body so hard I couldn't stand up. I had to bend over, keening, while bracing my hands on my knees, my pack so heavy on top of me, my ski pole clanging out behind me in the dirt, the whole stupid life I'd had coming out my throat.

It was wrong. It was so relentlessly awful that my mother had been taken from me. I couldn't even hate her properly. I didn't get to grow up and pull away from her and bitch about her with my friends and confront her about the things I wished she'd done differently and then get older and understand that she had done the best she could and realize that what she had done was pretty damn good and take her fully back into my arms again. Her death had obliterated that. It had obliterated me. It had cut me short at the very height of my youthful arrogance. It had forced me to instantly grow up and forgive her every motherly fault at the same time that it kept me forever a child, my life both ended and begun in that premature place where we'd left off. She was my mother, but I was motherless. I was trapped by her but utterly alone. She would always be the empty bowl that no one could fill. I'd have to fill it myself again and again and again.

Fuck her, I chanted as I marched on over the next few miles, my pace quickened by my rage, but soon I slowed and stopped to sit on a boulder. A gathering of low flowers grew at my feet, their barely pink petals edging the rocks. *Crocus,* I thought, the name coming into my mind because my mother had given it to me. These same flowers grew in the dirt where I'd spread her ashes. I reached out and touched the petals of one, feeling my anger drain out of my body.

By the time I rose and started walking again, I didn't begrudge my mother a thing. The truth was, in spite of all that, she'd been a spectacular mom. I knew it as I was growing up. I knew it in the days that she was dying. I knew it now. And I knew that was something. That it was a lot. I had plenty of friends who had moms who—no matter how long they lived—would never give them the all-encompassing love that my mother had given me. My mother considered that love her greatest achievement. It was what she banked on when she understood that she really was going to die and die soon, the thing that made it just barely okay for her to leave me and Karen and Leif behind.

"I've given you everything," she insisted again and again in her last days.

"Yes," I agreed. She had, it was true. She did. She did. She did. She'd come at us with maximum maternal velocity. She hadn't held back a thing, not a single lick of her love.

"I'll always be with you, no matter what," she said.

"Yes," I replied, rubbing her soft arm.

When she'd become sick enough that we knew she was really going to die, when we were in the homestretch to hell, when we were well past thinking any amount of wheatgrass juice would save her, I'd asked her what she wanted done with her body—cremated or buried—though she only looked at me as if I were speaking Dutch.

"I want everything that can be donated to be donated," she said after a while. "My organs, I mean. Let them have every part they can use."

"Okay," I said. It was the oddest thing to contemplate, to know that we weren't making impossibly far-off plans; to imagine parts of my mother living on in someone else's body. "But then what?" I pressed on, practically panting with pain. I had to know. It would fall on me. "What would you like to do with . . . what's . . . left over. Do you want to be buried or cremated?"

"I don't care," she said.

"Of course you care," I replied.

"I really don't care. Do what you think is best. Do whatever is cheapest."

"No," I insisted. "You have to tell me. I want to know what you want done." The idea that I would be the one to decide filled me with panic.

"Oh, Cheryl," she said, exhausted by me, our eyes meeting in a grief-stricken détente. For every time I wanted to throttle her because she was too optimistic, she wanted to throttle me because I would never ever relent.

"Burn me," she said finally. "Turn me to ash."

And so we did, though the ashes of her body were not what I'd expected. They weren't like ashes from a wood fire, silky and fine as sand. They were like pale pebbles mixed with a gritty gray gravel. Some chunks were so large I could see clearly that they'd once been bones. The box that the man at the funeral home handed to me was oddly addressed to my mom. I brought it home and set it in the cupboard beneath the curio cabinet, where she kept her nicest things. It was June. It sat there until August 18, as did the tombstone we'd had made for her, which had arrived the same week as the ashes. It sat in the living room, off to the side, a disturbing sight to visitors probably, but it was a comfort to me. The stone was slate gray, the writing etched in white. It said her name and the dates of her birth and death and the sentence she'd spoken to us again and again as she got sicker and died: *I'm with you always*.

She wanted us to remember that, and I did. It felt like she was with me always, metaphorically at least. And in a way it was literal too. When we'd finally laid down that tombstone and spread her ashes into the dirt, I hadn't spread them all. I'd kept a few of the largest chunks in my hand. I'd stood for a long while, not ready to release them to the earth. I didn't release them. I never ever would.

I put her burnt bones into my mouth and swallowed them whole.

By the night of my mother's fiftieth birthday, I loved her again, though I still couldn't bear to let the Judy Collins songs come into my head. It was cold, but not as cold as the night before. I sat bundled in my tent wearing my gloves, reading the first pages of my new book—*The Best American Essays 1991*. I usually waited until morning to burn whatever pages I'd read the night before, but on this night, when I was done reading, I crawled out of my tent and made a fire of the pages I'd read. As I watched them ignite, I said my mother's name out loud as if it were a ceremony for her. Her name was Barbara, but she'd gone by Bobbi, so that was the name I spoke. Saying *Bobbi* instead of *Mom* felt like a revelation, like it was the first time that I truly understood that she was my mother, but also more. When she'd died, I'd lost that too—the Bobbi she'd been, the woman who was separate from who she was to me. She seemed to come at me now, the full perfect and imperfect force of her humanity, as if her life was an intricately painted mural and I could finally see the whole thing. Who she'd been to me and who she hadn't. How it was she belonged to me profoundly, and also how she didn't.

Bobbi hadn't been granted her last wish, that her organs be used to help others, or at least not to the extent that she had hoped. When she died, she was ravaged with cancer and morphine, her forty-five-year-old body a toxic thing. In the end, they could use only her corneas. I knew that part of the eye was nothing but a transparent membrane, but when I thought of what my mother had given, I didn't think of it that way. I thought of her astounding blue, blue eyes living on in someone else's face. A few months after my mom died, we'd received a thank-you letter from the foundation that facilitated the donation. Because of her generosity someone could see, the letter said. I was mad with desire to meet the person, to gaze into his or her eyes. He or she wouldn't have to say a word. All I wanted was for whoever it was to look at me. I called the number on the letter to inquire, but was quickly brushed aside. Confidentiality was of the utmost importance, I was told. There were the recipient's rights.

"I'd like to explain to you about the nature of your mother's donation," the woman on the phone said in a patient and consoling voice that reminded me of any number of the grief counselors, hospice volunteers, nurses, doctors, and morticians who had addressed me in the weeks during which my mother was dying and in the days after she died—a voice full of intentional, almost overstated compassion, which also communicated that in this, I was entirely alone. "It wasn't the entire eye that was transplanted," the woman explained, "but rather the cornea, which is—"

"I know what the cornea is," I snapped. "I'd still like to know who this person is. To see him or her if I can. I think you owe me that."

I hung up the phone overcome with grief, but the small reasonable core that still lived inside of me knew that the woman was right. My mother wasn't there. Her blue eyes were gone. I'd never gaze into them again.

When the flames from the pages I'd burned had gone out and I'd stood to return to my tent, the sound of high and frenzied barks and howls came to me from the east—a pack of coyotes. I'd heard that sound in northern Minnesota so many times it didn't scare me. It reminded me of home. I looked up at the sky, the stars everywhere and magnificent, so bright against the dark. I shivered, knowing I was lucky to be here, feeling that it was too beautiful to go back into my tent just yet. Where would I be in a month? It seemed impossible that I wouldn't be on the trail, but it was true. Most likely I'd be in Portland, if for no other reason than that I was flat broke. I still had a small bit of money left over from Ashland, but nothing that wouldn't be gone by the time I reached the Bridge of the Gods.

I let Portland roll around in my mind through the days, as I passed out of the Sky Lakes Wilderness into the Oregon Desert—a high dusty flat plain of lodgepole pines that my guidebook explained had been smattered with lakes and streams before they were buried beneath the tons of pumice and ash that had fallen on them when Mount Mazama erupted. It was early on a Saturday when I reached Crater Lake National Park. The lake was nowhere in sight. I'd arrived instead at the campground seven miles south of the lake's rim.

The campground wasn't just a campground. It was a mad tourist complex that included a parking lot, a store, a motel, a little coin laundromat, and what seemed to be three hundred people revving their engines and playing their radios loud, slurping beverages from gigantic paper cups with straws and eating from big bags of chips they bought in the store. The scene both riveted and appalled me. If I hadn't known it firsthand, I wouldn't have believed that I could walk a quarter mile in any direction and be in an entirely different world. I camped there for the night, showering blissfully in the bathhouse, and the next morning made my way to Crater Lake.

My guidebook had been correct: my first sight of it was one of disbelief. The surface of the water sat 900 feet below where I stood on the rocky 7,100-foot-high rim. The jagged circle of the lake spread out beneath me in the most unspeakably pure ultramarine blue I'd ever seen. It was approximately six miles across, its blue interrupted only by the top of a small volcano, Wizard Island, that rose 700 feet above the water, forming a conical island upon which twisted foxtail pines grew. The mostly barren, undulating rim that surrounded the lake was dotted with these same pines and backed by distant mountains.

"Because the lake is so pure and deep, it absorbs every color of visible light except blue, so it reflects pure blue back to us," said a stranger who stood beside me, answering the question I'd nearly uttered out loud in my amazement.

"Thanks," I said to her. Because the water was so deep and pure it absorbed every color of visible light except blue seemed like a perfectly sound and scientific explanation, and yet there was still something about Crater Lake that remained inexplicable. The Klamath tribe still considered the lake a sacred site and I could see why. I wasn't a skeptic about this. It didn't matter that all around me there were tourists taking pictures and driving slowly past in their cars. I could feel the lake's power. It seemed a shock in the midst of this great land: inviolable, separate and alone, as if it had always been and would always be here, absorbing every color of visible light but blue.

I took a few photographs and walked along the lake's rim near a small gathering of buildings that had been built to accommodate tourists. I had no choice but to spend the day because it was a Sunday and the park's post office was closed; I couldn't get my box until tomorrow. It was sunny and finally warm again, and as I walked, I thought that if I'd continued with the pregnancy I'd learned about in that motel room in Sioux Falls the night before I decided to hike the PCT, I'd be giving birth to a baby right about now. The week of my mother's birthday would've been my due date. The crushing coalescence of those dates felt like a punch in the gut at the time, but it didn't compel me to waver in my decision to end my pregnancy. It only made me beg the universe to give me another chance. To let me become who I needed to before I became a mother: a woman whose life was profoundly different than my mother's had been.

Much as I loved and admired my mother, I'd spent my childhood planning not to become her. I knew why she'd married my father at nineteen, pregnant and only a tiny bit in love. It was one of the stories I'd made her tell when I'd asked and asked and she'd shaken her head and said, *Why do you want to know?* I'd asked so much that she finally gave in. When she'd learned she was pregnant, she'd pondered two options: an illegal abortion in Denver or hiding out in a distant city during her pregnancy, then handing over my sister to her mother, who'd offered to raise the baby as her own. But my mother hadn't done either of those things. She decided to have her baby, so she'd married my dad instead. She'd become Karen's mother and then mine and then Leif's.

Ours.

"I never got to be in the driver's seat of my own life," she'd wept to me once, in the days after she learned she was going to die. "I always did what someone else wanted me to do. I've always been someone's daughter or mother or wife. I've never just been me."

"Oh, Mom," was all I could say as I stroked her hand.

I was too young to say anything else.

At noon I went to the cafeteria in one of the nearby buildings and ate lunch. Afterwards, I walked through the parking lot to the Crater Lake Lodge and strolled through the elegantly rustic lobby with Monster on my back, pausing to peer into the dining room. There was a smattering of people sitting at tables, handsome groups holding glasses of chardonnay and pinot gris like pale yellow jewels. I went outside to the long porch that overlooked the lake, made my way along a line of grand rocking chairs, and found one that was set off by itself.

I sat in it for the rest of the afternoon, staring at the lake. I still had 334 miles to hike before I reached the Bridge of the Gods, but something made me feel as if I'd arrived. Like that blue water was telling me something I'd walked all this way to know.

This was once Mazama, I kept reminding myself. This was once a mountain that stood nearly 12,000 feet tall and then had its heart removed. This was once a wasteland of lava and pumice and ash. This was once an empty bowl that took hundreds of years to fill. But hard as I tried, I couldn't see them in my mind's eye. Not the mountain or the wasteland or the empty bowl. They simply were not there anymore. There was only the stillness and silence of that water: what a mountain and a wasteland and an empty bowl turned into after the healing began.

17

INTO A PRIMAL GEAR

Oregon was a hopscotch in my mind. I skipped it, spun it, leapt it in my imagination all the way from Crater Lake to the Bridge of the Gods. Eighty-five miles to my next box at a place called Shelter Cove Resort. One hundred and forty-three miles beyond that to my final box at Olallie Lake. Then I'd be on the homestretch to the Columbia River: 106 miles to the town of Cascade Locks, with a stop for a holy-shit-I-can't-believe-I'm-almost-there drink at Timberline Lodge on Mount Hood at the midpoint of that final stretch.

But that still added up to 334 miles to hike.

The good thing, I quickly understood, was that no matter what happened in those 334 miles, there would be fresh berries along the way. Huckleberries and blueberries, salmonberries and blackberries, all of them plump for the picking for miles along the trail. I raked the bushes with my hands as I walked, sometimes stopping to fill my hat, as I made my way leisurely through the Mount Thielsen and Diamond Peak Wildernesses.

It was cold. It was hot. The tree-bark-plucked-dead-chicken flesh on my hips grew another layer. My feet stopped bleeding and blistering, but they still hurt like hell. I hiked a few half days, going only seven or eight miles in an effort to alleviate the pain, but it did little good. They hurt deep. Sometimes as I walked, it felt like they were actually broken, like they belonged in casts instead of boots. Like I'd done something profound and irreversible to them by carrying all this weight over so many miles of punishing terrain. This, and yet I was stronger than ever. Even with that tremendous pack of mine, I was capable of hammering out the big miles now, though at day's end I was still pretty much shattered.

The PCT had gotten easier for me, but that was different from it getting easy.

There were pleasant mornings and lovely swaths of afternoon, ten-mile stretches that I'd glide right over while barely feeling a thing. I loved getting lost in the rhythm of my steps and the click of my ski pole against the trail; the silence and the songs and sentences in my head. I loved the mountains and the rocks and the deer and rabbits that bolted off into the trees and the beetles and frogs that scrambled across the trail. But there would always come the point in each day when I didn't love it anymore, when it was monotonous and hard and my mind shifted into a primal gear that was void of anything but forward motion and I walked until walking became unbearable, until I believed I couldn't walk even one more step, and I stopped and made camp and efficiently did all the tasks that making camp required, all in an effort to get as quickly as possible to the blessed moment when I could collapse, utterly demolished, in my tent.

That's how I felt by the time I dragged into the Shelter Cove Resort: spent and bored with the trail, empty of every single thing except gratitude I was there. I'd hopped another of my squares in the Oregon hopscotch. Shelter Cove Resort was a store surrounded by a rustic set of cabins on a wide green lawn that sat on the shore of a big lake called Odell that was rimmed by green forests. I stepped onto the porch of the store and went inside. There were short rows of snacks and fishing lures and a cooler with drinks inside. I found a bottle of Snapple lemonade, got a bag of chips, and walked to the counter.

"You a PCT hiker?" the man who stood behind the cash register asked me. When I nodded, he gestured to a window at the back of the store. "The post office is closed until tomorrow morning, but you can camp for free at a spot we've got nearby. And there are showers that'll cost you a buck."

I had only ten dollars left—as I'd now come to expect, my stops in Ashland and Crater Lake National Park had been pricier than I'd imagined they'd be—but I knew I had twenty dollars in the box I'd get the next morning, so when I handed the man my money to pay for the drink and the chips, I asked him for some quarters for the shower.

Outside, I cracked open the lemonade and chips and ate them as I made my way toward the little wooden bathhouse the man had pointed out, my anticipation tremendous. When I stepped inside, I was pleased to see that it was a one-person affair. I locked the door behind me, and it was my own domain. I'd have slept inside it if they'd let me. I took off my clothes and looked at myself in the scratched-up mirror. It wasn't only my feet that had been destroyed by the trail, but it seemed my hair had been too—made coarser and strangely doubled in thickness, sprung alive by layers of dried sweat and trail dust, as if I were slowly but surely turning into a cross between Farrah Fawcett in her glory days and Gunga Din at his worst.

I put my coins in the little coin box, stepped into the shower, and luxuriated under the hot water, scrubbing myself with the sliver of soap someone had left there until it dissolved completely in my hands. Afterwards, I dried off with the same bandanna I used to wash my cooking pot and spoon with lake and creek water and dressed again in my dirty clothes. I hoisted Monster on and walked back to the store feeling a thousand times better. There was a wide porch in front with a long bench that ran along its sides. I sat down on it and looked out at Odell Lake while brushing my wet hair with my fingers. Olallie Lake and then Timberline Lodge and then Cascade Locks, I was thinking.

Skip, hop, spin, done.

"Are you Cheryl?" a man asked as he came out of the store. Within a moment, two other men had stepped out behind him. I knew immediately by their sweat-stained T-shirts they were PCT hikers, though they didn't have their packs. They were young and handsome, bearded and tan and dirty, equal parts incredibly muscular and incredibly thin. One was tall. One was blond. One had intense eyes.

I was so very glad I'd taken that shower.

"Yes," I said.

"We've been following you a long way," said the blond one, a smile blooming across his thin face.

"We knew we were going to catch you today," said the one with the intense eyes. "We saw your tracks on the trail."

"We've been reading your notes in the trail register," added the tall one.

"We were trying to figure out how old you'd be," said the blond one.

"How old did you think I'd be?" I asked, smiling like a maniac.

"We thought either about our age or fifty," said the one with the intense eyes.

"I hope you're not disappointed," I said, and we laughed and blushed.

They were Rick, Josh, and Richie, all of them three or four years younger than me. They were from Portland, Eugene, and New Orleans, respectively. They'd all gone to college together at an insular Minnesota liberal arts school an hour outside the Twin Cities.

"I'm from Minnesota!" I exclaimed when they told me, but they knew that already, from my notes in the trail register.

"You don't have a trail name yet?" one of them asked me.

"Not that I know of," I said.

They had a trail name: the Three Young Bucks, which they'd been given by other hikers in southern California, they told me. The name fit. They were three young and buckish men. They'd come all the way from the Mexican border. They hadn't skipped the snow like everyone else. They'd hiked over it, right through it—regardless of the fact that it was a record snow year—and because they'd done so, they were at the back of the Mexico-to-Canada thru-hiker pack, which is how, at this late date, they'd met me. They hadn't met Tom, Doug, Greg, Matt, Albert, Brent, Stacy, Trina, Rex, Sam, Helen, John, or Sarah. They hadn't even stopped in Ashland. They hadn't danced to the Dead or eaten chewable opium or had sex with anyone pressed up against a rock on a beach. They'd just plowed right on through, hiking twenty-some miles a day, gaining on me since the moment I'd leapfrogged north of them when I'd bypassed to Sierra City. They weren't just three young bucks. They were three young extraordinary hiking machines.

Being in their company felt like a holiday.

We walked to the campsite the store set aside for us, where the Three Young Bucks had already ditched their packs, and we cooked dinner and talked and told stories about things both on and off the trail. I liked them immensely. We clicked. They were sweet, cute, funny, kind guys and they made me forget how ruined I'd felt just an hour before. In their honor, I made the freeze-dried raspberry cobbler I'd been carrying for weeks, saving it for a special occasion. When it was done, we ate it with four spoons from my pot and then slept in a row under the stars.

In the morning, we collected our boxes and took them back to our camp to reorganize our packs before heading on. I opened my box and pushed my hands through the smooth ziplock bags of food, feeling for the envelope that would contain my twenty-dollar bill. It had become such a familiar thrill for me now, that envelope with the money inside, but this time I couldn't find it. I dumped everything out and ran my fingers along the folds inside the box, searching for it, but it wasn't there. I didn't know why. It just wasn't. I had six dollars and twelve cents.

"Shit," I said.

"What?" asked one of the Young Bucks.

"Nothing," I said. It was embarrassing to me that I was constantly broke, that no one was standing invisibly behind me with a credit card or a bank account.

I loaded my food into my old blue bag, sick with the knowledge that I'd have to hike 143 miles to my next box with only six dollars and twelve cents in my pocket. At least I didn't need money where I was going, I reasoned, in order to calm myself. I was heading through the heart of Oregon—over Willamette Pass and McKenzie Pass and Santiam Pass, through the Three Sisters and Mount Washington and Mount Jefferson Wildernesses—and there'd be no place to spend my six dollars and twelve cents anyway, right?

I hiked out an hour later with the Three Young Bucks, crisscrossing with them all day; occasionally we stopped together for breaks. I was amazed by what they ate and how they ate it. They were like barbarians loose upon the land, shoving three Snickers bars apiece into their mouths on a single fifteen-minute break, though they were thin as sticks. When they took off their shirts, their ribs showed right through. I'd lost weight too, but not as much as the men—an unjust pattern I'd observed across the board in the other male and female hikers I'd met that summer as well—but I didn't much care anymore whether I was fat or thin. I cared only about getting more food. I was a barbarian too, my hunger voracious and monumental. I'd reached the point where if a character in one of the novels I was reading happened to be eating, I had to skip over the scene because it simply hurt too much to read about what I wanted and couldn't have.

I said goodbye to the Three Young Bucks that afternoon. They were going to push on a few miles past where I planned to camp because in addition to being three young incredible hiking machines, they were eager to reach Santiam Pass, where they'd be getting off the trail for a few days to visit friends and family. While they were living it up, showering and sleeping in actual beds and eating foods I didn't even want to imagine, I'd get ahead of them again and they'd once more be following my tracks.

"Catch me if you can," I said, hoping they would, sad to part ways with them so soon. I camped alone near a pond that evening still aglow from having met them, thinking about the stories they'd told me, as I massaged my feet after dinner. Another one of my blackened toenails was separating from my toe. I gave it a tug and it came all the way off. I tossed it into the grass.

Now the PCT and I were tied. The score was 5–5.

I sat in my tent with my feet propped up on my food bag, reading the book I'd gotten in my box—Maria Dermoût's *The Ten Thousand Things*—until I couldn't keep my eyes open anymore. I turned off my headlamp and lay in the dark. As I dozed off, I heard an owl in a tree directly overhead. *Who-whoo, who-whoo,* it hooted with a call that was at once so strong and so gentle that I woke up.

"Who-whoo," I called back to it, and the owl was silent.

"Who-whoo," I tried again.

"Who-whoo," it replied.

I hiked into the Three Sisters Wilderness, named for the South, North, and Middle Sister mountains in its boundaries. Each of the Sister peaks was more than 10,000 feet high, the third-, fourth-, and fifth-highest peaks in Oregon. They were the crown jewels among a relatively close gathering of volcanic peaks I'd be passing in the coming week, but I couldn't see them yet as I approached from the south on the PCT, singing songs and reciting scraps of poems in my head as I hiked through a tall forest of Douglas firs, white pines, and mountain hemlocks, past lakes and ponds.

A couple of days after I'd said goodbye to the Three Young Bucks, I took a detour a mile off the trail to the Elk Lake Resort, a place mentioned in my guidebook. It was a little lakeside store that catered to fishermen, much like the Shelter Cove Resort, only it had a café that served burgers. I hadn't planned to make the detour, but when I reached the trail junction on the PCT, my endless hunger won out. I arrived just before eleven in the morning. I was the only person in the place aside from the man who worked there. I scanned the menu, did the math, and ordered a cheeseburger and fries and a small Coke; then I sat eating them in a rapture, backed by walls lined with fishing lures. My bill was six dollars and ten cents. For the first time in my entire life, I couldn't leave a tip. To leave the two pennies I had left would've seemed an insult. I pulled out a little rectangle of stamps I had in the ziplock bag that held my driver's license and placed it near my plate.

"I'm sorry—I don't have anything extra, but I left you something else," I said, too embarrassed to say what it was.

The man only shook his head and murmured something I couldn't make out.

I walked down to the empty little beach along Elk Lake with the two pennies in my hand, wondering if I should toss them into the water and make a wish. I decided against it and put them in my shorts pocket, just in case I needed two cents between now and the Olallie Lake ranger station, which was still a sobering hundred miles away. Having nothing more than those two pennies was both horrible and just the slightest bit funny, the way being flat broke at times seemed to me. As I stood there gazing at Elk Lake, it occurred to me for the first time that growing up poor had come in handy. I probably wouldn't have been fearless enough to go on such a trip with so little money if I hadn't grown up without it. I'd always thought of my family's economic standing in terms of what I didn't get: camp and lessons and travel and college tuition and the inexplicable ease that comes when you've got access to a credit card that someone else is paying off. But now I could see the line between this and that—between a childhood in which I saw my mother and stepfather forging ahead over and over again with two pennies in their pocket and my own general sense that I could do it too. Before I left, I hadn't calculated how much my journey would reasonably be expected to cost and saved up that amount plus enough to be my cushion against unexpected expenses. If I'd done that, I wouldn't have been here, eighty-some days out on the PCT, broke, but okay—getting to do what I wanted to do even though a reasonable person would have said I couldn't afford to do it.

I hiked on, ascending to a 6,500-foot viewpoint from which I could see the peaks to the north and east: Bachelor Butte and glaciated Broken Top and—highest of them all—South Sister, which rose to 10,358 feet. My guidebook told me that it was the youngest, tallest, and most symmetrical of the Three Sisters. It was composed of over two dozen different kinds of volcanic rock, but it all looked like one reddish-brown mountain to me, its upper slopes laced with snow. As I hiked into the day, the air shifted and warmed again and I felt as if I were back in California, with the heat and the way the vistas opened up for miles across the rocky and green land.

Now that I was officially among the Three Sisters, I didn't have the trail to myself anymore. On the high rocky meadows I passed day hikers and short-term backpackers and a Boy Scout troop out for an overnight. I stopped to talk to some of them. *Do you have a gun? Are you afraid?* they asked in an echo of what I'd been hearing all summer. *No, no,* I said, laughing a little. I met a pair of men my age who'd served in Iraq during Desert Storm and were still in the army, both of them captains. They were clean-cut, strapping, and handsome, seemingly straight off a recruitment poster. We took a long afternoon break together near a creek, into which they'd placed two cans of beer to cool. It was their last night out on a five-day trip. They'd hauled those two cans the whole time so they could drink them on the final night to celebrate.

They wanted to know everything about my trip. How it felt to walk all those days; the things I'd seen and the people I'd met and what in the hell had happened to my feet. They insisted on lifting my pack and were stupefied to find that it was heavier than either of theirs. They got ready to hike away and I wished them well, still lounging in the sun on the creek's bank.

"Hey, Cheryl," one of them turned to holler once he was almost out of sight on the trail. "We left one of the beers for you in the creek. We did it this way so you can't say no. We *want* you to have it 'cause you're tougher than us."

I laughed and thanked them and went down to the creek to retrieve it, feeling flattered and lifted. I drank the beer that night near Obsidian Falls, which was named for the jet-black glass shards that wondrously cover the trail, making each step an ever-shifting clatter beneath me, as if I were walking across layers upon layers of broken china.

I was less wonder-struck the next day as I walked over McKenzie Pass into the Mount Washington Wilderness, and the trail became rockier still as I crossed the basalt flows of Belknap Crater and Little Belknap. These weren't pretty shiny shards of rock among spring green meadows. Now I was walking over a five-mile swath of black volcanic rocks that ranged in size from baseball to soccer ball, my ankles and knees constantly twisting. The landscape was exposed and desolate, the sun searing relentlessly down on me as I struggled along in the direction of Mount Washington. When I made it to the other side of the craters, I walked gratefully among the trees and realized the crowds had disappeared. I was alone again, just the trail and me.

The following day I hiked over Santiam Pass and crossed into the Mount Jefferson Wilderness, named for the dark and stately summit to my north. I hiked past the rocky multipeaked Three Fingered Jack, which rose like a fractured hand into the sky, and continued hiking into the evening as the sun disappeared behind a blanket of clouds and a thick mist slowly enveloped me. The day had been hot, but within thirty minutes the temperature dropped 20 degrees as the wind picked up and then suddenly stilled. I walked as quickly as I could up the trail, the sweat dripping from my body in spite of the chill, searching for a place to camp. It was precariously close to dark, but there was no place flat or clear enough to pitch my tent. By the time I found a spot near a small pond, it was as if I were inside a cloud, the air eerily still and silent. In the time it took me to pitch my tent and filter a bottle of water with my insufferably slow water purifier, the wind started up again in great violent gasps, whipping the branches of the trees overhead. I'd never been in a mountain storm. I'm not afraid, I reminded myself as I crawled into my tent without eating dinner, feeling too vulnerable outside, though I knew my tent offered little protection. I sat in expectant wonder and fear, bracing for a mighty storm that never came.

An hour after dark, the air went still again and I heard coyotes yipping in the distance, as if they were celebrating the fact that the coast was clear. August had turned to September; the temperatures at night were almost always bitingly cold. I got out of my tent to pee, wearing my hat and gloves. When I scanned the trees with my headlamp, they caught on something, and I froze as the reflection of two bright pairs of eyes gazed back at me.

I never found out whose they were. An instant later they were gone.

The next day was hot and sunny, as if the strange storm the night before had been only a dream. I missed a fork in the trail and later discovered that I was no longer on the PCT but on the Oregon Skyline Trail, which paralleled the PCT roughly a mile to the west. It was an alternate route my guidebook detailed adequately, so I continued on, unworried. The trail would lead back to the PCT the next day. The day after that I'd be at Olallie Lake.

Hop, skip, jump, done.

I walked in a dense forest all afternoon, once rounding a bend to come upon a trio of enormous elks, who ran into the trees with a thunderous clamor of hooves. That evening, only moments after I stopped to make camp near a trailside pond, two bow hunters appeared, walking southbound down the trail.

"You got any water?" one of them burst out immediately.

"We can't drink the pond water, can we?" asked the other, the desperation apparent on his face.

They both looked to be in their midthirties. One man was sandy-haired and wiry, though he had a little belly; the other was a redhead tall and meaty enough to be a linebacker. They both wore jeans with big buck knives hitched onto their belts and enormous backpacks that had bows and arrows slung across them.

"You can drink the pond water, but you need to filter it first," I said.

"We don't have a filter," said the sandy-haired man, taking his pack off and setting it near a boulder that sat in the small clear area between the pond and the trail where I'd planned to camp. I'd only just set down my own pack when they'd appeared.

"You can use mine, if you'd like," I said. I unzipped Monster's pocket, took out my water purifier, and handed it to the sandy-haired man, who took it, walked to the mucky shore of the pond, and squatted down.

"How do you use this thing?" he called to me.

I showed him how to put the intake tube in the water with the float and how to pump the handle against the cartridge. "You'll need your water bottle," I added, but he and his big red-haired friend looked at each other regretfully and told me they didn't have one. They were only up for the day hunting. Their truck was parked on a forest road about three miles away, down a side trail I'd recently crossed. They thought they'd have reached it by now.

"Have you gone all day without drinking?" I asked.

"We brought Pepsi," the sandy-haired man answered. "We each had a six-pack."

"We're headed down to our truck after this, so we only need enough water to get us another bit, but we're both dying of thirst," the red-haired man said.

"Here," I said, going to my pack to pull out the water I had left—about a quarter of one of my bottles. I handed it to the red-haired man and he took a long sip and handed it to his friend, who drank the rest. I felt sorry for them, but I was sorrier that they were here with me. I was exhausted. I ached to take off my boots and change out of my sweaty clothes, pitch my tent, and make my dinner so I could lose myself in *The Ten Thousand Things*. Plus, I got a funny feeling from these men, with their Pepsi and their bows and their big buck knives and the way they'd stormed right up to me. Something that gave me the kind of pause I'd felt way back in that first week on the trail, when I'd been sitting in Frank's truck and I thought that perhaps he meant me harm, only to have him pull out licorice instead. I let my mind settle on that licorice.

"We've got the empty Pepsi cans," said the red-haired man. "We can pump water into your bottle and then pour it into two of those."

The sandy-haired man squatted at the pond's shore with my empty water bottle and my purifier, and the red-haired man took his pack off and dug through it to get a couple of empty Pepsi cans. I stood watching them with my arms wrapped around myself, growing more chilled by the minute. The wet backs of my shorts and T-shirt and bra were now icy cold against my skin.

"It's really hard to pump," the sandy-haired man said after a while.

"You have to give it some muscle," I said. "That's just how my filter is."

"I don't know," he replied. "There's nothing coming out."

I went to him and saw that the float was all the way up near the cartridge and the open end of the intake tube had sunk into the muck at the shallow bottom of the pond. I took the purifier from him, pulled the tube up into the clear water, and tried to pump. It was entirely locked, jammed solid with muck.

"You weren't supposed to let the tube go into the mud like that," I said. "You were supposed to keep it up in the water."

"Shit," he said without apology.

"What are we going to do?" his friend asked. "I've got to get something to drink."

I went to my pack, took out my first aid kit, and pulled out the little bottle of iodine pills I carried. I hadn't used them since I was at that frog-ridden reservoir on Hat Creek Rim and half out of my head with dehydration myself.

"We can use these," I said, grimly understanding that I'd be drinking iodine water until I managed to repair my purifier, if it was even repairable.

"What are they?" asked the sandy-haired man.

"Iodine. You put them in and wait thirty minutes and then the water is safe to drink." I went to the lake and submerged my two bottles in the clearest-looking spot I could reach and put iodine pills in each of them, the men followed suit with their Pepsi cans, and I put a pill in each.

"Okay," I said, looking at my watch. "The water will be good to go at seven ten." I hoped that with that they'd hike away, but they only sat down, settling in.

"So what are you doing out here all by yourself?" asked the sandy-haired man.

"I'm hiking the Pacific Crest Trail," I said, and instantly wished I hadn't. I didn't like the way he was looking me, openly appraising my body.

"All by yourself?"

"Yeah," I said reluctantly, equal parts leery of telling the truth and afraid to concoct a lie that would only make me feel more jangled than I suddenly did.

"I can't believe a girl like you would be all alone up here. You're way too pretty to be out here alone, if you ask me. How long of a trip are you on?" he asked.

"A longish one," I answered.

"I don't believe that a young thing like her could be out here by herself, do you?" he said to his red-haired friend, as if I weren't even there.

"No," I said before the red-haired man could answer him. "Anyone can do it. I mean, it's just—"

"I wouldn't let you come out here if you were my girlfriend, that's for shit shock sure," the red-headed man said.

"She's got a really nice figure, don't she?" the sandy-haired man said. "Healthy, with some soft curves. Just the kind I like."

I made a complacent little sound, a sort of half laugh, though my throat was clotted suddenly with fear. "Well, nice to meet you guys," I said, moving toward Monster. "I'm hiking on a bit farther," I lied, "so I'd better get going."

"We're heading out too. We don't want to run out of light," said the red-haired man, pulling on his pack, and the sandy-haired man did too. I watched them in a fake posture of readying myself to leave, though I didn't want to have to leave. I was tired and thirsty, hungry and chilled. It was heading toward dark and I'd chosen to camp on this pond because my guidebook—which only loosely described this section of the trail because it was not in fact the PCT—implied that this was the last place for a stretch where it was possible to pitch a tent.

When they left, I stood for a while, letting the knot in my throat unclench. I was fine. I was in the clear. I was being a little bit silly. They'd been obnoxious and sexist and they'd ruined my water purifier, but they hadn't done anything to me. They hadn't meant harm. Some guys just didn't know any better. I dumped the things out of my pack, filled my cooking pot with pond water, lit my stove, and set the water to boil. I peeled off my sweaty clothes, pulled out my red fleece leggings and long-sleeved shirt, and dressed in them. I laid out my tarp and was shaking my tent out of its bag when the sandy-haired man reappeared. At the sight of him I knew that everything I'd felt before was correct. That I'd had a reason to be afraid. That he'd come back for me.

"What's going on?" I asked in a falsely relaxed tone, though the sight of him there without his friend terrified me. It was as if I'd finally come across a mountain lion and I'd remembered, against all instinct, not to run. Not to incite him with my fast motions or antagonize him with my anger or arouse him with my fear.

"I thought you were heading on," he said.

"I changed my mind," I said.

"You tried to trick us."

"No, I didn't. I just changed my—"

"You changed your clothes too," he said suggestively, and his words expanded in my gut like a spray of gunshot. My entire body flushed with the knowledge that when I'd taken off my clothes, he'd been nearby, watching me.

"I like your pants," he said with a little smirk. He took off his back-pack and set it down. "Or *leggings,* if that's what they're called."

"I don't know what you're talking about," I said numbly, though I could hardly hear my own words for what felt like a great clanging in my head, which was the realization that my whole hike on the PCT could come to this. That no matter how tough or strong or brave I'd been, how comfortable I'd come to be with being alone, I'd also been lucky, and that if my luck ran out now, it would be as if nothing before it had ever existed, that this one evening would annihilate all those brave days.

"I'm talking about liking your pants," the man said with a touch of irritation. "They look good on you. They show off your hips and legs."

"Please don't say that," I said as unfalteringly as I could.

"What? I'm complimenting you! Can't a guy give a girl a compliment anymore? You should be flattered."

"Thank you," I said in an attempt to pacify him, hating myself for it. My mind went to the Three Young Bucks, who perhaps weren't even back on the trail yet. It went to the world's loudest whistle that no one but the red-haired man would hear. It went to the Swiss army knife too far away in the upper-left-side pocket of my pack. It went to the not-yet-boiling water in the handleless pot on my little stove. And then it landed on the arrows that rose from the top of the sandy-haired man's pack. I could feel the invisible line between those arrows and me like a hot thread. If he tried to do anything to me, I'd get to one of those arrows and stab him in the throat.

"I think you'd better get going," I said evenly. "It'll be getting dark soon." I crossed my arms hard against my chest, acutely aware of the fact that I wasn't wearing a bra.

"It's a free country," he said. "I'll go when I'm ready. I got a right, you know." He picked up his Pepsi can and gently swirled around the water inside.

"What the hell are you doing?" a man's voice called, and a moment later the red-haired man appeared. "I had to hike all the way back up here to find you. I thought you got lost." He looked at me accusingly, as if I were to blame, as if I'd conspired with the sandy-haired man to get him to stay. "We got to go now if we're going to make it back to the truck before dark."

"You be careful out here," the sandy-haired man said to me, pulling on his pack.

"Bye," I said very quietly, wanting neither to answer him nor to rile him by not answering.

"Hey. It's seven ten," he said. "It's safe to drink the water now." He lifted his Pepsi can in my direction and made a toast. "Here's to a young girl all alone in the woods," he said, and took a sip and then turned to follow his friend down the trail.

I stood for a while the way I had the first time they left, letting all the knots of fear unclench. Nothing had happened, I told myself. I am perfectly okay. He was just a creepy, horny, not-nice man, and now he's gone.

But then I shoved my tent back into my pack, turned off my stove, dumped the almost-boiling water out into the grass, and swished the pot in the pond so it cooled. I took a swig of my iodine water and crammed my water bottle and my damp T-shirt, bra, and shorts back into my pack. I lifted Monster, buckled it on, stepped onto the trail, and started walking northward in the fading light. I walked and I walked, my mind shifting into a primal gear that was void of anything but forward motion, and I walked until walking became unbearable, until I believed I couldn't walk even one more step.

And then I ran.

18

QUEEN OF THE PCT

It was raining when I woke as the light seeped into the sky the next morning. I was lying in my tent in the shallow trough of the trail, its two-foot width the only flat spot I could find in the dark the night before. It had begun to rain at midnight, it had rained all night long, and as I walked through the morning, the rain came and went. I thought about what had happened with the men, or almost happened or was never really going to happen, playing it over in my mind, feeling sick and shaky, but by noon it was behind me and I was back on the PCT— the detour I'd inadvertently taken having wended its way up to the trail.

Water fell from the sky and dripped from the branches, streaming down the gully of the trail. I walked beneath the enormous trees, the forest canopy high above me, the bushes and low-growing plants that edged the trail soaking me as I brushed past. Wet and miserable as it was, the forest was magical—Gothic in its green grandiosity, both luminous and dark, so lavish in its fecundity that it looked surreal, as if I were walking through a fairy tale rather than the actual world.

It rained and rained and rained off and on through that day and all through the next. It was still raining in the early evening, when I reached the shores of the 240-acre Olallie Lake. I walked past the closed ranger station feeling a deep sense of relief, clomping over the mud and wet grass through a small cluster of picnic tables to the little collection of dark wooden buildings that constituted the Olallie Lake Resort. Until I'd hiked through Oregon, I'd had a profoundly different idea of what the word *resort* might suggest. No one was in sight. The ten primitive cabins scattered near the lake's shore all looked empty, and the tiny store amid the cabins was closed for the night.

It began to rain again as I stood under a lodgepole pine near the store. I pulled the hood of my raincoat up over my head and looked at the lake. The grand peak of Mount Jefferson supposedly loomed to the south and the squat rise of Olallie Butte sat to the north, but I couldn't see either of them, obscured as they were by the growing dark and the fog. Without the mountain views, the pines and wide lake reminded me of the northwoods of Minnesota. The air felt like Minnesota too. It was a week past Labor Day; autumn hadn't arrived yet, but it was close. Everything felt abandoned and forlorn. I dug inside my raincoat, pulled out the pages of my guidebook, and read about a place to camp nearby— a site beyond the ranger station that overlooked Head Lake, Olallie's much smaller neighbor.

I made camp there and cooked my dinner in the rain, then crawled into my tent and lay in my damp sleeping bag, dressed in my damp clothes. The batteries of my headlamp had gone dead, so I couldn't read. Instead, I lay listening to the spatter of raindrops against the taut nylon a few feet from my head.

There would be fresh batteries in my box tomorrow. There would be Hershey's chocolate kisses that I'd dole out to myself over the next week. There would be the last batch of dehydrated meals and bags of nuts and seeds that had gone stale. The thought of these things was both a torture and a comfort to me. I curled into myself, trying to keep my sleeping bag away from the edges of my tent in case it leaked, but I couldn't fall asleep. Dismal as it was, I felt a spark of light travel through me that had everything to do with the fact that I'd be done hiking the trail in about a week. I'd be in Portland, living like a normal person again. I'd get a job waiting tables in the evenings and I'd write during the day. Ever since the idea of living in Portland had settled in my mind, I'd spent hours imagining how it would feel to be back in the world where food and music, wine and coffee could be had.

Of course, heroin could be had there too, I thought. But the thing was, I didn't want it. Maybe I never really had. I'd finally come to understand what *it* had been: a yearning for a way out, when actually what I had wanted to find was a way in. I was there now. Or close.

"I've got a box," I called to the ranger the next morning, chasing him as he began to drive away in his truck.

He stopped and rolled down his window. "You Cheryl?"

I nodded. "I have a box," I repeated, still buried inside my putrid rain gear.

"Your friends told me about you," he said as he got out of his truck. "The married couple."

I blinked and pushed my hood off. "Sam and Helen?" I asked, and the ranger nodded. The thought of them sent a surge of tenderness through me. I pulled the hood back up over my head as I followed the ranger into the garage that was connected to the ranger station, which was connected to what appeared to be his living quarters.

"I'm going to town, but I'll be back later this afternoon, if you need anything," he said, and handed me my box and three letters. He was brown-haired and mustached, late thirties, I guessed.

"Thanks," I said, hugging the box and letters.

It was still raining and wretched outside, so I walked to the little store, where I bought a cup of coffee from the old man who worked the cash register on the promise I'd pay for it once I opened my box. I sat drinking it in a chair by the woodstove and read my letters. The first was from Aimee, the second from Paul, the third—much to my surprise—from Ed, the trail angel I'd met way back in Kennedy Meadows. *If you get this, it means you've made it, Cheryl. Congrats!* he wrote. I was so touched to read his words that I laughed out loud, and the old man by the cash register looked up.

"Good news from home?" he asked.

"Yeah," I said. "Something like that."

I opened my box and found not only the envelope that held my twenty dollars, but another envelope that held another twenty dollars— the one that was meant to have been in my box at the Shelter Cove Resort, which I must have mispacked months before. It was all the same now. I'd made it through with my two pennies, and my reward was that I was now rich with forty dollars and two cents. I paid for my coffee, bought a packaged cookie, and asked the man if there were any showers, but he only shook his head as I looked at him, crestfallen. It was a resort without showers or a restaurant, there was a driving, drizzling rain, and it was something like 55 degrees out.

I refilled my coffee cup and thought about whether I should hike on that day or not. There wasn't much reason to stay, and yet going back out to walk in the woods with all my wet things was not only dispiriting but possibly dangerous—the inescapable wet chill put me at risk of hypothermia. At least here I could sit in the warmth of the store. I'd been alternately sweating hot or freezing cold for going on three days. I was tired, both physically and psychologically. I'd hiked a few half days, but I hadn't had a full day off since Crater Lake. Plus, much as I looked forward to reaching the Bridge of the Gods, I wasn't in any hurry. I was close enough now that I knew I'd easily make it by my birthday. I could take my time.

"We don't have showers, young lady," said the old man, "but I can give you dinner tonight, if you'd like to join me and a couple of the staff at five."

"Dinner?" My decision to stay was made.

I returned to my camp and did my best to dry my things out in between rain showers. I heated a pot of water and hunched naked near it, bathing myself with my bandanna. I took apart my water purifier, shook out the muck that the sandy-haired man had sucked up into it, and ran clean water through my pump so I could use it again. A few minutes before I was going to walk to the small building where I'd been instructed to go for dinner, the Three Young Bucks appeared, soaking wet and dreamier than ever. I literally leapt with joy at the sight of them. I explained to them that I was off to have dinner and they could probably have dinner with me too and I'd be right back to get them if they could, but when I reached the little building and inquired, the woman in charge was unmoved by their arrival.

"We don't have enough food," she said. I felt guilty about sitting down to eat, but I was starving. Dinner was family fare, the kind I'd eaten at a thousand potlucks as a kid in Minnesota. Cheddar-cheese-topped casserole with ground beef, canned corn, and potatoes with an iceberg lettuce salad. I filled my plate and ate it in about five bites and sat politely waiting for the woman to cut the yellow cake with white frosting that sat enticingly on a side table. When she did, I ate a piece and then returned to discreetly take another—the biggest piece in the pan—and folded it into a paper napkin and put it in the pocket of my raincoat.

"Thank you," I said. "I'd better get back to my friends."

I walked across the wet grass, holding the cake very carefully inside my coat. It was only 5:30, but it was so dark and dreary it might as well have been the middle of the night.

"There you are. I was looking for you," a man called to me. It was the ranger who'd given me my box and letters that morning. He was blotting his lips with a dish towel. "I'm talking funny," he slurred as I approached him. "I had some surgery on my mouth today."

I pulled my hood up over my head because it had started to rain again. He seemed slightly drunk in addition to having the troubles with his mouth.

"So how about you come to my place for a drink now? You can get out of the rain," he said in his garbled voice. "My place is right there, the other half of the station. I got a fire going in the fireplace and I'll mix you up a nice cocktail or two."

"Thanks, but I can't. My friends just got here and we're all camped," I said, gesturing to the rise beyond the road, behind which my tent and probably by now the tents of the Three Young Bucks were erected. As I did so, I had a precise image of what the Three Young Bucks were likely doing at that very moment, the way they'd be crouched beneath their raincoats in the rain, trying to eat their loathsome dinners, or sitting alone in their tents because there was simply no other place to be, and then I thought of that warm fire and the booze and how if the men went with me to drink with the ranger I could use them to help me dodge whatever else he had in mind. "But maybe," I wavered, as the ranger drooled and then blotted his mouth. "I mean, as long as it's okay to bring my friends."

I returned with the cake to our camp. The Three Young Bucks were all zipped into their tents. "I have cake!" I called, and they came and stood around me and ate it with their fingers out of my hands, splitting it among themselves in the easy, unspoken way they'd honed over months of endless deprivation and unity.

In the nine days since I'd said goodbye to them, it seemed as if we'd grown closer, more familiar, as if we'd been together in that time instead of apart. They were still the Three Young Bucks to me, but they'd also begun to differentiate in my mind. Richie was hilarious and a little bit strange, with a dark edge of mystery I found compelling. Josh was sweet and smart, more reserved than the others. Rick was funny and incisive, kind and a great conversationalist. As I stood there with the three of them eating cake out of my hands, I realized that though I had a little crush on all of them, I had a bigger crush on Rick. It was an absurd crush, I knew. He was nearly four years younger than me and we were at an age when those nearly four years mattered, when the gap between what he had done and what I had done was large enough that I was more like a big sister than I was someone who should be thinking about being alone with him in his tent—so I didn't think about it, but I couldn't deny that to an increasing degree I got a little fluttery feeling inside me every time Rick's eyes met mine, and I also couldn't deny that I could see in his eyes that he got a little fluttery feeling too.

"I'm sorry about dinner," I said, after explaining what had happened. "Did you guys eat?" I asked, feeling guilty, and they all nodded, licking the frosting from their fingers.

"Was it good?" asked Richie in his New Orleans accent, which only increased his appeal, in spite of my crush on Rick.

"It was just a casserole and salad."

They all three looked at me like I'd injured them.

"But that's why I brought you the cake!" I cried from beneath my rain hood. "Plus, I have something else that might be of interest. A different sort of treat. The ranger here invited me to his place for a drink and I told him I'd come only if you guys came too. I should warn you that he's a little bit odd—he had mouth surgery today or something, so I think he's on painkillers and a bit drunk already, but he has a fireplace with a fire in it and he has drinks and it's *inside*. Do you guys want to go?"

The Three Young Bucks gave me their barbarians-loose-upon-the-land look and about two minutes later we were knocking on the ranger's door.

"There you are," he slurred as he let us in. "I was beginning to think you were going to stand me up."

"These are my friends Rick, Richie, and Josh," I said, though the ranger only looked at them with open disdain, his dish towel still pressed to his lips. It wasn't true he'd been entirely agreeable about my bringing them along. He'd only barely consented when I'd said it was all of us or none.

The Three Young Bucks filed in and sat in a row on the couch in front of the blazing fire, propping their wet boots up on the stone hearth.

"You want a drink, good-looking?" the ranger asked me as I followed him into the kitchen. "My name's Guy, by the way. Don't know if I told you that before or not."

"Nice to meet you, Guy," I said, trying to stand in a way that suggested I wasn't really with him in the kitchen so much as I was bridging the space between us and the men by the fire and that we were all one big happy party.

"I'm making something special for you."

"For me? Thanks," I said. "Do you guys want a drink?" I called to the Three Young Bucks. They answered in the affirmative as I watched Guy fill one gigantic plastic tumbler with ice and then pour various kinds of liquor into it and top it off with fruit punch from a can he took from the fridge.

"It's like a suicide," I said when he handed it to me. "That's what we used to call this kind of drink when I was in college, where you put all different kinds of liquor in it."

"Try it and see if you think it's good," said Guy.

I took a sip. It tasted like hell, but in a nice way. It tasted better than sitting out in the cold rain. "Yum!" I said too cheerfully. "And these guys—Rick and Richie and Josh—they'd like one too, I think. Would you guys like one?" I asked again as I bolted to the couch.

"Sure," they all said in a chorus, though Guy didn't acknowledge it. I handed Rick the tumbler of booze and wedged myself in beside him, all four of us in a row in the plush wonderland of the fireside couch without an inch to spare, the side of Rick's lovely body plastered against mine; the fire like our own personal sun before us, baking us dry.

"You want to talk about suicide, darling, I'll tell you about suicide," Guy said, coming to stand before me and lean against the stone mantel. Rick drank from the tumbler and handed it to Josh on the other side of him, then Josh took a sip and handed it to Richie on the far end. "We got some dealings with suicide around here, unfortunately. Now that's where this job gets interesting," Guy said, his eyes growing animated, his face hidden behind the dish towel from his mustache down. The tumbler made its way slowly back to me; I took a sip and handed it back to Rick, and so on, like we were smoking a gigantic liquid joint. As we drank, Guy told us in great detail about the scene he'd come across one afternoon when a man had blown his brains out in a Port-a-Potty in the woods nearby.

"I mean just absolutely brains fucking everywhere," he said through the towel. "More than you'd imagine. Think of the most disgusting thing that you can even picture, Cheryl, and then picture that." He stood staring only at me, as if the Three Young Bucks weren't even in the room. "Not just brains. But blood too and pieces of his skull and flesh. Just all over. Splattered all over the walls inside this thing."

"I can't even picture it," I said as I shook the ice in my tumbler. The Bucks had left me with sole custody of it now that it was empty.

"You want another one, hot stuff?" Guy asked. I handed it to him, and he took it into the kitchen. I turned to the men and we all looked at one another with meaningful expressions and then burst out laughing as quietly as we could while basking in the glow of the fire.

"Now there's this other time I got to tell you about," said Guy, returning with my drink. "Only this time it was murder. Homicide. And it wasn't brains, but blood. *Gallons* of blood, I mean *BUCKETS* of blood, Cheryl."

And so it went, all through the evening.

Afterwards, we walked back to our camp and stood around in a circle near our tents talking half drunk in the dark until it started to rain again and we had no choice but to disperse and say goodnight. When I got into my tent, I saw a puddle had formed at the far end. By morning it was a small lake; my sleeping bag was soaked. I shook it out and looked around the campsite for a place to drape it, but it was useless. It would only get wetter as the rain continued to pour down. I carried it with me when the Three Young Bucks and I walked to the store, holding it near the woodstove as we drank our coffee.

"So we came up with a trail name for you," said Josh.

"What is it?" I asked reluctantly from behind the scrim of my drenched blue sleeping bag, as if it could protect me from whatever they might say.

"The Queen of the PCT," said Richie.

"Because people always want to give you things and do things for you," added Rick. "They never give us anything. They don't do a damn thing for us, in fact."

I lowered my sleeping bag and looked at them, and we all laughed. All the time that I'd been fielding questions about whether I was afraid to be a woman alone—the assumption that a woman alone would be preyed upon—I'd been the recipient of one kindness after another. Aside from the creepy experience with the sandy-haired guy who'd jammed my water purifier and the couple who'd booted me from the campground in California, I had nothing but generosity to report. The world and its people had opened their arms to me at every turn.

As if on cue, the old man leaned over the cash register. "Young lady, I wanted to tell you that if you want to stay another night and dry out, we'd let you have one of these cabins for next to nothing."

I turned to the Three Young Bucks with a question in my eyes.

Within fifteen minutes, we'd moved into our cabin, hanging our sopped sleeping bags over the dusty rafters. The cabin was one wood-paneled room taken up almost entirely by two double beds that sat on antediluvian metal frames that squeaked if you so much as leaned on the bed.

Once we'd settled in, I walked back to the store in the rain to buy snacks. When I stepped inside, Lisa was standing there by the woodstove. Lisa, who lived in Portland. Lisa, who'd been mailing my boxes all summer long. Lisa, whom I'd be moving in with in a week.

"Hello!" she half screamed while we grabbed each other. "I knew you'd be here right about now," she said once we'd recovered from the shock. "We decided to drive up and see." She turned to her boyfriend, Jason, and I shook his hand—I'd met him briefly in the days before I'd left Portland for the PCT, when they'd first begun dating. It felt surreal to see people I knew from my old familiar world and a bit sad too. I was both happy and disappointed to see them: their presence seemed to hasten the end of my trip, underlining the fact that though it would take me a week to get there, Portland was only ninety miles away by car.

By evening we all piled into Jason's pickup truck and drove along the winding forest roads to Bagby Hot Springs. Bagby is a version of paradise in the woods: a trilevel series of wooden decks that hold tubs of various configurations on a steaming hot creek a mile-and-a-half walk back from a roadside parking area in the Mount Hood National Forest. It's not a business or a resort or a retreat center. It's just a place anyone can go for no charge at any hour of the day or night to soak in the natural waters beneath an ancient canopy of Douglas firs, hemlocks, and cedars. Its existence seemed more surreal to me than Lisa standing in the Olallie Lake store.

We practically had the place to ourselves. The Three Young Bucks and I walked to the lower deck, where there were long hand-hewn tubs as big as canoes made from hollowed-out cedars beneath a high airy wooden ceiling. We undressed as the rain fell gently down on the lush branches of the big trees that surrounded us, my eyes skating over their naked bodies in the half light. Rick and I got into neighboring tubs and turned on the spigots, moaning as the hot, mineral-rich water rose around us. I remembered my bath in that hotel in Sierra City before I hiked up into the snow. It seemed fitting that I was here now, with only a week left to go, like I'd survived a hard and beautiful dream.

I'd ridden up front with Lisa and Jason on the drive to Bagby, but on the return trip to Olallie Lake, I climbed in back with the Three Young Bucks, feeling clean and warm and blissed out as I clambered onto the futon that covered the truck's bed.

"That futon is yours, by the way," said Lisa, before she closed the camper hatch behind us. "I took it out of your truck and put it in here in case we decided to spend the night."

"Welcome to my bed, boys," I said in a mockingly lascivious tone to cover for the dislocation I felt at the prospect that this really was my bed—the futon I'd shared with Paul for years. The thought of him dimmed my ecstatic mood. I hadn't yet opened the letter he'd sent me, in contrast to the customary envelope-ripping glee with which I usually greeted mail. The sight of his familiar handwriting had given me pause this time. I'd decided to read it once I was back on the trail, perhaps because I knew that this would prevent me from mailing off an immediate reply, from saying rash and passionate things that weren't true any longer. "I'll always be married to you in my heart," I'd told him on the day we'd filed for divorce. It had been only five months ago, but already I doubted what I'd said. My love for him was indisputable, but my allegiance to him wasn't. We were no longer married, and as I settled alongside the Three Young Bucks into the bed I used to share with Paul, I felt a kind of acceptance of that, a kind of clarity where there'd been so much uncertainty.

The four of us lay wedged in across the futon's expanse as the truck bumped over the dark roads—me, Rick, Josh, and Richie, in that order across the truck's bed. There wasn't an inch to spare, just as it had been on the deranged ranger's couch the night before. The side of Rick's body was pressed against mine, ever so slightly tilted in my direction and away from Josh. The sky had finally cleared and I could see the almost full moon.

"Look," I said just to Rick, gesturing toward the window of the camper at the sky. We spoke quietly of the moons we'd seen on the trail and where we'd been when we'd seen them and of the trail ahead.

"You'll have to give me Lisa's number so we can hang out in Portland," he said. "I'll be living there too after I finish the trail."

"Absolutely, we'll hang out," I said.

"For sure," he said, and looked at me in this delicate way that made me swoon, though I realized that in spite of the fact that I liked him perhaps a thousand times more than a good number of the people I'd slept with, I wasn't going to lay a hand on him, no matter how deeply I longed to. Laying a hand on him was as far away as the moon. And it wasn't just because he was younger than me or because two of his friends were in bed with us, pressed up against his very back. It was because for once it was finally enough for me to simply lie there in a restrained and chaste rapture beside a sweet, strong, sexy, smart, good man who was probably never meant to be anything but my friend. For once I didn't ache for a companion. For once the phrase *a woman with a hole in her heart* didn't thunder into my head. That phrase, it didn't even live for me anymore.

"I'm really glad I met you," I said.

"Me too," said Rick. "Who wouldn't be glad to meet the Queen of the PCT?"

I smiled at him and turned to gaze out the little window at the moon again, intensely aware of the side of his body so warm against mine as we lay together in an exquisitely conscious silence.

"Very nice," said Rick after a while. *"Very nice,"* he repeated, with more emphasis the second time.

"What is?" I asked, turning to him, though I knew.

"Everything," he said.

And it was true.

19

THE DREAM OF A COMMON LANGUAGE

The next morning the sky was clear blue, the sun shimmering on Olallie Lake, views of Mount Jefferson framed perfectly to the south and Olallie Butte to the north. I sat on one of the picnic tables near the ranger station, packing Monster for the final stretch of my hike. The Three Young Bucks had left at dawn, in a hurry to reach Canada before the High Cascades of Washington were snowed in, but I wasn't going that far. I could take my time.

Guy appeared with a box in his hands, sober now, breaking me out of my contemplative trance. "I'm glad I caught you before you left. This just came," he said.

I took the box from him and glanced at the return address. It was from my friend Gretchen. "Thanks for everything," I said to Guy as he walked away. "For the drinks the other night and the hospitality."

"Stay safe out there," he said, and disappeared around the corner of the building. I ripped open the box and gasped when I saw what was inside: a dozen fancy chocolates in shiny twisted wrappers and a bottle of red wine. I ate some chocolate immediately while pondering the wine. Much as I wanted to open it that night on the trail, I wasn't willing to lug the empty bottle all the way to Timberline Lodge. I packed up the last of my things, strapped on Monster, picked up the wine and the empty box, and began to walk to the ranger station.

"Cheryl!" a voice boomed, and I turned.

"There you are! There you *are*! I caught you! *I caught you!*" shouted a man as he came at me. I was so startled, I dropped the box on the grass as the man shook his fists in the air and let out a joyous hoot that I recognized but couldn't place. He was young and bearded and golden, different and yet the same as the last time I'd seen him. "Cheryl!" he yelled again as he practically tackled me into an embrace.

It was as if time moved in slow motion from the moment that I didn't know who he was to the moment that I did know, but I couldn't take it into my consciousness until he had me all the way in his arms and I yelled, "DOUG!"

"Doug, Doug, Doug!" I kept saying.

"Cheryl, Cheryl, Cheryl!" he said to me.

Then we went silent and stepped back and looked at each other.

"You've lost weight," he said.

"So have you," I said.

"You're all broken in now," he said.

"I know! So are you."

"I have a beard," he said, tugging on it. "I have so much to tell you."

"Me too! Where's Tom?"

"He's a few miles back. He'll catch up later."

"Did you make it through the snow?" I asked.

"We did some, but it got to be too intense and we came down and ended up bypassing."

I shook my head, still shocked he was standing there. I told him about Greg getting off the trail and asked him about Albert and Matt.

"I haven't heard anything about them since we saw them last." He looked at me and smiled, his eyes sparkling to life. "We read your notes in the register all summer long. They motivated us to crank. We wanted to catch up to you."

"I was just leaving now," I said. I bent to retrieve the empty box I'd dropped in the excitement. "Another minute and I'd have been gone and who knows if you'd have caught me."

"I'd have caught you," he said, and laughed in that golden boy way that I remembered so vividly, though it was altered now too. He was grittier than he'd been before, slightly more shaken, as if he'd aged a few years in the past months. "You want to hang out while I organize my things and we can leave together?"

"Sure," I said without hesitation. "I've got to hike those last days before I get into Cascade Locks alone—you know, just to finish like I started—but let's hike together to Timberline Lodge."

"Holy shit, Cheryl." He pulled me in for another hug. "I can't believe we're here together. Hey, you still have that black feather I gave you?" He reached to touch its ragged edge.

"It was my good luck charm," I said.

"What's with the wine?" he asked, pointing to the bottle in my hand.

"I'm going to give it to the ranger," I replied, lifting it high. "I don't want to carry it all the way to Timberline."

"Are you insane?" Doug asked. "Give me that bottle."

We opened it that night at our camp near the Warm Springs River with the corkscrew on my Swiss army knife. The day had warmed into the low seventies, but the evening was cool, the crisp edge of summer turning to autumn everywhere around us. The leaves on the trees had thinned almost undetectably; the tall stalks of wildflowers bent down onto themselves, plumped with rot. Doug and I built a fire as our dinners cooked and then sat eating from our pots and passing the wine back and forth, drinking straight from the bottle since neither of us had a cup. The wine and the fire and being in Doug's company again after all this time felt like a rite of passage, like a ceremonial marking of the end of my journey.

After a while, we each turned abruptly toward the darkness, hearing the yip of coyotes more near than far.

"That sound always makes my hair stand on end," Doug said. He took a sip from the bottle and handed it to me. "This wine's really good."

"It is," I agreed, and took a swig. "I heard coyotes a lot this summer," I said.

"And you weren't afraid, right? Isn't that what you told yourself?"

"It is what I told myself," I said. "Except every once in while," I added. "When I was."

"Me too." He reached over and rested his hand on my shoulder and I put my hand on his and squeezed it. He felt like a brother of mine, but not at all like my actual brother. He seemed like someone I'd always know even if I never saw him again.

When we were done with the wine, I went to Monster and pulled out the ziplock bag that held my books. "You need something to read?" I asked Doug, holding *The Ten Thousand Things* up to him, but he shook his head. I'd finished it a few days before, though I hadn't been able to burn it because of the rain. Unlike most of the other books I'd read on my hike, I'd already read *The Ten Thousand Things* when I'd packed it into my resupply box months before. A densely lyrical novel set on the Moluccan Islands in Indonesia, it had been written in Dutch and published to critical acclaim in 1955, but mostly forgotten now. I'd never met anyone who'd read the book, aside from the college writing professor who'd assigned it to me in the fiction workshop I was enrolled in when my mother got sick. The title hadn't been lost on me as I'd sat dutifully reading it in my mother's hospital room, attempting to shut out my fear and sorrow by forcing my mind to focus on passages I hoped to refer to in the following week's class discussion, but it was useless. I couldn't think of anything but my mom. Besides, I already knew about the ten thousand things. They were all the named and unnamed things in the world and together they added up to less than how much my mother loved me. And me her. So when I was packing for the PCT, I'd decided to give the book another chance. I hadn't had any trouble focusing this time. From the very first page, I understood. Each of Dermoût's sentences came at me like a soft knowing dagger, depicting a far-off land that felt to me like the blood of all the places I used to love.

"I think I'm going to turn in," said Doug, holding the empty bottle of wine. "Tom'll probably catch up to us tomorrow."

"I'll put the fire out," I said.

When he was gone, I ripped the pages of *The Ten Thousand Things* from their gummy paperback binding and set them into the fire in thin clumps, prodding them with a stick until they burned. As I stared at the flames, I thought about Eddie, the same as I did just about every time I sat by a fire. It had been he who'd taught me how to build one. Eddie was the one who'd taken me camping the first time. He'd shown me how to pitch a tent and tie a knot in a rope. From him, I'd learned how to open a can with a jackknife and paddle a canoe and skip a rock on the surface of a lake. In the three years after he fell in love with my mother, he'd taken us camping and canoeing along the Minnesota and St. Croix and Namekagon rivers practically every weekend from June to September, and after we'd moved north onto the land my family had bought with the proceeds from his broken back, he'd taught me even more about the woods.

There's no way to know what makes one thing happen and not another. What leads to what. What destroys what. What causes what to flourish or die or take another course. But I was pretty certain as I sat there that night that if it hadn't been for Eddie, I wouldn't have found myself on the PCT. And though it was true that everything I felt for him sat like a boulder in my throat, this realization made the boulder sit ever so much lighter. He hadn't loved me well in the end, but he'd loved me well when it mattered.

When *The Ten Thousand Things* had turned to ash, I pulled out the other book in my ziplock bag. It was *The Dream of a Common Language*. I'd carried it all this way, though I hadn't opened it since that first night on the trail. I hadn't needed to. I knew what it said. Its lines had run all summer through the mix-tape radio station in my head, fragments from various poems or sometimes the title of the book itself, which was also a line from a poem: *the dream of a common language*. I opened the book and paged through it, leaning forward so I could see the words by the firelight. I read a line or two from a dozen or so of the poems, each of them so familiar they gave me a strange sort of comfort. I'd chanted those lines silently through the days while I hiked. Often, I didn't know exactly what they meant, yet there was another way in which I knew their meaning entirely, as if it were all before me and yet out of my grasp, their meaning like a fish just beneath the surface of the water that I tried to catch with my bare hands—so close and present and belonging to me—until I reached for it and it flashed away.

I closed the book and looked at its beige cover. There was no reason not to burn this book too.

Instead, I only hugged it to my chest.

We reached Timberline Lodge a couple of days later. By then it wasn't just Doug and me. Tom had caught up to us, and we'd also been joined by two women—a twenty-something ex-couple who were hiking Oregon and a small section of Washington. The five of us hiked together in duos and trios of various formations, or sometimes all of us in a row, making a leisurely party of it, the vibe festive because of our numbers and the cool sunny days. On our long breaks we played hacky sack and skinny-dipped in an icy-cold lake, incited the wrath of a handful of hornets and then ran from them while we laughed and screamed. By the time we reached Timberline Lodge 6,000 feet up on the south flank of Mount Hood, we were like a tribe, bonded in that way I imagined kids felt when they spent a week together at summer camp.

It was midafternoon when we arrived. In the lounge the five of us took over a pair of couches that faced each other across a low wooden table and ordered terribly expensive sandwiches, then afterwards sipped coffees spiked with Baileys while we played poker and rummy five hundred with a deck of cards we borrowed from the bartender. The slope of Mount Hood rose above us just outside the lodge's windows. At 11,240 feet, it's Oregon's highest mountain—a volcano like all the others I'd passed since I entered the Cascade Range south of Lassen Peak way back in July—but this, the last of the major mountains I'd traverse on my hike, felt like the most important, and not only because I was sitting on its very haunches. The sight of it had become familiar to me, its imposing grandeur visible from Portland on clear days. Once I reached Mount Hood I realized I felt ever so slightly like I was home. Portland—where I'd never technically lived, in spite of all that had happened in the eight or nine months I'd spent there over the past two years—was only sixty miles away.

From afar, the sight of Mount Hood had never failed to take my breath away, but up close it was different, the way everything is. It was less coolly majestic, at once more ordinary and more immeasurable in its gritty authority. The landscape outside the north windows of the lodge was not the glistening white peak one sees from miles away, but a grayish and slightly barren slope dotted with a few scraggly stands of pines and a smattering of lupine and asters that grew among the rocks. The natural landscape was punctuated by a ski lift that led to the crusty swath of snow farther up. I was happy to be protected from the mountain for a time, ensconced inside the glorious lodge, a wonderland in the rough. It's a grand stone-and-wood structure that was hand-hewn by Works Progress Administration workers in the mid-1930s. Everything about the place has a story. The art on the walls, the architecture of the building, the handwoven fabrics that cover the furniture—each piece carefully crafted to reflect the history, culture, and natural resources of the Pacific Northwest.

I excused myself from the others and walked slowly through the lodge, then stepped out onto a wide south-facing patio. It was a clear, sunny day and I could see for more than a hundred miles. The view included so many of the mountains I'd hiked past—two of the Three Sisters and Mount Jefferson and Broken Finger.

Hop, skip, spin, done, I thought. I was here. I was almost there. But I wasn't done. I still had fifty miles to walk before I reached the Bridge of the Gods.

The next morning I said goodbye to Doug and Tom and the two women and I hiked away alone, climbing up the short steep path that went from the lodge to the PCT. I passed under the ski lift and edged my way north and west around the shoulder of Mount Hood on a trail of what seemed to be demolished rock, worn down by the harsh winters into a pebbly sand. By the time I crossed into the Mount Hood Wilderness twenty minutes later, I had entered the forest again and I felt the silence descend on me.

It felt good to be alone. It felt spectacular. It was the middle of September, but the sun was warm and bright, the sky bluer than ever. The trail opened up into miles-wide views and then closed around me into dense woods before opening back up again. I walked for ten miles without pause, crossed the Sandy River, and stopped to sit on a small flat shelf looking over it from the other side. Nearly all the pages of *The Pacific Crest Trail, Volume 2: Oregon and Washington* were gone by now. What was left of my guidebook was folded into the pocket of my shorts. I took out the pages and read them again, letting myself go all the way to the end. I was thrilled by the prospect of reaching Cascade Locks and also saddened by it. I didn't know how living outdoors and sleeping on the ground in a tent each night and walking alone through the wilderness all day almost every day had come to feel like my normal life, but it had. It was the idea of not doing it that scared me.

I went to the river and squatted down and splashed my face. It was narrow and shallow here, so late in the summer and so high up, barely bigger than a stream. Where was my mother? I wondered. I'd carried her so long, staggering beneath her weight.

On the other side of the river, I let myself think.

And something inside of me released.

In the days that followed, I passed Ramona Falls and skirted in and out of the Columbia Wilderness. I caught views of Mounts St. Helens and Rainier and Adams far to the north. I reached Wahtum Lake and turned off the PCT and onto the alternate route the authors of my guidebook recommended, which would lead me down to Eagle Creek and into the Columbia River gorge and eventually to the river itself that ran alongside the town of Cascade Locks.

Down, down, down I went on that last full day of hiking, descending four thousand feet in just over sixteen miles, the creeks and streams and trailside seeps I crossed and paralleled going down and down too. I could feel the river pulling me like a great magnet below and to the north. I could feel myself coming to the end of things. I stopped to spend the night on the banks of Eagle Creek. It was five o'clock and I was only six miles away from Cascade Locks. I could have been in town by dark, but I didn't want to finish my trip that way. I wanted to take my time, to see the river and the Bridge of the Gods in the bright light of day.

That evening I sat next to Eagle Creek watching the water rush over the rocks. My feet were killing me from the long descent. Even after all this way, with my body now stronger than it had ever been and would likely ever be, hiking on the PCT still hurt. New blisters had formed on my toes in places that had gone soft from the relatively few extreme descents throughout Oregon. I put my fingers delicately to them, soothing them with my touch. Another toenail looked like it was finally going to come off. I gave it a gentle tug and it was in my hand, my sixth. I had only four intact toenails left.

The PCT and I weren't tied anymore. The score was 4–6, advantage trail.

I slept on my tarp, not wanting to shelter myself on that last night, and woke before dawn to watch the sun rise over Mount Hood. It was really over, I thought. There was no way to go back, to make it stay. There was never that. I sat for a long while, letting the light fill the sky, letting it expand and reach down into the trees. I closed my eyes and listened hard to Eagle Creek.

It was running to the Columbia River, like me.

I seemed to float the four miles to the little parking area near the head of the Eagle Creek Trail, buoyed by a pure, unadulterated emotion that can only be described as joy. I strolled through the mostly empty parking lot and passed the restrooms, then followed another trail that would take me the two miles into Cascade Locks. The trail turned sharply to the right, and before me was the Columbia River, visible through the chain-link fence that bordered the trail to set it off from Interstate 84 just below. I stopped and grasped the fence and stared. It seemed like a miracle that I finally had the river in my sights, as if a newborn baby had just slipped finally into my palms after a long labor. That glimmering dark water was more beautiful than anything I'd imagined during all those miles I'd hiked to reach it.

I walked east along a lush green corridor, the roadbed of the long-abandoned Columbia River Highway, which had been made into a trail. I could see patches of concrete in places, but the road had mostly been reclaimed by the moss that grew along the rocks at the road's edge, the trees that hung heavy and low over it, the spiders who'd spun webs that crossed its expanse. I walked through the spiderwebs, feeling them like magic on my face, pulling them out of my hair. I could hear but not see the rush of automobiles on the interstate to my left, which ran between the river and me, the ordinary sound of them, a great whooshing whine and hum.

When I emerged from the forest, I was in Cascade Locks, which unlike so many towns on the trail was an actual town, with a population of a little more than a thousand. It was Friday morning and I could feel the Friday morningness emanating from the houses I passed. I walked beneath the freeway and wended my way along the streets with my ski pole clicking against the pavement, my heart racing when the bridge came into view. It's an elegant steel truss cantilever, named for a natural bridge that was formed by a major landslide approximately three hundred years ago that had temporarily dammed the Columbia River. The local Native Americans had called it the Bridge of the Gods. The human-made structure that took its name spans the Columbia for a little more than a third of a mile, connecting Oregon to Washington, the towns of Cascade Locks and Stevenson on either side. There's a tollbooth on the Oregon side and when I reached it the woman who worked inside told me I could cross the bridge, no charge.

"I'm not crossing," I said. "I only want to touch it." I walked along the shoulder of the road until I reached the concrete stanchion of the bridge, put my hand on it, and looked down at the Columbia River flowing beneath me. It's the largest river in the Pacific Northwest and the fourth largest in the nation. Native Americans have lived on the river for thousands of years, sustained by its once-bountiful salmon for most of them. Meriwether Lewis and William Clark had paddled down the Columbia in dugout canoes on their famous expedition in 1805. One hundred and ninety years later, two days before my twenty-seventh birthday, here I was.

I had arrived. I'd done it. It seemed like such a small thing and such a tremendous thing at once, like a secret I'd always tell myself, though I didn't know the meaning of it just yet. I stood there for several minutes, cars and trucks going past me, feeling like I'd cry, though I didn't.

Weeks before, I'd heard on the trail grapevine that once I reached Cascade Locks I had to go to the East Wind Drive-In for one of their famously large ice-cream cones. For that reason, I'd saved a couple of dollars when I was at Timberline Lodge. I left the bridge and made my way along a busy street that ran parallel to the river and the interstate; the road and much of the town were sandwiched between the two. It was still morning and the drive-in wasn't open yet, so I sat on the little white wooden bench in front with Monster by my side.

I would be in Portland later that day. It was only forty-five miles away, to the west. I'd sleep on my old futon beneath a roof. I'd unpack my CDs and stereo and listen to any song I liked. I'd wear my black lace bra and underwear and blue jeans. I'd consume all the amazing foods and drinks that could be had. I'd drive my truck anywhere I wanted to go. I'd set up my computer and write my novel. I'd take the boxes of books I'd brought with me from Minnesota and sell them the next day at Powell's, so I'd have some cash. I'd have a yard sale to see me through until I got a job. I'd set out my thrift store dresses and miniature binoculars and foldable saw on the grass and get for them anything I could. The thought of it all astounded me.

"We're ready for you," a woman called, poking her head out of the sliding window that fronted the drive-in.

I ordered a chocolate-vanilla twist cone; a few moments later she handed it to me and took my two dollars and gave me two dimes in change. It was the last money I had in the world. Twenty cents. I sat on the white bench and ate every bit of my cone and then watched the cars again. I was the only customer at the drive-in until a BMW pulled up and a young man in a business suit got out.

"Hi," he said to me as he passed. He was about my age, his hair gelled back, his shoes impeccable. Once he had his cone, he returned to stand near me.

"Looks like you've been backpacking."

"Yes. On the Pacific Crest Trail. I walked over eleven hundred miles," I said, too excited to contain myself. "I just finished my trip this morning."

"Really?"

I nodded and laughed.

"That's incredible. I've always wanted to do something like that. A big journey."

"You could. You should. Believe me, if I can do this, anyone can."

"I can't get the time off of work—I'm an attorney," he said. He tossed the uneaten half of his cone into the garbage can and wiped his hands on a napkin. "What are you going to do now?"

"Go to Portland. I'm going to live there awhile."

"I live there too. I'm on my way there now if you want a ride. I'd be happy to drop you off wherever you'd like."

"Thanks," I said. "But I want to stay here for a while. Just to take it all in."

He pulled a business card from his wallet and handed it to me. "Give me a call once you settle in. I'd love to take you out to lunch and hear more about your trip."

"Okay," I said, looking at the card. It was white with blue embossed letters, a relic from another world.

"It was an honor to meet you at this momentous juncture," he said.

"Nice to meet you too," I said, shaking his hand.

After he drove away, I leaned my head back and closed my eyes against the sun as the tears I'd expected earlier at the bridge began to seep from my eyes. *Thank you,* I thought over and over again. *Thank you.* Not just for the long walk, but for everything I could feel finally gathered up inside of me; for everything the trail had taught me and everything I couldn't yet know, though I felt it somehow already contained within me. How I'd never see the man in the BMW again, but how in four years I'd cross the Bridge of the Gods with another man and marry him in a spot almost visible from where I now sat. How in nine years that man and I would have a son named Carver, and a year and a half after that, a daughter named Bobbi. How in fifteen years I'd bring my family to this same white bench and the four of us would eat ice-cream cones while I told them the story of the time I'd been here once before, when I'd finished walking a long way on something called the Pacific Crest Trail.

And how it would be only then that the meaning of my hike would unfold inside of me, the secret I'd always told myself finally revealed.

Which would bring me to this telling.

I didn't know how I'd reach back through the years and look for and find some of the people I'd met on the trail and that I'd look for and not find others. Or how in one case I'd find something I didn't expect: an obituary. Doug's. I didn't know I'd read that he'd died nine years after we'd said goodbye on the PCT—killed in a kite-sailing accident in New Zealand. Or how, after I'd cried remembering what a golden boy he'd been, I'd go to the farthest corner of my basement, to the place where Monster hung on a pair of rusty nails, and I'd see that the raven feather Doug had given me was broken and frayed now, but still there—wedged into my pack's frame, where I placed it years ago.

It was all unknown to me then, as I sat on that white bench on the day I finished my hike. Everything except the fact that I didn't have to know. That it was enough to trust that what I'd done was true. To understand its meaning without yet being able to say precisely what it was, like all those lines from *The Dream of a Common Language* that had run through my nights and days. To believe that I didn't need to reach with my bare hands anymore. To know that seeing the fish beneath the surface of the water was enough. That it was everything. It was my life—like all lives, mysterious and irrevocable and sacred. So very close, so very present, so very belonging to me.

How wild it was, to let it be.

ACKNOWLEDGMENTS

Miigwech is an Ojibwe word I often heard growing up in northern Minnesota, and I feel compelled to use it here. It means thank you, but more—its meaning imbued with humility as well as gratitude. That's how I feel when I think about trying to thank all of the people who helped me make this book: humbled as well as grateful.

It is to my husband, Brian Lindstrom, that I owe my deepest *miigwech,* for he has loved me beyond measure, in both my writing and my life. Thank you, Brian.

I'm indebted to the Oregon Arts Commission, the Regional Arts and Culture Council, and Literary Arts for providing me with funding and support while I wrote this book and also throughout my career; to Greg Netzer and Larry Colton of the Wordstock Festival for always inviting me to the show; and to the Bread Loaf Writers' Conference and the Sewanee Writers' Conference for giving me meaningful support along the way.

I wrote most of this book while sitting at my dining room table, but crucial chapters were written away from home. I'm grateful to Soapstone for the residencies they provided me, and especially to Ruth Gundle, the former director of Soapstone, who was particularly generous to me in the early stages of this book. A profound thank you to Sally and Con Fitzgerald, who hosted me so graciously while I wrote the final chapters of *Wild* in their beautiful, silent "wee house" in Oregon's Warner Valley. Thanks also to the incomparable Jane O'Keefe, who made my time in the Warner Valley possible, and both loaned me her car and did my grocery shopping.

Thank you to my agent, Janet Silver, and also to her colleagues at the Zachary Shuster Harmsworth Agency. Janet, you are my friend, champion, and literary kindred spirit. I will always be grateful to you for your support, smarts, and love.

I'm indebted to the many people at Knopf who believed in *Wild* back in the early stages and have worked to bring it into the world. I'm especially grateful to my editor, Robin Desser, who never stopped pushing me to make this the best book it could be. Thank you, Robin, for your intelligence and your kindness, for your generous spirit and your incredibly long, single-spaced letters. Without you, this book wouldn't be what it is. Thanks also: Gabrielle Brooks, Erinn Hartman, Sarah Rothbard, Susanna Sturgis, and LuAnn Walther.

A deep bow to my children, Carver and Bobbi Lindstrom, who endured with grace and good humor all those times I had to go off alone to write. They never let me forget that life and love matter most.

Thanks also to my stellar writers' group: Chelsea Cain, Monica Drake, Diana Page Jordan, Erin Leonard, Chuck Palahniuk, Suzy Vitello Soulé, Mary Wysong-Haeri, and Lidia Yuknavitch. I'm indebted to each of you for your wise counsel, honest feedback, and killer pinot noir.

I'm deeply grateful to the friends who have nurtured and loved me. There are too many to name. I can only say you know who you are and I'm so fortunate you're in my life. There are some people I'd like to thank in particular, however—those who helped me in specific and numerous ways as I wrote this book: Sarah Berry, Ellen Urbani, Margaret Malone, Brian Padian, Laurie Fox, Bridgette Walsh, Chris Lowenstein, Sarah Hart, Garth Stein, Aimee Hurt, Tyler Roadie, and Hope Edelman. I'm humbled by your friendship and kindness. Thanks also to Arthur Rickydoc Flowers, George Saunders, Mary Caponegro, and Paulette Bates Alden, whose early mentorship and endless goodwill has meant the world to me.

Thank you to Wilderness Press for publishing the guidebooks that were and still are the definitive texts for those hiking the Pacific Crest Trail. Without the guidebooks' authors Jeffrey P. Schaffer, Ben Schifrin, Thomas Winnett, Ruby Jenkins, and Andy Selters, I'd have been utterly lost.

Most of the people I met on the PCT passed only briefly through my life, but I was enriched by each of them. They made me laugh, they made me think, they made me go on another day, and most of all, they made me trust entirely in the kindness of strangers. I am particularly indebted to my fellow 1995 PCT alumni CJ McClellan, Rick Topinka, Catherine Guthrie, and Joshua O'Brien, who responded to my inquiries with thoughtful care.

Lastly, I would like to remember my friend Doug Wisor, whom I wrote about in this book. He died on October 16, 2004, at the age of thirty-one. He was a good man who crossed the river too soon.

Miigwech.

BOOKS BURNED ON THE PCT

The Pacific Crest Trail, Volume 1: California, Jeffrey P. Schaffer, Thomas Winnett, Ben Schifrin, and Ruby Jenkins. Fourth edition, Wilderness Press, January 1989.

Staying Found: The Complete Map and Compass Handbook, June Fleming.

* The Dream of a Common Language, Adrienne Rich.

As I Lay Dying, William Faulkner.

** The Complete Stories, Flannery O'Connor.

The Novel, James Michener.

A Summer Bird-Cage, Margaret Drabble.

Lolita, Vladimir Nabokov.

Dubliners, James Joyce.

Waiting for the Barbarians, J. M. Coetzee.

The Pacific Crest Trail, Volume 2: Oregon and Washington, Jeffrey P. Schaffer and Andy Selters. Fifth edition, Wilderness Press, May 1992.

The Best American Essays 1991, edited by Robert Atwan and Joyce Carol Oates.

The Ten Thousand Things, Maria Dermoût.

*Not burned. Carried all the way.
**Not burned. Traded for *The Novel.*

NOTE ON THE AUTHOR

Cheryl Strayed is the author of the critically acclaimed novel *Torch* and the collection of essays *Tiny Beautiful Things: Advice on Love and Life from Someone Who's Been There*. Her work has appeared in numerous magazines and journals, including the *New York Times Magazine*, *Washington Post Magazine*, *Allure* and *The Rumpus*. She lives in Portland, Oregon.

MEET AN AGONY AUNT LIKE NO OTHER

If you loved *Wild*, you can read more from Cheryl Strayed in her latest book,

Tiny Beautiful Things

Life can be hard: your lover cheats on you, you lose a relative,
you can't pay the bills. But it can be pretty great, too: you've had
the hottest sex of your life, you get that plum job, you muster the courage
to write your novel. Everyday across the world, people go through the full
and glorious gamut of life's possibilities – but, sometimes, things go awry . . .

For a few years, tens of thousands of Americans have turned to Cheryl Strayed,
internet agony aunt 'Dear Sugar'. Unlike most agony aunts, Sugar's advice was
spun from genuine compassion and informed by a wealth of personal experience –
experience that was sometimes tragic and sometimes tender, often hilarious and
often heartbreaking. Having successfully battled her own demons – as told
in her bestselling memoir, *Wild* – Cheryl Strayed sat down to answer the letters
of the frightened, the anxious, the confused; and with each gem-like
communication – of which the best are collected in this volume –
she proved to be the perfect guide for those who have got lost in life.

'Nothing short of dynamite . . . We're reading the columns with boxes of tissues
and raised fists of solidarity, shaking our heads with awe and amusement' *Salon*

Tiny Beautiful Things: Advice on Love and Life from Someone Who's Been There
is available online or in any good bookshop.

© Joni Kaba

To find out more
visit www.cherylstrayed.com,
follow Cheryl on Twitter @CherylStrayed
or watch her videos at www.youtube.com/AtlanticBooks